STRANGERS IN BLOOD

STRANGERS IN BLOOD

FUR TRADE COMPANY FAMILIES IN INDIAN COUNTRY

JENNIFER S. H. BROWN

UNIVERSITY OF BRITISH COLUMBIA PRESS
VANCOUVER

STRANGERS IN BLOOD

Fur Trade Company Families in Indian Country

Second Printing 1985

Canadian Cataloguing in Publication Data

Brown, Jennifer S. H., 1940-
Strangers in blood

Bibliography: p.
Includes index.
ISBN 0-7748-0251-0 (pbk)

1. Northwest, Canadian—Social life and
customs. 2. Fur traders—Northwest, Canadian.
3. Frontier and pioneer life—Northwest,
Canadian. 4. Hudson's Bay Company. 5. North
West Company. I. Title.
FC3207.B76   971.03   C80-091104-0
F1060.7.B76

International Standard Book Number 0-7748-0251-0 (pbk)

Printed in Canada

This book has been published with the help of a gift to scholarly publishing made in honour of Dr. Harold S. Foley for his distinguished services to the University of British Columbia and with the assistance of the Canada Council.

Contents

Photographic Credits

Plate 7 is reproduced by courtesy of the Rare Book Room of the Northern Illinois University Library, DeKalb, and is from Louis Armand de Lom d'Arce, baron de Lahontan, *Nouveaux voyages de Mr. le baron de Lahontan dans l'Amérique Septentrionale,* vol. 2 (The Hague, 1703). Plate 8 was furnished by Edgar S. Oerichbauer, Archaeologist, the State Historical Society of Wisconsin, Madison. Plates 9, 14, and 18 are from the iconographic collections of the State Historical Society of Wisconsin. Plate 10 is from Charles Bert Reed, *Masters of the Wilderness,* Chicago Historical Society, Fort Dearborn Series (Chicago: University of Chicago Press, 1914), opp. page 58. Plates 11, 12, 19, 22, and 23 are from the privately owned lantern slide collection of the Rev. Egerton R. Young, courtesy of the Rev. H. Egerton Young, as are the cover illustration and plates 1–6. Plate 13 is from a steel engraving in the J. M. Longyear Research Library of the Marquette County (Michigan) Historical Society; the original oil painting is in the Glenbow-Alberta Institute Museum, Calgary. Plates 15, 17, and 21 are from the Provincial Archives of Manitoba. Plate 20 is from Beckles Willson, *The Life of Lord Strathcona and Mount Royal* (London: Cassell, 1915), opp. page 272. Plate 16 is from Sketchbook 44 in the Frank B. Mayer Papers, Ayer Collection, the Newberry Library, Chicago.

Illustrations

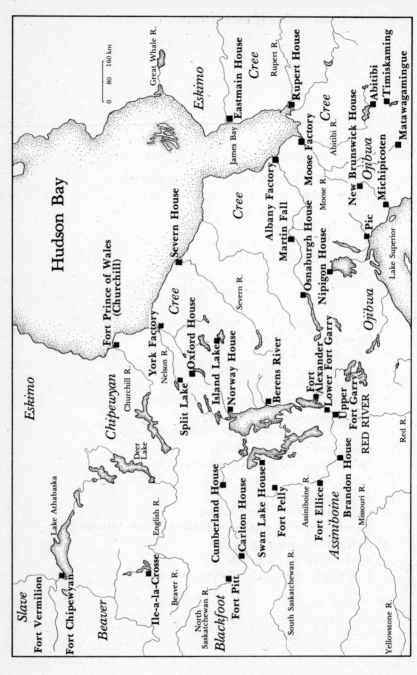

COMPANY POSTS AND INDIAN GROUPS FROM HUDSON BAY TO THE SASKATCHEWAN COUNTRY

Slave
Fort Vermilion

Lake Athabaska

Eskimo

Fort Chipewyan

Beaver

Deer Lake

Churchill R.

Chipewyan

Ile-a-la-Crosse

English R.

Beaver R.

North Saskatchewan R.

Blackfoot
Fort Pitt

South Saskatchewan R.

Cumberland House

Carlton House

Swan Lake House

Fort Pelly

Assiniboine R.

Fort Ellice

Assiniboine

Brandon House

Missouri R.

Yellowstone R.

Split Lake

Nelson R.

York Factory

Fort Prince of Wales (Churchill)

Hudson Bay

Severn House

Oxford House

Island Lake

Norway House

Berens River

Severn R.

Cree

Fort Alexander

Lower Fort Garry

Upper Fort Garry

RED RIVER

Red R.

Ojibwa

Nipigon House

Osnaburgh House

Martin Fall

Albany Factory

Cree

Moose Factory

James Bay

Eastmain House

Cree

Great Whale R.

Eskimo

Rupert R.

Rupert House

0   80   160 km

Abitibi R.

Moose R.

New Brunswick House

Pic

Lake Superior

Ojibwa

Michipicoten

Abitibi

Timiskaming

Matawagamingue

Preface

On 2 May 1670, King Charles II of England granted to his "Deare and entirely Beloved Cousin Prince Rupert" and seventeen others a Royal Charter establishing them as "the true and absolute Lordes and Proprietors" of an area vaster than any European of the time realized. These eighteen founders of the Hudson's Bay Company, having "at their owne great cost and charge undertaken an expedicion for Hudsons Bay in the north West part of America for the discovery of a new Passage into the South Sea and for the finding some Trade for Furrs Mineralls and other considerable Commodityes" were to receive the "sole Trade and Commerce of all those Seas Streightes Bayes Rivers Lakes Creekes and Soundes . . . within the entrance of the Streightes commonly called Hudsons Streightes together with all the Landes and Territoryes upon the Countryes Coastes and confynes of the Seas Bayes Lakes Rivers Creekes and Soundes aforesaid that are not actually possessed by or granted to any of our Subjectes or possessed by the Subjectes of any other Christian Prince or State."

This privileged monopolistic company was not to keep its rights to the "sole Trade" without facing challengers who sometimes threatened its very survival. Early French competition for furs was vigorous and ended only with the British conquest of New France in 1763. The conquest opened the Canadian fur trade to British entrepreneurs (largely, in fact, Highland Scots), who soon created a much more serious rival, the North West Company, from their flexible business partnerships. Eventually the two were to merge, and in 1821, a new Hudson's Bay Company with a substantial component of North West Company officers in its councils assumed economic and administrative control of the fur trade.

This volume undertakes a comparative study of these companies as organizations that differed conspicuously in their origins and characteristics and of the social and domestic relations that developed within them. The traders of these firms constituted a bipartite community of both anthropological and historical interest. They were not colonists. Unlike many Europeans who came to the New World, they arrived in the fur trade country with the intention of returning to their homelands, *cum animo revertendi,* as the Montreal lawyers in the Connolly case of the 1860s put it. Until the late period and then only in certain restricted areas, their employers did not wish them to settle in the Northwest; settlements, except on limited scales, conflicted with the trading and fur extraction purposes for which these men came. Nor did they come to Christianize or civilize the Indians—aims that many others of their background thought they should have had. Rather they came as traders, to reside for periods ranging from a few years to (despite original intentions) the rest of a lifetime, in small, widely separated, fort-like structures built mainly for trade and for housing at most a few dozen men and their furs and supplies during long, rigorous, northern winters.

In the 1820s, these few hundred men and their families occupied a web of posts spread over most of what is now northern and western Canada and the northwest corner of the United States. Many of them were almost totally isolated from what they called "civilization" and even from each other for most of the year. Yet they formed a community in some important respects, exhibiting a shared cultural background (albeit with some notable internal variations), common values, aims, and concerns, mutual kin ties originating in Europe or else from the family connections and friendships they formed in the fur trade country, and a feeling of unity and understanding among themselves combined with a sense of separateness and isolation from their homelands. Not long after the 1821 coalition, Henry Hallet, an Englishman with a large native family and twenty-nine years' experience in the fur trade, received an "intimation" from company governor George Simpson that his services were no longer required and appealed his dismissal to the governor and council in terms reflecting this sense of distinctness:

> You are aware Sirs, that by remaining in the Indian country such a length of time, the Customs and habits we imbibe are so different to those of the Civilized world, add to which the attachment most people form to it, that it will be almost impossible for me to return to my native Country. Therefore I humbly beg that you will take my Case into Consideration and trust that . . . you will allow me to be retained in the service (HBCA, D. 4/116, f.60, 25 June 1822).

Paradoxically, the geographical remoteness of the traders from each other is precisely what now facilitates studying them as a group; lacking other means, they communicated through letters and post journals, and many of the documents they intended for each other and for their employers survive. If they had resided in a single settlement or "community" in its usual concrete sense, communications to and about their kin, friends, and colleagues would have been largely oral and lost. Their literacy thus became a vehicle for maintaining the community and now aids the study of it. The risks of fur trade life and travel also impelled traders to another use of literacy—will-making; and these wills, of which two or three by the same author sometimes survive, are invaluable indicators, not only of wealth, but also of the author's involvements in and attitudes toward their personal and family relations. If a will happened to become subject to litigation among heirs with conflicting claims (as in Montreal when the half-Cree son of North Wester William Connolly successfully sued to claim his mother's share of the Connolly estate), still more documentary records of fur trade life were generated as witnesses testified and lawyers gathered evidence.

Valuable documentation on the fur trade also comes from outside observers—the missionaries, explorers, scientists, government officials, and others who, in increasing numbers, particularly in the nineteenth century, visited or resided for varying periods in the Northwest. Artist Paul Kane, botanist David Douglas, scientist Henry Lefroy, arctic explorer John Franklin, and the first missionaries to Oregon are a small sampling of the people whose writings furnish records to supplement those authored by the traders themselves.

Of course, while these documentary sources make this study possible, the need to rely solely on them (with the exception of some oral traditions preserved by traders' descendants) limits its scope and precludes certain kinds of investigation. "Informants" cannot be questioned about gaps or bias in their testimony, and their face-to-face interactions cannot be observed. The investigator, unable to achieve the anthropologist's ideal of ethnographic participant-observation, must explore many scattered sources to gather enough data about enough individuals to form bases for generalization. On the other hand, such materials provide an opportunity for close study of social change over many decades, a kind of study not possible during the usually limited timespans of ethnographic work. There is another advantage, too, for the user of historical materials; even though our informants cannot correct us and even though their records may have undergone subsequent censorship, the remaining evidence from them is not skewed, nor are they disconcerted, by our presence. Such collections as the Hargrave and Ermatinger papers are rich in data and opinions that would hardly be readily communicated to an outsider; their personal and firsthand quality survives without their having been reshaped for transmission to a probing researcher.

The character and sequence of some particularly influential historical events furnish a skeletal structure that shapes the organization of this study. The broadest span of time that might define its scope is well marked at both ends—the founding of the Hudson's Bay Company in 1670, and the Confederation of Canada and the company's deed of surrender of its lands to the British Crown, and thereby to Canada, in the years 1869-70, at which point company rule in the fur trade country yielded to political control by the Canadian government. The uneven amount of evidence available within that timespan, however, and the salience of certain events after the 1770s in respect to the topics at hand, combine to dictate the focussing of attention on a much narrower period than two hundred years. For one thing, the evidence for the early years of the British fur trade into Hudson Bay is patchy indeed. Early company papers had no permanent home and were kept in such places as a "great Trunke" in a room rented by the Hudson's Bay Company for its meetings in London. The surviving collection of reports from the main posts in the Bay begins to be complete only from 1723, more than fifty years after the chartering of the company (Davies 1965: xiii–xiv). Later in the century, records improved and increased in numbers, yet they were still primarily official; the private letter-writing among traders so valuable to this study is mainly a nineteenth-century phenomenon. The earliest mission registers for the area also date from the early nineteenth century, and their data on traders' native families and interconnections can be related with confidence only to the decades from the 1780s on. The spotty character of early evidence thus fosters an emphasis on the better documented and eventful decades from the 1780s to the 1860s.

Several important occurrences supply a framework for organizing the plethora of materials on the traders of these later decades. In 1779, the first North West Company co-partnership was formed in Montreal, replacing earlier, less unified French and Canadian fur-trading in the Northwest with new, vigorous, and sometimes violent competition between the London-based and Montreal-based traders. Four decades later came a cluster of events that exerted powerful influences on the lives of traders and their families. In 1821, the two companies resolved their destructive differences by merging under the name of the older but numerically smaller Hudson's Bay Company. By a Deed Poll of that year, thirty-two former North Westers and twenty-one senior Hudson's Bay officers were commissioned as shareholding chief factors and chief traders in the new concern. This arrangement brought into a sometimes uneasy association the two groups whose comparison is central to this study— Hudson's Bay men consisting largely of protestant Englishmen and Scots (drawn mostly from the Lowlands and the Orkney Islands), and North Westers consisting mainly of Highland Scots and Canadians, many with Roman Catholic and French-Canadian affiliations and with extensive kin links among themselves. The year 1820 also saw the arrival on the scene of a dynamic new personality, George Simpson, who soon became company governor in the Hudson's Bay territories. His personal influence on the fur trade and its traders was to be powerfully felt for the next forty years.

In these years too, the Red River Colony in Manitoba, an emigration and settlement project initiated in 1811–12 by Thomas Douglas, fifth Earl of Selkirk, in co-operation with the Hudson's Bay Company, was becoming established on a permanent footing after some serious reversals and troubles with North West Company opposition. By the 1820s, the infant settlement was attracting not only the Scottish farmers and Hudson's Bay Company traders' native families for whom it was originally intended, but also missionaries who made it their headquarters. Representatives of the Roman Catholic

Church and the Church of England began work there in 1818 and 1820 respectively, bringing European Christianity to Indians and to fur trade families long isolated from its influences and pressures. The arrival of Selkirk's settlers and of protestant clergy also inevitably meant the introduction of another force for change in this eventful period—European women, whose interest in bringing Christian civilization to the domestic scene in the fur trade country would lend support to the larger-scale efforts of the churchmen in that direction.

Beginning in the 1820s, traders began occasionally to find white wives among the Red River settlers' families; and in 1830, Hudson's Bay Governor Simpson and a few colleagues tried the experiment of importing their own chosen brides from Britain. The news of their novel marriages sent shock waves through fur trade social networks all across the Northwest and seemed to herald a new era in which native-born women, who for several decades had been the customary marital choices of traders, would be rejected as unsuitable mates for officers and gentlemen. The comments of several traders—James Hargrave, Donald Ross, and others—show the degree to which 1830 was a benchmark year in their changing social and domestic lives. By 1840, when he congratulated James Hargrave on his marriage to the Scottish-born niece of Chief Factor J. G. McTavish, Chief Trader James Douglas could succinctly summarize the changing patterns in fur trade marital unions during the preceding decades:

> There is a strange revolution in the manners of the country; Indian wives were at one time the vogue, the half breed supplanted these, and now we have the lovely tender exotic torn from its parent bed, to pine and languish in the desert (PAC, Hargrave Papers, 26 February 1840).

There are some indications that this "revolution" was, like most, followed by a period of readjustment and re-evaluation. Newly imported British wives did indeed, in the cases of Mrs. Simpson and others, "pine and languish in the desert," and in the 1840s and 1850s, Simpson himself became more favourably disposed toward native-born wives (and their children) as the people best adapted to domestic life and work in the fur trade country. When the Wesleyan missionary George Barnley brought his British wife to live at Moose Factory in the mid-1840s, Simpson found that he became "latterly . . . a most troublesome man" and complained to the company's London secretary, W.G. Smith, in January 1848 that:

> When these missionaries choose to marry in the Country, there can be

no great objection to it, because native women are tolerably manage-
able; but imported wives, fancy themselves such great women that there
is no possibility of pleasing them (HBCA, D.4/115, ff. 116–17).

The native wives whom Simpson was prepared to accept in the 1840s
differed from their predecessors of the 1820s and before in respects that
doubtless aided their acceptance as mates for officers and gentlemen. No
longer were there Indians among them; all were of mixed descent, and they
had generally been exposed, even if brought up in the Northwest, to the
"civilizing" influences of white religious and educational agencies. Geneti-
cally, culturally, and in their social affiliations, they exhibited far fewer Indian
traits. And accordingly, fur trade social and domestic life was for some years
before the end of Hudson's Bay Company control over the Northwest losing
the distinctiveness that had for many years set it apart from European society
or what the traders commonly described as the "Civilized world."

One major question that arises in fur trade social history is to define the
relationships between fur trade "society" and the social spheres or systems
centred outside it. Clearly the traders never constituted a wholly independent
or separate social system. They were hired and paid by distant enterprises and
could be recalled or dismissed by them. With the exception of traders' native
sons who entered company employ, they were born and brought up outside
the fur trade country and usually maintained some social ties with the home-
land. They were subject to company rules and decisions governing their
behaviour and places of residence, and their wills were typically proved and
their estates settled in the British or Canadian courts. And, on the other hand,
especially in the earlier phases of the trade, their need for the assistance and
co-operation of the Indians who supplied the furs, consumed their trade
goods, and helped them survive in a harsh northern environment, made them
pay attention to Indian demands and codes of conduct.

This picture of traders' lack of independence as a group can be overdrawn,
however. They were not simply mirrors of their European backgrounds,
slaves to their employers, or hostages to Indian codes and demands; their
position was more complex than that. They may be seen, in the term Louis
Hartz used in *The Founding of New Societies,* as a "fragment" of European
society, drawn only from certain sectors of that society and going abroad to
engage, as many Europeans did, in a specialized activity related to European
economic and colonial expansion. Such fragments did not carry with them,
represent, or introduce into their foreign settings anywhere near the totality of

ate 1. Norway House, a major HBC post north of Lake Winnipeg, showing the factor and his wife and ethnically diverse company
ployees in the post compound in the late nineteenth century. The borders of the original coloured lantern slide, which was
parently based on a photograph, have been peeled back to reveal the process of paint application.

Plate 2. A meeting of fur traders during winter travel, when periods of solitude were long and chances for sociability much welcomed. Age and heat, perhaps from the acetylene lamp, have caused the paint on this slide to crack.

Plate 3. J. E. Laughlin's lantern slide painting of Indians arriving at Rossville mission near Norway House in the 1840s, to ask missionary James Evans for a visit to their settlement.

Plate 4. Described as Bull Bear and squaw, Blackfoot Indians, this photograph was copied onto a lantern slide and then coloured. It indicates the mixture of HBC blankets and Indian accoutrements that characterized nineteenth-century Indian dress in northern fur trade areas.

Plate 5. If a sled dog's foot was injured on rough or sharp ice, a thick woollen dog-shoe was tied onto the paw with a soft deerskin thong. Experienced dogs stopped when injured and waited for shoes to be applied.

Plate 6. At Methodist and other mission schools such as this one in the Canadian West, children of both Indian and mixed parentage assumed European dress and learned the practical arts of civilization, centring particularly upon agriculture.

These lantern slides are part of a large collection made in the 1890s and early 1900s by the Methodist missionary Egerton R. Young to illustrate lectures on Indian missions for audiences in North America, Great Britain, and Australia. Each slide consists of two layers of glass taped together; the image was either painted in translucent oil or water colours on the inner surface of one of the layers or reproduced photographically thereon. The pictures were projected using a brass magic lantern with an acetylene flame. These brilliant images must have been especially striking in the days before movies and television.

European institutions, ways, and social structures. Correspondingly, then, the traders' collective position as a fragment separated from a whole could lead both to a sense of isolation and to a certain feeling of semi-autonomy vis-à-vis the home society. The influences of childhood ties and upbringing and the formal constraints of company rules and policies persisted, but fur traders might live for considerable periods in relative seclusion and freedom from these forces. During these times they might also lose some of the cultural baggage they had brought; in the late 1700s David Thompson of the Hudson's Bay Company observed that his colleague George Hudson, who had spent thirteen years at the inland post of Cumberland House, "had lost all his education, except reading and writing, and the [a?] little of this, for the accounts of the trade appeared labor to him" (Hopwood 1957: 28).

Such isolation or semi-autonomy did not, however, necessarily mean that traders were immersed in Indian cultures and societies to the point that they lost social and cultural independence. As studies of immigrant or "stranger" traders in other foreign settings have shown, substantial economic and social relations may persist among diverse groups, even when they are drawn into the same society or polity, without cultural assimilation following. Lloyd Fallers has observed that "Clearly, persons who share a common system of social relations—who trade with each other for example—. . . must also have some common understanding of the significance of their interaction. But . . . this shared understanding may be far from complete without seriously disrupting social life." What Fallers calls "this lack of complete 'fit' between the deeper cultural commitments and the superficial sets of common understandings" (1967: 8) was a readily visible phenomenon in the fur trade country, where traders maintained a marked degree of separateness and social distinctness from their Indian associates as well as from Europe.

The fur trade itself may be conceptualized as a partial or incomplete social sphere. In the decades between the 1770s and 1821 it contained two major subfields of growing importance, the Hudson's Bay and North West Companies. The European influences from the two somewhat differing contexts of these companies had great significance, but they were in turn mediated and modified by the differing internal organizational and personnel characteristics of the firms. The dynamics of the isolated, foreign environment in which they operated also influenced these patterns; distinctive fur trade rules and customs appeared in response to distinctive fur trade conditions, and they were themselves modified later as colonists and missionaries grew in numbers and importance, bringing pressures that finally eclipsed this social sphere.

Within this sphere, the trader found himself in a complex and ambiguous position. His career success depended upon the favour and friendly interest (or what he himself sometimes called the "patronage") of his employers and superiors. Although he could play the role of independent and authoritative patron to the Indians and to his men in the isolation of his own post, he was obliged to show loyalty, deference, and respect to "their Honors" in London or to the North West Company partners in Montreal and to his senior colleagues. When Chief Trader James Hargrave, who had for several years been in charge of York Factory, a major company depot, wrote to Chief Factor John Dugald Cameron asking the latter's support for his promotion, he became the humble client:

> Should you consider my services and my poor merits deserving of your patronage may I presume to solicit your vote and to beg that you will use your influence with those mutual friends who are so likely to listen favorably to your recommendation (PAC, Hargrave Papers, 1 February 1840).

Thus, men who played the patron in one social context became clients in others, accepting and showing loyalty to the values circulated by other actors.

Fur traders were not, however, confined to playing the alternate roles of patron and client. Patronage implies a two-sided social relationship, while in many circumstances the traders also played the role of middlemen or brokers between their employers and their native fur suppliers. The broker role is often and understandably assimilated to or confused with that of the patron, since the broker too exhibits leadership and initiative, as Robert Paine has noted in reference to recent studies of the Canadian arctic. As "a middleman attracting followers who believe him able to influence the person who controls the favours" (1971: 19–20), he acts as patron to those followers while simultaneously being the intermediate party in a triad and the purveyor rather than originator of the dominant values circulated. As a processor of information, he looks in two directions, interpreting and translating communications between the other parties and representing one to the other according to his own lights. When, for example, the Hudson's Bay Company tried to increase its trade returns in the early 1800s, William Auld, in charge at York Factory, was at the nexus of communication between the company's London directors and the Indians of his area; and he was well situated in his role as mediator to modify the emphases and contents of the transmissions and transactions between them. On 26 September 1811, he wrote to the directors humanely, but perhaps with highly selected emphasis, of the Indians' plight in the face of rising prices for company trade goods:

> I see the progressive rise in the price of every article of your Exports In common with my fellow labourers I bitterly feel the decline of the value of your Imports Identifying myself with the Natives of these Territories

your legitimate subjects I am irresistibly pressed forward to advocate their Cause and to proclaim their wrongs . . . your Chief Factors and Traders alike with myself are utterly disqualified for wringing from the bloody sweat of these poor Creatures any more advantages worth a moments consideration and we recoil with horror at the thought of these *advantages* being rejected at the judgment seat of Heaven . . . you must see we have very little chance of obtaining any great benefit from lowering the value of Indian Barter we who set so high a value on experience may pause before we step beyond the limits it prescribed as safe We may drive them to desperation by depriving them of the means of a wretched existence (HBCA, A. 11/118, ff. 25–26).

The company directors, with their inferior, second-hand knowledge of Hudson Bay, were not in a good position to question either Auld's accuracy or his sincerity, and his modern readers are similarly handicapped. One can only note that Auld, whatever his private motives may have been, likely stood to benefit if the company accepted his evaluation of the trade and of the Indians' condition. Lower prices for trade goods would improve relations with the Indians and probably encourage them to bring more furs, in turn raising the production figures for York Factory and enhancing Auld's own standing as chief officer there. Whether or not he was fully sensitive to these possibilities, his position as broker gave him the opportunity to exploit and influence company-Indian social and trade relations for his own benefit aside from that of the other parties. Aware of the various reciprocities involved in the fur trade, transmitting and emphasizing selected information, Auld administered but could also help to shape policies for which he was not, however, ultimately "responsible." Fur traders, situated in a semi-autonomous yet intermediate position between two very different worlds, required a diversity of such role-playing skills and strategies for their success and even, at times, survival. These various kinds of patronage and brokerage relationships were of great importance in both Hudson's Bay and North West Company social life, although their characteristics and orientations differed somewhat between the two companies.

As they trace two centuries of variation and change in fur trade social and domestic life, the following chapters also focus on institutionalization as a major phenomenon. The French and British fur traders in the Canadian Northwest early began to exhibit the social organization and cultural content that distinguished them from other spheres of colonial life. Of course, traders brought with them European instructions, models, and experience that affected their behaviour in the fur trade country, and they encountered Indians whose expectations and ways of life demanded their consideration and accommodation. But within those constraints, individuals could make decisions, innovate, and experiment to a degree; and in learning from their successes and failures, they built up new social patterns adapted to their distinctive situations. Fredrik Barth has described this kind of process well:

> I find it reasonable to see social institutions and customs as the outcome of a complex aggregation of numerous micro-events of behaviour, based on individual decisions in each person's attempt to cope with life . . . individual behaviour produces experience, a confrontation with reality which may or may not seem consistent with preexisting conceptualizations and thus may sometimes tend to confirm, sometimes to falsify them (1973: 5).

And his paradigm of the process of institutionalization or "how individual experience feeds back on cultural standardization" presents a useful model in terms of which to view the growth and accretion of distinguishably fur trade social patterns over time.

As applied to historical periods, this approach encourages the study of individual decisions and actions through time and of their aggregation into social patterns that in turn influence and constrain the choices and actions of succeeding individuals as they become normal and accepted in a community. The approach also suggests a macrobiographical method of organizing historical materials that in their raw form are unwieldy and of uneven quality and helpfulness regarding specific individuals and details. Macrobiography, here taken to include the collection, organization, and comparison of biographical materials on temporally and/or socially distinct groups of individuals, is a means of tracing the structuring of social life over extended periods. It has proved a useful method for elucidating the social and domestic patterns of Hudson's Bay and North West Company traders early and late, before and after coalition.

The historical fact of internal contrast in the fur trade country, that is, the presence of two distinct European-derived enterprises with the same purpose in the same environment, gives this study an analytical dimension it otherwise would not have. If all traders had been employees solely of one company, their fur trade social patterns might have simply been taken as adaptive responses of white men to the context of the Indian country; and the social environment created by the company itself through its personnel selection procedures, codes, and organizational structure might, for lack of visible contrasting alternatives, have been neglected rather than recognized as a significant variable. The combined Hudson's Bay and North West Company presence, however, highlights this variable and calls for comparative study of the two trading companies, so that traders may be viewed in the contexts of the restricted and distinctive environments of the companies that hired them, as well as in their broader fur trade setting.

Within these two companies, the traders here studied were predominantly officers, or at least men who attained a clerkly or higher rank at some point in their careers. There are two reasons for this "upper class" bias, one practical, and one of some theoretical importance. On the practical side, far more information can be compiled about men who were literate (or if not, who left some imprint on the records because of their special duties, explorations, or other work) than about particular labourers, voyageurs, and others who remained in low positions—although this study finds numerous occasions to refer to specific occurrences and social patterns that involved the participation of these men.

The theoretical interest of focussing on the upper ranks emerges in both the earlier and later periods covered by this volume. Particularly in the eighteenth-century Hudson's Bay Company, given the vertical emphasis of its social organization, the role models provided by officers in familial and other spheres proved of much importance as the numbers of Hudson's Bay families grew, officers typically having been the first to acquire such families. Then too, in the difficult period after the 1821 merger, officers' families hold special interest precisely because of their rank, their various and changing perceptions of rank and its ingredients, and their varied assessments and treatment of the social placing and ranking of their native-born wives and offspring. While the standing of low-ranked "servants" of both companies remained much the same after 1821 (in fact, even more frozen than before, given the increased stratification of the period), officers and their native wives, sons, and daughters had much to lose as well as to gain, as diverse social and moral values were articulated by their superiors, by colleagues, and by clergy and other newcomers to the fur trade country and as new policies and prejudices took shape. The study of social ranking is perhaps most interesting when focussed on those whose rank is ambiguous, changing, and variously defined within their social order—in this instance, officers' native families and those officers themselves as husband-fathers of such families after 1821.

The title of this book derives from a British legal category that was sometimes invoked when the legitimacy of traders' native families was called into question. If a trader's heirs could not attain legal recognition as his relatives, they paid the same legacy duty as other "strangers in blood"—hence the need for law courts to assess their status. The phrase also succinctly highlights broader themes of this volume—the interracial encounters brought about by the fur trade and the problems that their participants and progeny faced, early and late.

For ease of reference, the anthropological style of documentation is used; in-text citations are keyed directly to the list of sources at the back of the book. Factual biographical information given in the text is, unless specific citations indicate otherwise, documented in readily accessible printed sources. The reader is referred particularly to the published volumes of the *Dictionary of Canadian Biography* (University of Toronto Press) and the extensive data compiled in relevant publications of the Hudson's Bay Record Society and the Champlain Society.

The permission of the Hudson's Bay Company to reprint those portions of my text that appeared in *The Beaver* in Spring 1977, pp. 39–45 ("A Colony of very Useful Hands"); and Winter 1977, pp. 4–10, and Spring, 1978, pp. 48–55 ("Ultimate Respectability: Fur Trade Children in the Civilized World") is gratefully acknowledged. I also thank the National Museum of Man, National Museums of Canada, for permission to reprint portions of my article, "Two Companies in Search of Traders: Personnel and Promotion Patterns in Canada's early British Fur Trade," from Canadian Ethnology Service Paper No. 28 (1975), pp. 623–45.

Several people and institutions have contributed to the research and writing of this study. Of central importance to my research were the Hudson's Bay Company Archives in Winnipeg, along with the microfilms of their contents in the Public Archives of Canada, Ottawa; and I thank the Hudson's Bay Company for permission to use and publish from their archives. Shirlee Anne Smith, in her capacity as librarian at Hudson's Bay House in Winnipeg and later as archivist of the Hudson's Bay Company, was unfailingly helpful.

Much valued assistance also came from John Bovey and his staff at the Provincial Archives of Manitoba, from Hugh MacMillan, liaison officer of the Archives of Ontario, from Barbara Wilson of the Public Archives of Canada, and from other staff members at these repositories, as well as from St. John's Anglican Cathedral in Winnipeg, the Missouri Historical Society in St. Louis, the Newberry Library in Chicago, the Wisconsin State Historical Society in Madison, and the McCord Museum in Montreal. The many contributions of the staff and readers of the University of British Columbia Press deserve special mention; particular thanks go to Jane C. Fredeman, senior editor, for her helpfulness, interest, and skilled editorial labours. The early phases of my research, in 1971–73, were supported by a research fellowship from the National Institute of Mental Health, U.S. Department of Health, Education, and Welfare.

Several faculty members of the University of Chicago, most particularly George W. Stocking, Jr., Raymond D. Fogelson, and Bernard S. Cohn, made many valued criticisms and suggestions on earlier versions of the manuscript. I also wish to thank several fellow students of the fur trade whose ideas and comments have been much appreciated—among them Irene Spry, John E. Foster, Charles Bishop, William J. Eccles, Arthur J. Ray, and especially Sylvia Van Kirk, whose vast knowledge, sound perspectives, and suggestions on subjects of mutual interest have been of immense value.

Finally, I wish to express special appreciation to Wilson and Matthew

Brown, my husband and son, who were patient and encouraging supporters throughout; and to Harcourt and Dorothy Stacey Brown, who with parental devotion opened to me the pathways of learning and scholarship and built me the foundations of my Canadian heritage. They have waited long enough for a superstructure to appear.

1

The Backgrounds and Antecedents of the British Traders

In the 1780s, when the North West Company was beginning to emerge as the Hudson's Bay Company's strongest rival, each of these firms was already operating on the basis of persisting cultural traditions that influenced its behaviour and organization. The distinctive origins and configurations of these traditions help to explain why these two fur trade rivals of the late eighteenth and early nineteenth centuries showed the broad social differences that they did, despite their common British (and heavily Scottish) façade.

One important contrast sprang from the differing character of the early French and British fur trade presence in the Canadian Northwest. The French predecessors of the North West Company had operated from a colonial base, while the Hudson's Bay Company operated directly from Europe. French fur trade activities were inextricably linked with colonial economic and political affairs and with the growing pains of a youthful and expanding settlement. The British, in contrast, were spared the complications and costs of colonization in Hudson Bay. But they faced other problems in conducting their trade from so great a distance. Lacking an established New World base, the early company directors were much handicapped by their unfamiliarity with local conditions and native peoples. Accordingly, while both the British and the French initially attempted to conduct the fur trade through royally chartered, monopolistic companies, these companies followed differing courses to differing fates. In the case of New France, a series of such firms arose and declined, leaving the field to other more successful organizational forms that developed after Canada became a royal province in 1663 and eventually, after the conquest, to the personalized and kin-based partnerships of the early North Westers and their rivals. England's chartered monopoly was to survive much longer as a highly structured organization whose field officers, if not their London superiors, studied and slowly learned to adapt to the conditions of trade and life in Hudson Bay.

THE FRENCH BACKGROUND

A conspicuous feature of both the early French and British spheres was the separation and distance between the trader, notably the seventeenth-century coureur de bois, and his colonial military and religious authorities on one hand; and the Bay trader and his London directors on the other. These divisions were rather different in character, however. The French opposition and tension between administrator and trader was not strictly one between high-ranked authority and low-ranked rebel, but may be in part reflective of older divisions within French society itself. Historical geographer Edward Whiting Fox has analyzed these divisions in terms that seem transferable, to some extent, to the context of New France. He notes that two quite different socio-economic systems co-existed in France for several centuries. One was the agriculturally based territorial monarchy with its administrative, military and religious hierarchy and its peasants, market towns, and short-range overland trade networks. The other system was based in expanding ports and riverine cities with international and transoceanic connections and emphasized the linear extension of waterborne commercial transport and trade organizations, rather than territorial expansion.

Maritime commerce tended to create its own society, "relatively discrete and self-contained"; and there are some indications that its merchants "were by no means persuaded of the necessity of belonging to any administrative state at all" (Fox 1972: 34, 38, 68). Because this society was characterized by linear rather than areal extent and lacked a formal political administration, it had a certain invisibility, even though it maintained itself "by an active exchange of goods and messages, as well as a highly developed sense of common purpose" (ibid., 39). The men of commerce conducted their affairs by means of consultation, negotiation, and compromise. By placing a premium on record-keeping and writing, commerce also provided "special incentives and opportunities" for the spread of literacy and other intellectual skills. It developed its own hierarchy in which entrepreneurs, bourgeois, and tradesmen, rather than landed aristocrats and peasants, were conspicuous groups. And whereas administrative monarchies were chronic consumers (and borrowers) of capital, commerce generated profits to feed the growth of an "economic system capable of indefinite rationalization and expansion" (ibid., 66, 57, 147, 37).

In New France of the seventeenth century, a corresponding split existed between the representatives of continental monarchy and the merchants and traders whose waterborne fur trade activities were so important to the colony's support. On a small scale, early New France seemed to replicate France in the divisiveness of its two sub-societies, both seeking dominance, yet each having its own objectives, special interests, terms of reference, and organization. Its royally chartered companies, highly regulated and subordin-ated to colonial aims, eventually failed as effective fur trade organizations. And the administrative and religious powers of the colony had great difficulty in managing the traders themselves, who commonly lacked commitment to the established order and to agricultural settlement.

The independent behaviour of many traders was a continuing subject for comment. Jean Talon wrote that they were men "without Christianity, without sacraments, without religion, without priests, without magistrates, sole masters of their own actions and of the application of their wills" (Diamond 1961: 10). Other observers noted the extent to which they adopted Indian ways when among the Hurons and other Indian groups around the Great Lakes. Some violated Indian conventions in their eagerness to cast off their own. And numbers found within the framework of Indian society a more ample freedom than that offered within the confines of their own colony—a phenomenon that was not uncommon among whites in early North America (Hallowell 1963; Axtell 1975). The youthfulness of these men may have exacerbated the tension; as of 1663, the average age of all males in the colony was 22.2 (Trudel 1973: 260).

Of much concern to the colonial authorities was the sexual freedom shown by the early traders when in the Indian country and by the Indians themselves. The Hurons, the most important trading partners of Champlain and his followers in the first half of the seventeenth century, considered premarital sexual relations and multiple companionships normal, and girls as well as men could initiate such relationships. Stable marriages were not considered to begin until children were produced (Trigger 1969: 66). The French mission-aries' efforts to change these patterns were hindered by the behaviour of their trading compatriots. The morality of Huron women would be improved, wrote the missionary Gabriel Sagard,

> if the French who went up with us did not, out of frenzied malice, tell them the opposite (of what we did), defaming and taxing wickedly the honor and modesty of the women and girls . . . so that they could continue their infamous and evil life with more liberty. Hence those who should have aided and served us in the education and conversion of

these peoples by their good examples were the very ones who hindered us and destroyed the good which we went to establish (Saunders 1939: 26).

When the priests tried to urge upon the Indians the virtues of chastity, the Indians were unimpressed and "pointedly asked why, if chastity were such a fine thing, all the French Christians did not practice it" (Eccles 1969: 52).

Such problems, and the fear that more settlers would be attracted from agricultural pursuits to a disorderly fur trade life, led the colonial authorities to promulgate laws and decrees to restrict fur trade activities (ibid., 104-5). A rule that all adult men enter into a Christian marriage relationship or suffer penalties was one solution offered against turbulence and immorality. In 1668, Colbert proposed to Intendant Talon that all "who may seem to have absolutely renounced marriage would be made to have additional burdens and be excluded from all honors; it would be well even to add some mark of infamy." Talon responded by forbidding bachelors "to hunt, fish, trade with the Indians, and even to enter the woods" (Diamond 1961: 10). Both officials also hoped to speed population growth by promoting marriage; and to this end, the French government later undertook to import large numbers of white women to New France. For a while too, Christian intermarriage with Indians was encouraged. In the mid 1600s, the Jesuits favoured intermarriage as an aid to converting the Indians and doubtless also as a means of coping with the six to one ratio of marriageable male to female colonists that still existed in 1663 (Trudel 1973: 261). While formerly Indian mates had been taken by Frenchmen eager to "become barbarians, and to render themselves exactly like them," such degrading unions would, they hoped, be replaced by "stable and perpetual" ones that would spread knowledge of God and his commandments (Saunders 1939: 29). Talon was amenable to Indian marriages, and although he was concerned that the fertility of Indian women was reduced by their custom of nursing their children longer than necessary, he felt that "this obstacle to the speedy building up of the colony can be overcome by a police regulation" (Diamond 1961: 9). By the early 1700s, however, through migration and internal growth, the colony had become better supplied with white women; and civil and religious authorities began to discourage Indian-white marriages (Eccles 1969: 91).

Efforts to promote marriage as a means of reducing disorder, spreading Christianity, and increasing the population may have had some of their desired effects within the boundaries of New France. But they scarcely slowed the stream of men to the fur trade country each year or modified their behaviour in that distant area. Indeed, even as the authorities tried to contain the traders by social legislation, their own economic measures encouraged more settlers to enter the fur trade. Beginning in 1675, beaver prices were fixed by ministerial decree, a measure that benefited mainly the traders; "the law of supply and demand was held in abeyance; and at the established prices profits were guaranteed, regardless of how much beaver was brought to the bureau of the company. Nothing could have been better contrived to bring about expansion in the fur trade, or of the numbers engaged in it." By 1680, over eight hundred coureurs de bois were off in the Indian country (although many of these would have gone on a seasonal basis only), and the intendant Duchesneau was complaining, "I have been unable to ascertain the exact number because everyone associated with them covers up for them" (Eccles 1969: 105, 110). The social mobility that fur trade wealth could confer offered another incentive. A man with financial resources could apply for a seigneury and for the privilege of attaching a *de* to his name, as did Médard Chouart, Sieur Des Groseilliers, as a consequence of his fur trade gains.

Fur traders might on occasion become seigneurs, but seigneurial families also became involved in the fur trade themselves. Young men of gentlemanly background, "not accustomed to hold the plow, the pick, or the ax . . . spend their lives in the woods, where there are no priests to restrain them nor fathers, nor governors to control them," wrote the Marquis de Denonville, governor general in the late 1680s. Some intendants themselves also profited from the fur trade, against orders, while illegal trading continued (Diamond 1961: 25, 31).

In 1681, governmental authorities attempted to place more direct controls on the trade. A licensing system was established, whereby up to twenty-five trading permits a year were to be granted, each entitling its holder to send one canoe with three men to trade with the Indians. No one would receive a permit two years in succession; while applicants waited their turns, they would be usefully employed in the colony (Eccles 1969: 113). Enforcement was continually a problem, however. At the end of the century, a glut on the European beaver markets caused the authorities to impose new regulations and attempt stronger measures against contraband traders; but as one officer sent to the post of Michilimackinac to implement the new rules soon learned, the traders on the Great Lakes and beyond were little inclined to co-operate. Writing to his superior in 1702, he complained, "It is very fine and Honourable for me, Monsieur, to be charged with your orders but it is also very vexatious to have only ink and paper as means to enforce them" (ibid., 128). Variously revised licensing systems persisted, however, as the major, if imperfect, means of controlling the fur traders.

The trade, after all, could not be eliminated; it remained of critical economic importance. In the first half of the eighteenth century, it was also becoming clear that the presence of French traders in the Northwest had a broader political significance—they maintained Indian-French alliances and a French presence in lands that might otherwise be taken over by British Hudson's Bay Company traders to the north and Anglo-American traders to the south. The French had lost any claim to Hudson Bay with the signing of the Treaty of Utrecht in 1713; but they still could, and did, make their influence felt in the areas around and beyond the Great Lakes.

The city of Montreal, upriver and inland from Quebec, became the main centre from which about a hundred canoes were licensed to depart each spring for the Great Lakes and beyond—eventually reaching the Lake Winnipeg and Saskatchewan River areas. This city had been founded in 1642 as a religious centre for seminaries and Indian mission activities. But the site was soon observed to be one of the best locations available for trading with the Indians upriver and inland. By the early 1700s it was a commercial centre whose citizens prospered from their ready access to networks of water transport. And by the 1740s, its important residents were members of what Eccles has called "a coterie of interrelated, wealthy families forming a military and commercial colonial aristocracy" (ibid., 147). The fur trade had become a respectable as well as essential occupation, dominating its own growing community.

This aristocracy was largely displaced from its high position after the British conquest of Canada. But a certain structural continuity carried over into the new regime. The British North Westers who took over the Montreal fur trade were also to form, with a few of the French, a similar coterie of wealthy, largely interrelated families. These too were linked in flexible partnerships built up by the kind of negotiation and compromise that Fox has found so typical of commercial societies engaged in long-range trade. And their enterprises grew and flourished on the basis of experience, skills, and labour contributed mainly by voyageur descendants of the early traders of New France.

THE BRITISH IN HUDSON BAY

The British Hudson Bay fur trade and its context were rather distinct in character. England had moved a considerable distance away from traditional monarchy toward parliamentary government by the mid-1600s and was emerging as "the communications center of an oceanic commercial society." Half of England lay within reach of navigable waterways, accessible to water-borne trade. And this nation, as an emerging commercial society, seemed to exhibit less of the dualism and opposition between commerce and territorial monarchy that appeared so prominent in seventeenth- and eighteenth-century France (Fox 1972: 83, 108). The Hudson's Bay Company, although founded as a royally privileged, colonial as well as trade venture, rose to maturity in a moderate monarchical context and was not driven toward failure by governmental overregulation or royal insistence that it fulfil the aims of colonization and territorial expansion that its original courtier-founders had in mind. The main political pressure placed on it came more from liberal entrepreneurs and parliamentarians seeking free trade and access to its resources than from a restrictive royal bureaucracy.

The Royal Charter granted to the Hudson's Bay Company in 1670 was a direct consequence of a successful voyage made to Hudson Bay in 1668 by the ship *Nonsuch* and sponsored by a small group of investors or "Adventurers" with close ties to the court of King Charles II. That voyage was in turn an indirect result of some events in New France a few years earlier. Médard Chouart, Sieur Des Groseilliers, had made an important contribution to the fur trade of New France by trading firsthand with the Cree. Living far to the north of the Great Lakes, they were the original suppliers of many of the furs coming to New France in that period. In doing so, he bypassed the regular conveyors of these furs from the Cree to the French—Indian middlemen who had been benefiting from their intermediary positions between these parties.

Groseillier's initial rewards for bringing prime furs directly from the Cree to Quebec in 1656 were considerable; his efforts were appreciated after the colony's economic losses from Indian wars and the Iroquois destruction of the Hurons in 1649. He became a captain of militia and a landowner. Two years later, he and his brother-in-law, Pierre Esprit Radisson, left on a trading expedition without the official sanction of the governor. On their return in 1660, with sixty Indian canoes and a large load of furs, they were punished with severe fines despite the fact that "they had brought a stream of life-giving furs to the colony; they had proved the wealth of the north and they had pioneered a new and efficient approach to it" (Rich 1961, I: 28).

This clash between coureurs de bois and colonial administrators in New France was to assume far more historic importance than other similar conflicts. Discouraged by their treatment, Groseilliers and Radisson decided to leave the colony and find another base from which to pursue their new-found trade. In 1664, they attracted the attention of a British commissioner in Boston who was delighted at their optimistic accounts of northern fur trade and exploration possibilities and intrigued by their talk of "a passage from the West Sea to the South Sea, and of a great trade of beaver in that passage." Thinking them "the best present he could possibly make His Majesty," he sent them home to the court of King Charles II (ibid., I: 24).

The commissioner's comments on the Northwest Passage and a "great trade of beaver" reflected British interest in Hudson Bay and northern Canada as arenas for trade and exploration rather than settlement. The British had hoped for many decades to find a route to China around North America; and Henry Hudson, Thomas Button, and others had kept these hopes alive with their discoveries of so large a bay of salt water north of the continent. Groseilliers and Radisson revived interest in this prospect and stirred high expectations for trade as well.

Before the Hudson's Bay Company was chartered in 1670, colonization emerged as a third motive for establishing a British enterprise in northern Canada. The two French fur traders were not responsible for this development; its origin lay with the royal courtiers and nobility who decided to finance Groseilliers' and Radisson's 1668 voyage from England to the Bay and who later became the shareholders listed in the charter. Several of these men, the First Earl of Shaftesbury, the Duke of Albemarle, and others, were involved in colonizing projects in Carolina, the Bahamas, and elsewhere; and it was natural that they should hope to extend these activities to Canada as well.

In sum, then, the shareholders' pursuit of three objectives stimulated the founding of the company and influenced the charter's phrasing of their goals and expectations. They hoped to discover "a new Passage into the South Sea," to find "some trade for Furrs Mineralls and other considerable commodityes," and to establish their chartered territories of Rupert's Land (later so named after Prince Rupert, first company governor) as "one of our Plantacions or Colonyes in America" (ibid., I: 31, 54).

For some years after the company's chartering, however, there was reason to doubt whether it would achieve any of these objectives, and even to question whether it would survive. Severe problems arose in those early decades—French threats and attacks by land and sea, the defections of the two independent-minded coureurs de bois who had at first encouraged and helped the new enterprise, and the paucity of early returns (no dividends were paid until 1684 and none from 1691 to 1717) (ibid., I: 59, 69, 99). It was only after the Treaty of Utrecht in 1713 that the company became assured of maintaining a consistent presence at any of the posts it had established in James Bay and on the west coast of Hudson Bay. And by that time, company objectives had narrowed to focus only upon trade. Exploration had become an auxiliary activity carried on to seek new fur sources and trading partners; colonization was no longer discussed, except by critics objecting to the company's slight use and non-improvement of the lands it monopolized and challenging its royal privilege in the parliamentary inquiries of 1690 and 1749.

This progressive narrowing or specialization of company goals and activities in the Bay requires some examination, since it had great significance in determining the nature of Hudson's Bay Company social patterns. The company's loss of interest in the Northwest Passage was predictable as further coastal explorations failed to reveal any viable westward route; and advocacy of the search for such a passage was eventually left to men who knew the Bay less well and who sought to invalidate the company's monopoly on the grounds that it had, by neglecting the search, not fulfilled the terms of its charter (Dobbs 1744, Ellis 1748, Great Britain 1749). A growing knowledge of the local geography doubtless also sped the decline of company interest in colonization, as it became clear that the arctic and subarctic climates of Hudson Bay were not suitable for agriculturally based settlement. However, human and social factors were also significant in causing this goal to fade away. The difficulties of defending Hudson Bay against the continuing dangers of military attack would effectively have depressed interest in colonizing activity for many years. But more importantly, the company's ownership had largely changed hands by 1680, and its management passed to men whose interests and objectives were different from those of its founders.

The proprietors of 1670 had included a prince, a duke, an earl, two lords, and nine knights. These courtier stockholders were interested in colonizing as well as trading into Hudson Bay, and their charter gave them the right to do both. But by the end of 1679 several of the most prominent owners—the Earl of Shaftesbury, the Earl of Arlington, Sir Peter Colleton, Sir George Carteret, and Sir John Kirke—had sold their company stock, discouraged by general economic and political uncertainties, by the company's failure to yield dividends, and by the difficulties facing any colonization scheme in Hudson Bay. Company leadership and control passed to a small group of City financiers led by James Hayes, who as private secretary to Prince Rupert, an expert at finance, and a man "thoroughly at home in the profitable border territory between private trade and government concession," had had growing involvement in the company since its beginning (Rich 1961, I: 33, 86–87). Hayes and the City men were willing to forego colonization ventures and concentrate their efforts on the building of a profitable trade. They and their successors in fact laid the basis of a long persisting company resistance to the planting in its territories of settlements that would, it was argued, be heavy financial burdens and strain the meagre subsistence resources of the north. As a result, no colonization was attempted until Lord Selkirk won company support for the settlement of Red River in 1811, and even that project was strictly circumscribed and regulated so that it would not interfere with the fur trade.

Although the company did not send colonists to Hudson Bay, there were three other options available for occupying its chartered lands; and these were pursued with varying degrees of seriousness and success in the early years. The first, and earliest one used, was a kind of "maritime transhumance" whereby ships sailed to the Bay each spring to trade with the Indians and departed before the early winter ice closed in. To vary the pattern, a post might be occupied for a winter at a time by a staff who would arrive one summer and depart the next, but still the traders did not venture far from the coast. In 1668 the first company traders, led by Groseilliers, built a small post, wintered there, and sailed back to England the following summer. In 1670–71, Groseilliers and Radisson and their ships again wintered in the Bay, returned to England for the following winter, and were evidently back at their post for the 1672–73 season, establishing the back-and-forth, dominantly maritime character of the company's fur trade venture in its early years (MacKay 1936: 26–27, 48).

But there were strong reasons to build up more extensive, if more costly, land-based establishments with resident staffs. As capital investments in the Bay increased, posts required maintenance and protection against the French and, occasionally, other interlopers. Additionally, trade results were better if company men were present the year round to maintain relationships with local Indian groups. And the best furs were to be had, not in summer when fur-bearing animals had shed their heavy pelts, but in late winter and early spring when their coats were still thick for protection against cold. Thus, while maritime transport of furs, trade goods, personnel, and information remained a critical activity linking Britain to Hudson Bay, the company found itself obliged to occupy the Bay coast in a more substantial way and to explore the feasibility of other modes of organizing and maintaining its presence there.

The next method, first briefly tried in the 1680s, might be described as "company familism," whereby servants' families were supported as dependents within the posts. Once employees, and particularly senior officers, were expected to serve and reside for lengthy periods in the Bay, questions about whether their families might join them began to arise. The economic implications of this issue were considerable; if wives, children, and personal servants of officers were allowed to travel to the Bay, the company would bear the costs of their passage and of supplying the residences, amenities, and educational, religious, medical, and other services that they might require. And in times of military danger, their safety would be an added concern.

Despite these problems, in the early 1680s the London directors were evidently persuaded in two instances to consider allowing officers' families to join them during their terms of service. The outcome of these cases and of the directors' subsequent policy decisions was far-reaching in its implications for later Hudson's Bay Company social life. In 1683 Henry Sergeant was sent out as governor of the posts in James Bay, accompanied by his wife, her companion Mrs. Maurice, and a maidservant, along with one John French, the first clergyman to serve with the company (Thorman 1966). From the committee minutes of 12 April 1684, it momentarily appeared that such domesticity might be allowed to spread; on that day Mrs. Hugh Verner was granted permission to join her husband at Rupert's River, on the understanding that he would pay her passage and "£12 a year for her Diett." Sixteen days later, however, this permission was withdrawn, the minutes noting only that "upon divers good Considerations it is the opinion of this Committee She Shall not goe this expedition nor any other woman" (Rich 1945, II: 224, 230). In 1687, Governor Sergeant and the "whole parcell of women appertaining to him" were recalled from the Bay, their scheduled return (with the clergyman) in 1686 having been delayed by French attack. The "considerations" leading the Committee to forbid other white women to follow Mrs. Sergeant are not enumerated in the minutes, but they certainly had to do with the perceived costs and inconvenience of their presence.

This prohibition became regular policy after 1684 and was consistent with the London committee's increasing emphasis on fur-trading rather than on colonization. Beginning in that year, not even its traders' own dependents were to be allowed into the fur trade country to settle as temporary residents. The rule barring white women from the Bay saved money, and it was readily enforceable. Since the company controlled passage rights on its ships, it was in a position to keep European women out of Hudson Bay for as long as it pleased, and it effectively did so until the first Red River settlers and families arrived at York Factory on their way to their new home. A known exception is the Orkney Islands girl who in 1806 successfully disguised herself as a labourer to follow her lover to Albany in James Bay. She maintained her disguise until she bore a child in December, 1807 (Bolus 1971).

The London committee's rejection of colonization, "maritime transhumance," and company familism left them with basically one alternative. This mode, which might be characterized as "military monasticism," involved posting men to the Bay without the encumbrances of families or settlers to carry out their duties in orderly, quasi-military fashion, in forts meant to be defensible against attack. Establishing a land base did not originate as one unified plan of action; rather it developed in part as a result of the committee's rejections of other possibilities, in part from the constraints imposed by economic and military problems, and in part out of some specific proposals and complaints sent home by officers in the Bay. From these various sources, celibacy and firm discipline, the conspicuous features of this organizational structure, grew to become long-term tenets of company policy.

In the same period in which the directors were confronted with deciding whether to allow officers' wives to the Bay, they were discovering that their married men's families, even remaining in Britain, could become burdensome. On several occasions, for example, the committee minutes of the early years recorded the petitions of wives asking that their husbands be sent home from the Bay (Rich 1945, I: xxxiv, 55, 170, 212). These requests were generally granted if the men themselves wished to return; the committee doubtless wished to avoid both the lowering of morale among Bay employees and the responsibility for aggravating their domestic problems. But their granting meant a higher turnover of employees and the expenditure of more energy on recruiting replacements. The families of married employees could also consume the committee's time in cases where a man's return was not solicited. On 23 November 1681 Elizabeth, wife of Richard Nalridge, applied for her husband's wages. The committee denied her request on grounds indicating one kind of marital problem that might arise during a husband's long absence. Thomas Wilkinson, lately returned from the Bay, reported "that she hath had several Bastards since her said Husband went away and that he did desire him [Wilkinson] when he came out of the Country to request the Committee to pay no more of his wages to his said wife" (ibid., I: 151).

It is not surprising, then, that the committee early expressed a preference for hiring bachelors, hoping to increase employees' efficiency and commitment and to reduce its costs and responsibilities. And if these bachelors did marry, it was hoped that they would marry late and not allow their domestic attachments to interfere with the company interest and their loyalty to it. In this respect, the company position resembled traditional British army attitudes that persisted into the twentieth century. Domesticity could wait; the first obligations of the subaltern were to his trade and his superiors. Later his commanding officer might grant permission to marry. "But even then the army and his regiment, that is to say his duty, must come before his family; and if he were suddenly required to leave his wife for a long time, then he might not complain and indeed would not have dreamed of doing so." Army celibacy was not to be identified, however, with army chastity; and the lack of the latter made the former easier to bear. The subaltern was expected to understand "that if he must have a woman then there were plenty available, and that it was the part of a gentleman to keep his assigned bachelor role in affairs, not to cause trouble and dislocation by premature nuptials" (Raven 1961: 154, 157).

The Hudson's Bay Company, in contrast, demanded both celibacy and chastity from its Bay employees, seeking to impose monastic as well as military order upon their lives there. Marriage might distract a man from his fur trade work and involve the company in undesirable complications and expense. But non-marital sexual relations in the Bay were viewed as at least equally threatening and disruptive to company business. The only women present in Hudson Bay were members of the Indian groups on whose goodwill and co-operation the trade depended. And these groups were as yet largely strangers who might be influenced by the French to menace the security of the posts. Even if they posed no military threat, the Indians might still reduce a post's provisions or embezzle its goods if they were allowed too much freedom on the premises or too much personal familiarity with its men. Added to these concerns, there was worry over the consequences of the "licentiousness" of the company's servants, so remote from their employers' control.

The London directors' safest course seemed therefore to be to enjoin formality and circumspection in trader-Indian interactions, to avoid offending the natives, to reduce the danger from any Indian-French collusion and infiltration, and to reduce other social and economic costs. In the 1680s, an important decade for policy-making, the committee sent out several orders on these matters. Governor John Nixon was instructed on 29 May 1680, "to endeavour to make such Contracts wth. the Indians in all places where you settle as may in future times ascertain to us all liberty of trade and commerce and a league of friendship and peaceable cohabitation" (Rich 1945, I: 73–74). For the British proprietors, this "friendship" was a matter of formal diplomacy and appropriate symbols (the "Union Flagg" and the dividing of "tallys of wood" in this case) and did not include the forming of close personal contacts between traders and Indians. The instructions to Governor Geyer at Port Nelson in June, 1688, included the order "that you trust noe Indians or Strangers within your Fort upon any pretense whatsoever"; and orders sent out in 1682 and 1683 warned more particularly that Indian women were not to be admitted within the posts (Rich 1957: 102, 145). Correspondingly, company men were not supposed to venture outside the posts except to perform specific, authorized duties such as gathering supplies of fuel and hunting local game to augment provisions.

As a mode for the company's occupation of Hudson Bay, such monastic insularity and discipline turned out to be little more practicable than the colonialist and other options. The company was overly optimistic about the degree of regulation that could be imposed from London. Although it could effectively dictate the hiring of bachelors, forbid women to travel to the Bay, and enforce or encourage celibacy at home, the behaviour of its men was much less readily controlled once they arrived in Hudson Bay; and the ideals of monastic discipline and sexual abstinence were soon shown to be difficult to realize. In the early 1700s, for example, the London committee was obliged to censure the men at Albany in James Bay not only for their "Excessive Hard Drinking" but for their involvements with Indian women; and the Albany situation stimulated the sending forth of a general order to "hinder as much as Possible the detestable Sin of Whoring, which we are informed is practised in the Factory [Albany] notwithstanding what we have so often ordered" (Rich 1961, I: 496). The phrasing used here is interesting; the flat prohibitions of the 1680s have yielded to the less sanguine "hinder as much as possible," as though later committee members were prepared, like the British army, to recognize that total abstinence was unlikely. They may also have realized by then that the Indians were probably even less supportive of the ideal of abstinence than were their own men.

Company hopes for establishing military order were also subjected to compromise in the face of the environmental, human, and social conditions of Hudson Bay. The rise and decline of company hopes of building up military organization and discipline with their concomitant physical structures—forts and fortifications—in the Bay, provide ample illustration of the varied obstacles facing the concern. The development of the fur trade presented unfamiliar challenges to the company directors. The problem of distance was aggravated because few men with actual fur trade experience ever served on the committee; trader James Knight's election to it as a substantial stockholder in the early 1700s (Davies 1965: 400–401) was an unusual occurrence. The committee naturally tended to fill the resulting information vacuum with the incomplete, commonly outdated, and sometimes biased data conveyed to them by the ships returning annually from the Bay.

The isolation of "Their Honors" in London and their lack of firsthand knowledge were continuing subjects of concern to the men they sent out to conduct the trade. In 1682, John Nixon, the second governor appointed to the Bay, warned in the earliest surviving account of the trade sent to London that, "It is not possible for your Honnours to knowe in England by guess what is most convenient for your intrest, as it is for me to knowe heere by experiance, by this yow may see in parte what is the cause that your concerns have thriven no better." He also complained that returning sea captains and other employees could, because they were able to meet directly with the committee, wield considerable power as carriers and controllers of information. Anxious over the misrepresentations of his performance that might be given them by a company ship captain with whom he had clashed and who had sailed home while he remained in the Bay, Nixon told the committee:

> If I doe all things well he will rob me of the credit of it, and if badly I am sure to have all the disgrace heaped upon my back, for this advantage all my adversaries have above me, that they come first home, who by fraud and flatterie, can have their tale first tould, and they can be heard by yow though it proves to your loss (Rich 1945, I: 278, 275).

Although Nixon would himself later return to London to correct the imbalances and distortions that he perceived in the information presented to the committee, his views were partisan too. And particularly in the early decades, officers' knowledge might be insufficient to provide reliable guidance for committee actions. Nixon and his colleagues of the period generally served in the Bay for relatively short terms. Their knowledge of the trade, Indians, and country therefore could not have been as extensive as that possessed by later eighteenth-century governors and officers who, in most cases, reached their high positions only after long service. While Nixon made several perceptive observations and recommendations to the committee in his report and could, as he said, write from "experiance" rather than "guess," his governorship had lasted only three years and ended the following year.

As a consequence, compared to later officers, even Nixon had a relatively limited knowledge of the novel and in many ways unique conditions in the Hudson Bay fur trade. But on the other hand, both he and the committee shared at least a secondhand familiarity with the conduct of other European enterprises abroad. They were therefore drawn to introduce into the Bay strategies founded on their interpretations of events elsewhere as well as on their acquaintance with the Bay itself. A tendency to extrapolate in this manner is clearly present in Nixon's 1682 report; his plans and proposals for the trade are frequently buttressed with examples drawn from other parts of the world. In urging the company to build up its military strength and to provide him with the needed tools and workmen, for example, he spoke not of French attack from Quebec but of the Amboyna Massacre of 1623, in the East Indies: "I have been in the East-india and heard from the natives themselves how the English lost Ambonia, which is now the best flower in the hollanders gardine, which might have been ours if wee had had the care and foresight which we aught." And while expressing his hopes for the "prosperity of the Northwest," he cited other examples of the "loss and dishonoure of oure natione":

one of loosing St. christophers [St. Kitts in the West Indies] to the Frensh, the other for loosing New-york to the dutch. besides the sur-prysing of many small tradeing forts in New-England, by the Indians there, those that shoulde have kept them being ignorant marchants, haveing their forts unprovided, and evrything out of order, the men undissiplined, and the Indians seemingly their friends, and when they saw their opportunity surprised their factories (Rich 1945, I: 252–53, 284–85).

Although there is no record that he ever served the East India Company, Nixon also showed some familiarity with it. And while he does not mention them, conditions in Carolina may also have influenced his thinking; he was apparently a magistrate there in the 1670s and had entered the Hudson's Bay Company on the suggestion of two of its founders who were also Carolina proprietors, the Earl of Shaftesbury and Sir Peter Colleton (Davies 1966).

To compensate, then, for his relatively limited experience in the fur trade, Nixon called upon his knowledge of enterprises in other areas and slanted his solutions to its problems accordingly. Particularly impressed by the military problems that beset previous British commercial ventures, Nixon saw the solutions to his Bay difficulties mainly in military terms and urged the establishment of stronger martial authority not only for defence but also for the better internal control of his men, whose indiscipline dismayed him:

My commission is to governe after the lawes of England, but which of them, military or sivill, and if I were capable of both I have not power to put them in practice . . . if their be not some lawes put in practice heare, there will be unavoydably some notable dissaster befall the country, and I am sure no government at present can stand with the constitution of this country, but military and no law but martiall (Rich 1945, I: 272).

Military order was also, Nixon felt, an appropriate pattern for the organization of work in the posts. His proposed complement of twenty-three men for Albany included (besides a factor, a surgeon, two tailors, an armourer, gunner, and calker), "one man that hath been ane ould souldier, whose office shall be to keep the men in order, and traine them up in marshall dissipline, and keep them to their worke, and to watch and ward, In the time of trading when wee have a greate many Indians about the factorie" (ibid., 250).

The London committee seemed to agree with these principles and for several decades tried to build up its posts, physically and organizationally, as effective military structures. Until well into the eighteenth century, posts on the Bay shores were still conceived of as forts as well as trading places. However, those who sought to organize them along military lines faced considerable obstacles—as Joseph Robson, a mason hired to construct the stone fort at Churchill, learned when he was obliged to work under the command of Governor Richard Norton. Norton had no notion of how to construct a fortification strong enough to withstand bombardment; and his incompetence provoked a frustrated Robson to sail home in 1736, where later he wrote his *Account of Six Years' Residence in Hudson's Bay* (1752). Both men's descriptions agree that Norton directed the fort to be built with rough laying of stone in clay instead of mortar, with ramparts filled with earth and gravel. It disintegrated by itself from the effects of frost and erosion, without the help of attack. Although some of Robson's criticisms proved unfounded, his contempt for Norton's military qualifications and for his fort as a military bastion was apparently deserved.

Broadly, the problems in modelling fur trade establishments on a military pattern sprang from the fact that company personnel were not trained in military arts or architecture and were not readily assimilated to military forms and discipline. Officers such as Richard Norton might be skilled at Indian languages and arctic travel, but, as K.G. Davies (1965: lx) said of Norton, they were often out of their depth as commanders or builders of forts. In both their backgrounds and primary occupations, fur traders were civilians. In addition, it was difficult to maintain the posts in a perpetual state of military preparedness when, with occasional exceptions, long decades passed without attacks. Everyday life centred on trading, maintaining and provisioning the posts, keeping accounts, and enduring long winters. Governor Nixon and the London committee might try to consolidate the company's position by drawing upon the military-style governance and control that they had seen to be relevant elsewhere; but these were not necessarily applicable or workable in the context of Hudson Bay. And the infrequent communications between London and the Bay gave the company's servants a degree of autonomy inconsistent with maintaining a tight military chain of command.

In combination with other factors, this semi-autonomy allowed traders to devise some of their own ways of adapting to local conditions. While these employees remained "servants" of "Their Honors" in London, they also shared the informal daily routine of a life that was often uncomfortable, difficult, and even dangerous to a degree that they felt was not well understood in London. It was to be expected, then, that London's control over their attitudes and actions would be imperfect and that the geographical gulf between London and the Bay would become a social one as well, as the traders formed common values and ways of coping with fur trade life.

This gulf became conspicuous first in the realm of opinion, when Governor Nixon sent home his blunt, critical assessments of the state of affairs in the Bay and of the committee's inadequacies in handling its problems there. Later, the committee's ignorance of fur trade working conditions was often to be complained of still more forthrightly. In 1717–18, James Knight and his men were engaged in founding Fort Prince of Wales on the northwest coast of Hudson Bay in most difficult circumstances, on the spot where numerous members of a Danish exploring expedition had died a century before. Recalling that he had heard several committee members say that they had "a good mind to Come over here," Knight wished that

> They and all the rest of the Committee had took their summer campaign [country trip] here. Then I believe they would set a little more Value upon mens Lives & their goods not to expose all to this Hazard & wee to such hardships. Were they but here to see the Sculls & bones of Men as Lyes Scatter'd . . . It would put them into a feavor to think how they should Secure Themselves (MacKay 1936: 72).

Some ninety years later, William Auld, an officer with twenty-one years' experience, effectively reiterated the traders' concern over the committee's limited perspectives. His 1811 report from York Factory strongly emphasized that local conditions should not be conceived of in externally derived terms. Discussing the length of time needed to train boatmen, for example, Auld informed the London committee that their perceptions of the matter were too much guided by images of British life:

> Your rivers never freeze ours are only a short time open were our people perpetually during *three* full years constantly working among the Rapids no question but they would in that time become expert and able *Voyageurs* but they may fairly be said not to spend more than 1 month among the Rapids exclusively the rest of the summer they are in smooth Current or tranquil streams and Lakes . . . I intreat you to dismiss from your mind the spancaly-dressed wherry-man with his plush breeches and

his silver badge nor conceive the *descent* of the solitary bargeman at London Bridge with that through the shallow horrors of rocky chasms as at all *synonimous.* Here the slightest mistake is big with fate allow a wrong impulse and the vessel is overwhelmed in an instant (HBCA, A. 11/118, ff. 22–23).

During the eighteenth century, while their sense of distance from London sharpened, the traders began to acquire distinctive attitudes toward life at the posts. After the peace treaty between England and France in 1713, these men were more likely to remain in the Bay for considerable periods without being captured or removed. As their occupation became more permanent and as they lost need for or interest in military preparedness, their posts came to be seen less as forts and more as places of business and residence—in short, as "house and home."

Certain developments in place-names help to chart the course of this change. Early company posts were typically known as "Forts," according with their founders' military preoccupations. During the eighteenth century, however, the gradual demilitarization of the posts was reflected in the different names assigned to them. New posts built in that century and later were commonly called "Houses," although some "Forts" were still built in westerly areas where Indian attacks or aggressive trade rivalry might occur (Fort Chipewyan, Fort Vancouver). And beginning in the 1700s Bay establishments such as York and Moose generally became known as "Factories" rather than "Forts"; their older designation eventually disappeared.

The expanding usage of "House" and "Factory" corresponded with the settling of fur traders into a land-based civilian business routine in the Bay. As in other areas reached by British trade, "factories" were the places where "factors" traded with the natives, while "House" was at first a designation used mainly for lesser centres. The earliest houses such as Henley House were subsidiary outposts of the larger fort-factory establishments on the Bay, but in later years many major inland posts went by that name.

Two other terms found in traders' vocabularies from an early period also developed distinctive fur trade meanings. Eighteenth-century post officers typically described the cleared and open area around a fort or factory as "the plantation"; here the Indians lived while they were trading, hunting locally, or depending on post supplies in times of hardship. In this area too, traders might plant small gardens of hardy vegetables such as collards and turnips (although such gardens were also sometimes inside the post enclosure). The term turns up most frequently in the context of recording how many Indians were "Tenting upon the Plantation" at particular times (e.g., HBCA, B. 239/a/13–23). When company critics used the term, however, in the 1749 parliamentary inquiry, they clearly had in mind the substantial agricultural developments achieved in other colonial areas. The company, they charged, had not tried "to settle any Plantation or Colony, in any Part of that vast Tract of Land" and had "not improved or cultivated above 4 Acres of Land about all their Factories" (Great Britain 1749: 26, 10).

By the early eighteenth century, company men were also making idiosyncratic use of another British place term. The Cree who tented on the "plantations," helped to provision the posts, and came to rely on British assistance when food was scarce, early became known as the "Home" or "Homeguard" Indians—distinguished from more distant and less frequently seen "Upland" groups. The term describes well the Indians' treatment of a post as a "home base," a permanent place of resort, and in many cases, a temporary residence. The York Fort journal for 1730–31 demonstrates some uses that the York Home Indians made of this post as a focus for their activities and not simply a place for trade. On 4 April 1730, when word came to the post that "Deer" (doubtless caribou—Davies 1965: xviiin) had been sighted inland, three Indians and their wives immediately left for the hunt, "leaving their Children at the Factory." On 30 January 1731, during an arduous winter, an "Antient Woman and Widow-Daughter, with 4 small Children, came here from the North River, almost famished, the Uncle of the said Children sent them to ye Factory, by reason he designs farther up in the Countrey to Look for Deer and Beaver." On 23 March, there were "68 Indians Young and Old" on the plantation; "it has been a very hard winter with all the home Indians that has come here as yet." By 17 April "122 Indians . . . whose daily maintenance is from the Factory" were awaiting the beginning of the great spring goose hunt (HBCA, B. 239/a/12, f. 18; /13, ff. 13, 17, 20). Other journal entries repeat these themes. The post was a place to leave the young, weak, sick, or elderly while more active Indians pursued their hunts and travels; and in time of danger, it could provide relief with European staples such as oatmeal.

If the post and "plantation" served as home base for the Indians in the area, the post itself served even more as "home" to the traders. It became a focus for domestic life as well as a place of work. And in numbers of cases it became a final resting place; deaths from sickness, accident, and exposure were not infrequent, and each major post came to have its cemetery. Accordingly, the posts became social entities rather different in character from what the London committee had deliberately planned in its early efforts at policy-making and problem-solving. The committee's rules still imposed broad constraints, controlling the posts' organizational structures and the selection of their personnel. But the traders themselves found means of synthesizing and reconciling these constraints with the experiential models that they imported from Britain and with their local circumstances.

They did not do so, however, by the kinds of conscious planning or goal-oriented business decisions recorded by the London committee as it deliberated over various formal organizational options in the Bay. In their case, the operative process more closely resembled institutionalization in Barth's sense—the "complex aggregation of numerous micro-events of behaviour" (1973: 5) over a considerable period. Such a process is difficult to reconstruct; it was never explicitly set forth in committee minutes or post journals as were formal decisions and policies. But much evidence, early and late, from the fur trade and from Britain, suggests that the Bay posts developed semi-independently over the years following an older British organizational form that was neither military nor monastic.

The company post took shape as a large-scale "household," a unit of social and economic organization basic to seventeenth-century English society (Laslett 1965). As an organizational mode well known to both traders and company directors of the late 1600s and early 1700s, the household provided an implicit model for structuring Bay posts and, as such, could readily have been imported to the Bay by traders arriving not as social planners but simply as carriers of British social patterns and values. The parallels between British household organization of the 1600s and the social organization of company posts in Hudson Bay are of great interest; and it seems likely that certain internal hierarchical, marital, and familial arrangements that evolved in the Bay posts were derived from established patterns in British domestic economic life. These parallels, briefly stated here, have been independently remarked by historian John E. Foster (1975). Their relevance to Hudson Bay social life will emerge in greater detail in the following chapters.

In the 1600s, England consisted of a series of status groups; classes in the sense of "groups of people which act in championship of their conflicting aims" or "people banded together in the exercise of collective power, political and economic" were not yet prominent. Working men, rather than being aggregated into large industrial work places, were commonly integrated into small households that were both familial units (centred on the householder and his immediate family but also including apprentices and servants as "family" members) and units of work and production. Many non-householders were therefore "held apart from each other by the social system. Many or most of them were subsumed . . . within the personalities of their fathers and masters" (Laslett 1965: 22, 51–52). The head of the people grouped in a household was "father to some of its members and in place of father to the rest," as well as its entrepreneur, employer, or manager; his domestic and economic functions were not sharply distinguished. He was married, his wife being a subordinate partner in the activities of the household. Servants, apprentices, and offspring were generally unmarried until they could provide for a family by assuming headship of a comparable unit. Upon the death of the head, the household might survive as a viable economic unit if there were a son to succeed him. Or "an apprentice might fulfil the final function of apprenticehood, substitute sonship, that is to say, and marry his master's daughter or even his widow" (ibid., 2, 8).

There are intriguing resemblances between these units and the Hudson's Bay Company posts that slowly spread along the coasts and interior waterways of the Northwest. Clearly the company did not plan these posts to be households, for there were to be no women or children. But other elements of British household organization, notably its closely integrated vertical social relationships, condensed as they were into the apprenticeship system, found their way to Rupert's Land. The scale of fur trade social units also bears comparison with older British household patterns. Three or four major Bay posts, holding at times forty or fifty servants, were comparable in size and standing to British noble households; their leading officers were the aristocracy of the fur trade. Other posts, inland houses with their masters and a few servants, were on a scale with ordinary English households that usually numbered a dozen or so persons at the most.

The apparent parallels between household and post with regard to those members who married and those who did not are also interesting. Households were commonly headed by one married couple, while subordinate and junior members remained unmarried. Perhaps significantly, much of the eighteenth-century evidence on Hudson Bay fur trade domesticity centres on the marital or quasi-marital relations of the governors, chief factors, or masters of posts—those of Governor Sergeant who tried the experiment of bringing a British wife to the Bay, Governor James Isham and his "woman" in the 1740s, the masters of inland posts as characterized by Philip Turnor, and others. Andrew Graham confirmed in his *Observations,* that by the 1760s the heads of posts held privileged positions in this regard, claiming for themselves a broader right to constant female companionship than they would grant to their fellow officers:

> The Factors for the most part at proper times allows an officer to take in an Indian lady to his apartment, but by no means or on any account whatever to harbour her within the Fort at night. However the Factors keep a bedfellow within the Fort at all times and have carried several of their children home [to England] as before observed (Williams 1969: 248).

It is likely, of course, that heads of posts were under greater Indian pressure to cement trade alliances by accepting offers of women than were the lower ranks of men, since they had greater control over the trade and access to trade goods. And some bias is to be expected in the historical record, more data generally being preserved regarding the highest ranking officers. Nonetheless, it is

possible that the pattern described by Graham may also have seemed acceptable to traders in the Bay because it in some ways mirrored a familiar pattern
where bachelorhood and dependency (along with a notable degree of sexual
abstinence) were the rule until a man could assume leadership of an economically productive household, however small (Laslett 1965: 130, 90).

"The political and social organization brought by a Western country to the
territories it has colonized, its methods of imposing and maintaining that
organization . . . all of these reflect closely, as in an enlarged sketch, its own
patterns of social organization" (Crozier 1964: 263-64). The growth of fur
trade domesticity in Hudson Bay was not, of course, the result of deliberate
policy; in fact, it spread and flourished despite the efforts of a non-colonial
company to suppress it. But it may be that the traders brought to Hudson Bay
some powerful and basic British domestic organizational patterns that were
then reinforced because they offered means of coping with post life. The
resemblances between older British social forms and those of the Hudson Bay
posts are strong enough, however, to suggest some continuity between the
two. It is surely true that while traders gained a certain social autonomy in
Rupert's Land, it was narrowed not only by Indian-imposed restraints,
company rules at-a-distance, and the exigencies of fur trade life, but also, in all
probability, by their being subject to the hold of British organizational models
they brought with them unawares, as part of their cultural baggage.

2

Company Men with a Difference:
The London and Montreal
Britishers

The Hudson's Bay Company and the British fur trade partnerships of post-conquest Montreal differed as strikingly in their personnel selection patterns as they did in their origins and early organizational structures. Correspondingly, the social and ethnic backgrounds of the traders chosen to join these concerns were also distinctive. And their leading officers typically followed rather different paths from Britain to the Indian country and from lower to higher rank. These contrasting hiring and promotion practices were important determinants of the domestic relations that developed in the Hudson's Bay and Canadian fur trades between the 1760s and 1821.

COMPANY MEN IN HUDSON BAY

The Hudson's Bay Company first began to establish regular recruiting procedures and personnel and wage policies in the early 1680s. In the 1670s its Bay operations had been small-scale and tenuous; it had simply taken its servants "as it could find them," with "no system for training up its own men for the peculiar tasks which they would have to perform" (Rich 1961, I: 295). The inadequacy of this approach was soon evident. When Groseilliers and Radisson absconded to the French in the mid-1670s, the company had no officers of comparable experience to replace them. There was no consistent wage policy, and conspicuous inequities caused complaints and discipline problems among the men. Governor Nixon noted in his 1682 report the "one great cause of the mens discontent . . . they see other men have 20 or 30 *lib*. pr. ann., who can doe no more for it than one of 6 pound pr. annum," and added, "I can not blame them much considdering how confusedly they have been served." Not only were the underpaid men discontented; the overpaid ones were unruly. Nixon would gladly have sent the latter home for "their wages would serve double their number," but having no replacements for them, he found that they exploited the security of their positions; "I must humor them lyke childrine, which makes them still the more insolent" (Rich 1945, I: 256).

The urban backgrounds of many of these early employees also contributed to difficulties with them. The London committee, hiring men as they were needed, naturally tended to draw upon inhabitants of the London area. The early ships' captains, William Bond and Nehemiah Walker, and presumably Walker's two brothers, who also served the company for short periods, were, for example, residents of the Thameside parish of Rotherhithe, and it does not appear that the company went much farther afield for its other early recruits. But such city men as Bond and Walker had access to other employment if they became displeased with company terms and were given to suing for higher salaries if they stayed in its service.

Londoners could not only exploit their city's competitive labour market; they also often brought to the Bay its licentiousness and liquor problems, as John Nixon warned. His dismay at their immorality and indiscipline soon led him to urge the committee to change its hiring practices and to request "Some country lads, that are not acquainted, with strong d[r]ink, that will woorke hard, and faire hard, and are not debauched with the voluptwousness of the city." His advice was to "send over yearely 5 lykly country lads of 17 or 18 years of age, and let their tyms be 7 years, so that before their tymes be out they will be lusty younge-men, and fit for your service both at sea, and land, and at small wages." He further urged that hiring Scots along with country appren-tices would help "to brydle all mutanous, licentious, and factious spirits"; and he recommended to the committee a man who could "informe youre honoures how yow may get men out of Scotland."

> if England can not furnish you with men, Scotland can, for that countrie is a hard country to live in, and poore-mens wages is cheap, they are hardy people both to endure hunger, and could, and are subject to obedience, and I am sure that they will serve for 6 pound pr. yeare, and be better content, with their dyet than Englishmen (Rich 1945, I: 251, 280, 277).

Nixon himself may have been a Scot; his background is not known. In any case, his recommendations appear to have influenced subsequent practices. Although Londoners never completely disappeared, they came to be outnumbered by Scots and apprenticed "country lads" hired for terms of several years. Certainly his suggestions were well-timed; by the early 1680s the committee was beginning to appreciate the need for officers and men willing to serve long terms in the Bay.

Within two years of Nixon's report, the first signs of an apprenticeship system began to appear. In 1684, ten apprentices were listed for Bay service, including Henry Kelsey, later a distinguished explorer and trader; and thereafter, the employees at Hudson Bay posts regularly included numbers of apprentices.

Many apprentices began service even younger than Nixon had proposed. It was not unusual to indenture fourteen-year-olds for seven-year terms, and some, such as John Hinson and Richard Norton, were younger still (Davies 1965: 87n, 376n). Many of these boys became the expert linguists and canoemen that the company needed to travel inland and conduct the trade. Since so large a portion of their upbringing and education occurred in the country, they more easily adapted to that life than did older tradesmen trained in Britain. Their commitment to a fur trade career was also doubtless facilitated in many cases by the relative weakness of their ties to Britain. Many were poor or marginal members of British society even before they were indentured. Some were "parish boys." John Hinson, for example, was born in Woodford, Essex, "in Wm. Thomson's Barn May 7th 1699," and bound by the churchwardens of that place as apprentice to the company beginning in 1708. In that decade Joseph Adams from Woodford, another charity ward, began his company career in the same way (Davies 1965: 76n, 33n).

In 1689 other apprentices began to be drawn from Christ's Hospital (the "Blue-coat School"), a charitable institution especially for children lacking one or both parents. Christ's Hospital boys were usually older and better educated than parish boys. In 1722 when former parish boy Joseph Adams was in his early twenties, the London committee was telling him that "wee would have you . . . at your leisure time, learn to write, whereby you may be capable of Preferment (Davies 1965: 79n). In contrast, Samuel Hopkins, "A Blew Coat Boy," began his seven-year apprenticeship in 1715 by keeping accounts at Albany Fort. The committee's hopes for the quality of service that Hopkins and his like might furnish, compared to that of other types of employees, are reflected in the instructions sent out with him to James Knight:

We would have you be very kind to him, & give him all the Encouragemt. you Can, And if you are desirous of such another, pray inform us, & we will take care to send you one, because there are but few but what are Wilde that offer their Service to us for that Employment.

Replying in September 1716, Knight encouraged the sending of more "Hospital boys," saying "It will do very well to have one at each factory that writes well and is brought up to accounts" (Davies 1965: 63,63n). Later in the century, the company also began to draw apprentices from the Grey Coat Hospital at Westminster, choosing boys trained in surveying and mapping to help its inland exploration and trade efforts in the face of Canadian competition.

In sum, apprentices were attractive candidates for Bay employment. Because their initial commitment was commonly for seven years, in contrast to the three-year terms of many other early employees, they formed a nucleus of experienced men. Being unmarried and usually without strong family ties, they were free of domestic responsibilities in Britain. In addition, many apprentices themselves found that their best chances for economic security and social mobility lay in a career within the company. By the time he made his will in 1737, Joseph Adams was literate and described himself as "Gentleman lately returned from Albany Fort in Hudson's Bay"; he had held some important positions there, succeeding, for example, to the charge of Albany when its governor died in 1730 (ibid., 152, 233n). And numerous other apprentices and "writers" (apprentice clerks) rose to high positions as the company expanded its operations and found that its best officers were those men already accustomed to life in Hudson Bay.

Even before the first ten apprentices were hired, there were signs that the London committee was beginning to share Nixon's high opinion of Scotsmen as recruits. Although a few Scots had early been listed as seamen in company books, the first hint of a deliberate effort to secure their services appeared in the minutes of a meeting on 16 March 1683. On that date four of the seven men taken into the service were Scots. One of them, a man "bred up at sea," was hired for five years at six pounds a year. Two were Edinburgh tradesmen hired for four years at starting wages of six pounds with annual increments of two pounds. The fourth was a cooper from Leith hired for four years at fifteen pounds annually (Rich 1945, II: 86). In some instances at least, Nixon's prediction that Scots could be hired at six pounds a year was being substantiated. Further efforts to recruit Scotsmen were stimulated in part by manpower shortages felt in England as a result of French-British conflict in the 1690s. In 1691 some of the Scots recruited for land service in the Bay were nearly lost to Navy press gangs on their arrival in London. In 1693 the company was again seeking about a dozen able Scotsmen aged between twenty and thirty years (Rich 1957: xxii). Some of these early Scots who accepted low-paying contracts eventually profited well in the service. John Fullartine, one of the Edinburgh tradesmen hired in 1683, was appointed a "Governor & Cheife Commandr." in 1701 at a salary ranging up to £300 a year. Later, after leaving Bay service, he became a stockholder and committee member. William Stuart carried out significant exploration toward the Great

Slave Lake area far inland from the Bay and was second in command at York in 1717; he died there in 1719 (Davies 1965: 361–68; 413–17).

The beginning of the eighteenth century marked a new phase in the enlistment of Scots. By this time, company ships had formed a habit of stopping at Stromness in the Orkney Islands for last-minute supplies before starting their transatlantic crossings; and because of labour shortages in England, the islands' human resources soon attracted the company's attention. Isolated and poor, Orcadians, with their Norse inheritances, were accustomed to a harsh environment and familiar with boat-building and other water-related occupations. Although their main eighteenth-century activities were reported to be agriculture and sheep-raising, many found work in the British Navy and the Greenland and Iceland fisheries (Scott 1912–13: 360–61; Rich and Johnson 1951, II: xlviii); and they readily accepted employment in the Hudson's Bay Company. In 1702, the company's ship left London with orders to hire ten or twelve young Orkneymen when it stopped there (Rich 1961, I: 377); and this method of engaging men became an established custom, carried on with the help of an agent in Stromness. By the year 1799, over three-quarters of the 529 servants in the Bay were from the Orkneys (Rich and Johnson 1951, I: xxxvii, lxxiv).

Orkneymen found advantages in company service. Men who entered as low-paid labourers might leave after twenty years wealthy by Orkney standards, and able to buy their own farms (ibid., II: xlviii; J. Nicks 1979); Isaac Cowie, a trader with personal knowledge of the Orkneys in the mid-nineteenth century, wrote that some retired employees had been residing in comparative opulence on the island of Harray where they were known as the "Peerie (Little) lairds o' Harray" (1913: 62–63). The broader contribution of company-derived income to the islands' economy was also noted by an earlier writer who observed that the £2,000 to £3,000 paid out by the company agent in Stromness in 1795–98 "no doubt greatly tends to quicken the little trade of this place" (Rich and Johnson 1951, II: lvii).

The company in its turn found several advantages in hiring Orkneymen. Not only would they accept lower wages and a lower living standard than Londoners; they also apparently shared Scotland's relatively high literacy rates. Many of these men were able to handle simple fur trade accounts and record-keeping. When the company expanded from 181 servants in 1772 to nearly three times that number in the 1790s to meet North West Company competition, it could remedy the resulting shortages of qualified English officers by promoting certain experienced Orkney labourers to higher ranks.

The moral qualities of the Orkneymen were also attractive. In 1727 Joseph Myatt, in charge at Albany, expressed his pleasure that the company had hired some Orkneymen, because they would not bring their own brandy into the country like the London men, who were "so well acquainted with the ways and debaucheries of the town that I even despair ever of reclaiming them, for there is not one labouring man that came over the last year but what are sots to a man" (Davies 1965: 123). Edward Umfreville, onetime company employee, commented in 1790 on other distinctive traits of Orkney morality in the Bay:

> a close prudent quiet people, strictly faithful to their employers, and sordidly avaricious. When these people are scattered . . . among the Indians . . . their behaviour is conducted with so much propriety, as not only to make themselves esteemed by the natives, and to procure their protection, but they also employ their time in endeavouring to enrich themselves, and their principals, by their diligence and unwearied assiduity (Wallace 1954: 109–10).

As apprentices, Orkneymen, and other Scots (mostly Lowlanders like the two Edinburgh tradesmen hired in 1683) began to join Londoners in the service, the Hudson Bay posts were increasing in size and becoming centres of a wide variety of activities. Now they needed not only commanding officers, factors, ships' crews, armourers, and other men for trade and defence, but also specialists in construction, maintenance, and subsistence activities. When new servants reached the Bay, they found themselves in communities of at most four or five dozen men, many of them engaged in familiar trades. But while the social and occupational hierarchies of the posts were recognizable, employees had opportunities to learn "country" skills, rise to higher ranks, and in sum, pursue careers considerably different from those open to them in Britain.

The servants' lists of such large posts as York Factory indicate the diversity of occupations that came to be represented in the Bay. In the ranks of the officers (commonly including the chief factor, second, masters of inland houses, and ship's captain when present), there was generally a surgeon whose medical skills served the needs of both traders and Home Indians. There might also be a steward, tailor, cooper, mason, joiner or carpenter, and smith. Several positions reflected the importance of water-related activities—among them shipwright, sloop or craft master, boat builder, canoeman (with sub-categories of steersman, bowsman, and middleman according to level of skill), and fisherman. At York in 1786 there were listed fifty-one servants; their occupations included chief, surgeon, sloop master, writer, linguist, pateroon (duties unclear), carpenter, bricklayer, armourer, carpenter's assistant, hunter and labourer, sailor, and simply (in fourteen cases) labourer (HBCA, B. 239/f/1, ff. 15–16).

The wages of these men varied according to their skills, experience, seniority, and rank. In the 1780s young labourers were still beginning service at £6 a year, the wage that John Nixon had recommended for Scots a century before, reflecting in part an absence of inflation during that period. Some servants eventually advanced considerably, particularly if they took up a trade or acquired country skills that were seasonally useful. At York in the 1780s, men in the joint position of "canoeman and laborer" were receiving £16 to £20 annually. A skilled bowsman might become a steersman, having the charge of his vessel and the responsibility for safe delivery of its goods. Bowsmen generally went "a few years in that capacity before they attempt[ed] to steer a Canoe," and steersmen's wages were correspondingly higher. Tradesmen too might become canoeists or take on two trades; one man at York was a "Bowsman and Taylor" and another was listed as both carpenter and shipwright (ibid., ff. 13–14, 25, 43).

As inland posts were established to reach farther into the Indian country to meet Canadian competition, active labourers and canoemen with country experience were strong candidates to be masters of the new houses, even if they lacked the usual literacy of officers. Sometimes, in fact, a servant might be offered more upward mobility than he wished to accept. When Joseph Colen reported to London from York in June, 1794, that one Edward Wishart had declined to serve as summer master at Sepawish House, he commented with some sympathy on the matter:

> he cannot write his own name and being obliged to apply to the men to read his Letters of Instruction exposes him to their ridicule and contempt. . . . It has been long remarked in this Country that the men who are active and expert, at the same time ignorant of Letters are the most ready in learning the Indian Tongue—here are several clever men in this service who scarcely know a Letter in the Alphabet are good Linguists and good servants—consequently would be proper for the station of Master, yet they are fearful to undertake it knowing that they would expose themselves to the Ridicule of their fellow Servants (HBCA, B. 239/a/95, f. 30).

Numerous men did accept opportunities for advancement however; and they acquired the needed skills with varying degrees of success, often from senior officers who trained and encouraged them. Important positions might be reached from a variety of lowly beginnings. Several overseas governors and other senior officers were recruited from the ranks; James Knight, John Fullartine, Henry Kelsey, Richard Staunton, Thomas McCliesh, Joseph Adams, Richard Norton, William Tomison, and others began as tradesmen, labourers, or apprentices and retired as governors or chief factors. This was not, of course, a typical pattern in the earliest years when the company was too young to have raised up its own leaders; Governors Charles Bayly, John Nixon, and Henry Sergeant all lacked Bay experience before their appointments in the 1670s and 1680s. But it soon became an entrenched practice strongly supported, naturally enough, by aspiring Bay servants; and those few outsiders later appointed at high levels became liable to failure as much because of the hostility of their fellow-employees as on account of their own inexperience. One such instance was John Newton, who was sent from England in 1748 to replace James Isham as chief at York. The London committee later regretted the appointment because of his mismanagement; and his "distance and severity" did not win the new arrival much support from the career men he was sent to command (Craig 1974: 482–83). In later years company men made explicit their concern at the committee's other occasional efforts to appoint unseasoned officers. In 1811 William Auld at York was much displeased with his new recruits of officers' rank:

> the very considerable time which is requisite to form Steersmen Guides and Interpreters is equally requisite to qualify as an officer to perform with success the duties of his station . . . many of those whom you have named and are come this year are utterly incompetent to a charge among Indians of whose language and customs they are alike strangers to (HBCA, A. 11/118, f. 24; see also Joseph Colen in ibid., B. 239/a/95, f. 30).

Internal recruitment of officers was thus fostered as company practice both by country conditions and by the attitudes of senior officers who had themselves benefited from the mobility it offered and appreciated its objective utility. Yet mobility was in some respects restricted, particularly from the late 1700s on, and with regard to one ethnic group. After 1750, numerous entrants began service as literate "writers," as did Humphrey Marten, Matthew Cocking, John Thomas, and George Gladman, Sr.; and these youths were with growing frequency favoured for promotion. By the early nineteenth century, however, social stratification sharpened and ordinary apprentices, tradesmen, and labourers found fewer chances for advancement. After the 1821 coalition, the distinctions between "gentlemen" and "servants" rigidified further, in accord with North West Company social patterns and the predilections of the new régime. But the company had already been losing its willingness to offer its recruits an almost complete on-the-job education since the numbers of previously trained young men were growing at home and also since its needs for office or "white-collar" personnel were increasing. Where older values and expectations persisted, as among officers' native-born sons who sought the upward mobility that their fathers had found, frustration developed and found lively expression in the 1820s to 1840s as later sections will show.

Some men also suffered a certain exclusion from advancement because of their ethnic origin. Despite the rapidly growing numbers of Scottish servants during the eighteenth century, Englishmen retained a hold on most senior positions. This is not to say that the Scots were collectively subject to discrimination; although the English servants may have been favoured for promotion by the dominantly English London committee, there were no expressions of prejudice against Scots in general. It is clear, however, that while the Lowland Scots were not viewed as particularly distinct from the English ethnically or socially, the Orkneymen acquired considerable visibility as a separate group, both in their own view and that of others. Coming from small isolated islands, many were already friends or relatives with common backgrounds (J. Nicks 1979). They were not systematically denied advancement; at least twenty-eight Orkneymen became either governors, chief factors, chief traders, or district masters between the early 1700s and the mid-1800s (Bailey 1971: 200). But loyalties to one another sometimes led them to join together against their superiors. Although their dispersal at the different posts weakened the effectiveness of any effort at unity or collective action, they became known as a sometimes troublesome group with a potentially subversive concern for its own interests—a reputation sustained by their conduct on various occasions.

In 1777, for example, Humphrey Marten at York recorded the arrival from the inland posts of an Orkneyman who "gave several broad hints, that a kind of Combination was entered into by some of the Orkney-Men; that they would stick up for 15£/Annum." Marten took away his duties and restricted him to a pound of bread a day; within three weeks, the man agreed to return inland at "6£ and 40s gratuity" (Rich and Johnson 1951, I: 142n). Similar "combinations," perhaps more successful, were reported from York in 1811. William Auld (himself a Lowland Scot) observed to the London committee that the Orkneymen "are never to be complained against except in cases where a great number of them happen to have their contracts expiring at the same time then they unite to reduce us to their terms" (HBCA, A. 11/118, f. 29). In 1787, Joseph Colen at York was sufficiently concerned about the inland Orkneymen's loyalty to the company that he suggested a reduction in their numbers in favour of "some careful steady Englishmen of fair Character"; there was fear that the Orkneymen were becoming "too closely connected" with the Canadian traders (ibid., A. 11/117, f. 9; Johnson 1967: xv–xvi). In apparent response to his request, an unusually large number of Englishmen were sent to the Bay in 1788; but by 1794, Colen was complaining of both the low quality and the inexperience of some of the English recruits. Orkneymen, despite their occasional lapses of loyalty, were to remain an important part of the work force until well into the nineteenth century.

Although the Orkneymen suffered some disadvantages as a group and although the distance between literate gentlemen and uneducated servants was growing in the late 1700s, two related characteristics of company social organization in the fur trade country remained particularly important for more than a century after its founding: the conspicuous vertical integration of social relations among the differently ranked men at the posts and the significant opportunities for vertical mobility within the company. The vertical integration of the posts was a trait readily borrowed from English social organization and was probably reinforced by the special conditions of Bay life itself. In seventeeth- and eighteenth-century England, master-servant ties were still dominantly primordial status relationships rather than contractual arrangements; and company master-servant relations within the Bay as well as between London and the Bay preserved much of this flavour. While company employees were servants of their London masters, the highest-ranked men were also masters of those placed beneath them. And even though many men were contracted to practise specific trades, their roles at the posts were far more diffuse than those of later industrial workers. They lived co-residentially in large enclosed compounds separated from the outside world and owed their masters a complete allegiance that left little room for any private life. The company and its officers might be characterized in the same terms as the master and his family in England—as a "greedy organization" whose ideal servant was loyal, unmarried, and asexual, with no conflicting claims to distract him from absorption in this vertical relationship (Coser 1973: 31–32, 35).

It follows that in a company post, as in a large English household, there were few opportunities for servants to establish significant horizontal relationships with their peers; even the Orkneymen had difficulty in their occasional efforts to organize for collective purposes. In master-servant relationships "*By definition* the subordinate group within each pair had few other links to the wider society. . . . there were no alternatives to challenge the system" (Davidoff 1974: 407, 411). In eighteenth-century Hudson Bay, such a "wider society" was not only inaccessible but also practically absent, reinforcing the importance of vertical linkages and making the fur trade sub-field an exaggerated yet fragmentary version of its home society.

"The system" did, however, have its compensations and, as it developed in Hudson Bay, its potential benefits. The master provided food, housing, and other services and a regular cash wage that, even if small, might be largely saved over the years. There was considerable employment security; although a few men were dismissed for conspicuous misconduct such as desertion or indulging in private trade, disabled or marginally useful servants commonly were paternally supported by the company for some time and granted pensions upon retirement.

Additionally, while strong personal enmities could develop in the small world of the fur trade, friendships could grow equally strong. Because many servants arrived young and with little previous training, senior men might assume the roles not only of master but of patron, teacher, adviser, and even surrogate father. These asymmetrical relationships had considerable importance in strengthening the vertical social integration of the posts, and probably in reinforcing the attachment of their participants to company service as the locus of their strongest personal ties. On one occasion, Humphrey Marten vividly expressed the mixed sentiments of friendship and kinship that might be present in such associations, as he recorded his sorrow at the "Shocking news of the Death of my beloved Friend and I may truly say Father Mr. James Isham, who paid the Grand debt on the 13th Instant" (Rich 1949: 325).

In Hudson Bay, probably more than in Britain itself, this integration was accompanied by selective opportunities for the vertical mobility of the subordinate members. Senior men often aided the careers of their juniors considerably by training and encouraging them and by recommending them to the attention of the London committee. The committee itself fostered such relationships as the best method of raising up successful field officers, having no other means of training them.

The relationship of Richard Norton and Thomas McCliesh demonstrates some elements of such a pattern. Norton was apprenticed to the company in 1714, at age thirteen. After a decade of varied service, he found himself, as the result of the death of a superior officer, in charge of Fort Prince of Wales (Churchill), which fell under the jurisdiction of McCliesh, then governor at York. Norton's four years in this position were not successful; his management was poor and his profits low. Accordingly, the company sent him to York for four years as "second" to McCliesh to improve his knowledge of trade methods and accounts. The degree of friendship that developed between them is suggested by the fact that on a visit to England in 1730–31 Norton married McCliesh's daughter; the following year he also recovered the command of Churchill (Johnson 1974: 414–15, 489–90).

Thus, a senior colleague might offer a subordinate both direct career assistance and helpful kinship ties. The father-surrogate might also be the father-in-law; and, as in older English households, an apprentice might eventually become a substitute son by marrying his patron-master's daughter. While this early case involved the taking of a British wife, it later became common for senior company men with native families to encourage or arrange matches between their daughters and younger employees who seemed acceptable both as future officers and as husbands and sons-in-law.

These alliances often served their participants and the company well. But they might also at times work against the company's interest. Thomas McCliesh had another company son-in-law, William Coats, who commanded a ship to the Bay each summer from 1726 to 1751—until the discovery that he had regularly been engaging in illicit trade brought about his dismissal (Williams 1974: 127–28). Another case of apparent favouritism was recorded by Miles Macdonell, leader of the Red River colonists temporarily residing at York Factory in 1812. Macdonell found one John McNab "quite unfit for the Company's service, being as deficient of intellect as industry." McNab, he wrote to Lord Selkirk, could "only be kept on the list by the interest of his friends being son of a late, and married to a daughter of the present chief of YF" (PAC, Macdonell Papers, 29 May 1812).

From these relations and other evidence emerges the unified image of the "company man" as found in the Hudson's Bay Company. He was a distinctive social type in several respects. Because his kinship ties in Britain were generally not strong or extensive, those that became most significant tended to derive from the company and often from his friendship ties with a senior patron within the fur trade. As a result, his company membership rather than his social class or occupation dominated his life and career.

This kind of company man recurs in association with similar patterns of social and economic organization elsewhere. The characteristics of this social type and his relationships suggest comparison with Japanese society, which offers certain striking parallels. There the "frame" (*ba*)—the institution of which a person is a member—is far more important than membership in a class, caste, or occupational category. The Japanese terms *ie* and *kaisha* help to express the pervasiveness of the frame concept in Japanese society:

> *Kaisha* is "my" or "our" company, the community to which one belongs primarily, and which is all-important in one's life . . . it provides the whole social existence of a person, and has authority over all aspects of his life; he is deeply emotionally involved in the association . . . *ie,* the household, is a concept which penetrates every nook and cranny of Japanese society . . . a corporate residential group and, in the case of agriculture or other similar enterprises . . . a managing body . . . a social group constructed on the basis of an established frame of residence and often of management organization (Nakane 1970: 3–5).

Membership in the *ie* or *kaisha* may be achieved through the fortunes of personal contacts and associations and is commonly not based on prior ties of kinship. Servants and clerks were regularly incorporated into traditional agricultural and merchant households and might marry the daughters of their households; an adopted son could then carry on the enterprise as successor to the head.

A modern Japanese company too is conceptualized as *ie*, as consisting of members of one household headed by their employer. Its members typically enter it right after school at the lowest levels. They then rise through the ranks, commonly with the help of a parent-master-patron figure or *oyabun* with whom a close bond is formed that may quite override considerations of merit or of the company's best interests (ibid., 5-7, 16-17, 42). Employees expect to remain for their lifetime. The company commonly provides housing (separate from other residential sectors), along with recreational facilities, health care, and in some cases, a cemetery. Loyalties and in-group feelings against those in parallel organizations are strong; no horizontal ties link men of similar occupation in different companies. Accordingly the functional group always consists of heterogeneous elements linked vertically. Hierarchy tends to dominate, and "the small isolated segments become subject to the workings of the institutional group of which they form part" (Nakane 1970: 7, 17, 21, 25; Abegglen 1958).

Such parallels as these between Japanese social organization and that of the Hudson's Bay Company suggest that understanding of this British fur trade concern may be facilitated not only by tracing historical antecedents in the English household and master-servant complex but also by examining similar social structures and their consequences in other societies.

THE BRITISH NORTH WESTERS: PARTNERS, KINSMEN, AND FRIENDS

While the traders of Hudson Bay were settling into established patterns of social life at their forts, factories, and houses, changes that would be of critical importance for their company's future were occurring in eastern Canada. Although New France was not formally ceded to the British until the Peace of Paris in 1763, the fall of Quebec and other events in 1759-60 had already allowed numbers of Britishers to penetrate the Canadian economy and society. In 1761, over 200 voyageurs were sent inland from the Montreal region to the Indian country to pursue the fur trade. This number was not unlike figures for earlier years; what was novel was that 7 of the 12 merchants who hired them had English or Scottish names. By the end of the 1700s, British merchants were sending out over 450 men. Fur trade merchants with French-Canadian names, in contrast, had decreased to about a dozen and their voyageurs totalled 76 (Eccles 1969: 186-87). The Montreal fur trade became dominated by British management and capital. And its social organization was characterized, not by the vertical integration of the pre-nineteenth-century Hudson's Bay Company, but by horizontal division—the split between the Britishers who occupied or could aspire to occupy the highest positions and the French Canadians who, while contributing knowledge and technical skills that the British needed, continued in the fur trade largely as voyageurs and other low-rank employees.

Accompanying this transfer of control was a trend toward consolidation; "The number of individual traders and companies licensed to carry goods to the upper country in 1790 was only about half the number to which passports were issued in 1777." Small traders yielded to larger enterprises that in turn coalesced into the North West Company, which effectively monopolized the Montreal trade after 1804. And by 1811, the North Westers were unsuccessfully petitioning the British Privy Council for chartered rights to a large area reaching from the Rocky Mountains to the Pacific (Stevens 1926: 142-43).

The British merchants and wintering partners who took control of the Montreal fur trade between the 1760s and 1800 were largely Scots. Of 128 men having some importance in the trade in those four decades, 77 were of Scottish background, at least 55 being born in Scotland itself, and the rest in the United States or Canada. Of the remainder, 27 were of other British or Irish descent, 19 were French Canadians, and 5 of other backgrounds (Wallace 1934: appendix).

The many kin and friendship ties among these Scots strengthened their unity in business enterprises. Unlike their Hudson's Bay Company rivals, the men whose partnerships became aggregated into the North West Company had no corporate charter; their organizational solidarity was largely based on personal and familial associations shared, reinforced, and built up in the process of emigrating from Scotland and finding new footholds in North America. In entering the fur trade, they resembled in some respects other ethnic trader groups known in various parts of the world—"groups with strong kin ties, but with insufficient economic opportunity in their home areas, that have slipped into the trader role in so many peasant societies." A group of this type is "productive of associations"; since it lacks "satisfying and reliable moral ties with the indigenous local community," it is "typically a socially segregated and hostilely-regarded community of kinship units, knit together and defended by associational ties" (Fallers 1967: 12-13). The eighteenth-century Scottish migrants to North America did not necessarily arrive as traders. But their tendency to form close kinship-based communities and frequently to enter joint trade and business pursuits has been remarked by students of their migration patterns.

The magnitude of these migrations cannot be precisely known, but there are some estimates. Apparently nearly 25,000 Scots emigrated between 1763 and 1775, over 20,200 of them in the years 1768 to 1775 (Graham 1956: 188-89). In the New World, their settlement became conspicuously localized. Those established in Canada and in New York's Mohawk and upper Hudson valleys before the American Revolution are of particular relevance to this study because of the later fur trade roles of some of their members.

In 1773, a substantial body of migrant Highlanders, largely Roman Catholic Macdonells or Macdonalds from Glengarry and other parts of Inverness-shire, arrived to take up residence on the large estates (some 100,000 acres) of Sir William Johnson in the Mohawk Valley. Johnson, an Irishman, had emigrated to New York in the late 1730s to manage the landholdings of

Peter Warren, his mother's brother (Flexner 1959: 11, 17). Here Johnson became a dominant political figure, skilled in difficult dealings with the French and Indians. The Mohawks adopted him; and the British recognized his services by making him a baronet and appointing him "Colonel, Agent, and sole supervisor of the Six Nations and other Northern tribes" in 1756, as well as supervisor of the fur trade in the northern colonies which, beginning in 1764, included British Canada (ibid., 40, 160; Stevens 1926: 23).

Johnson's economic role in the Mohawk Valley became as important as his political one. Besides supplying goods for the fur trade in the area, he expanded agricultural settlement on his growing estates, largely by bringing in tenant farmers from his own home, County Meath, and elsewhere. The Scottish Highlanders whom Johnson welcomed in 1773 doubtless fitted easily into this context. Certainly their social situation in Johnson's frontier domains more closely resembled that of the agriculturists on Scottish chiefly estates (or, for that matter, on French-Canadian seigneuries) than that of the small freeholders who populated the newly opened areas of Pennsylvania and other American colonies. They immediately became part of a paternalistic economic unit. Johnson provided cleared land, seed, horses, and cows to support them until they could clear their own farms, which they rented free for the first five years. They brought their grain and wood to his gristmills and sawmills and were expected to contribute a few days annually to road work and maintenance. Johnson also imported "tradesmen and artificers" to serve their needs—a shoemaker, tanner, hatter, surveyor, and others; and his sister's son, Dr. John Dease, arrived from Ireland to serve as the local physician (Flexner 1959: 298–99; Pryde 1935: 152). Dease, later an administrator of Indian affairs, had four sons, John Warren, Francis Michael, Peter Warren, and Charles Johnson Watts, who collectively served a total of nearly seventy years in the Montreal fur trade and the Hudson's Bay Company.

Like other Highland groups, Johnson's Macdonells were led to their new homes by men of the tacksman (or intermediate landholding) class. In 1773, one of their leaders, Allan Macdonell, wrote to Johnson that he and his fellows had a "great desire of Settling under your Wing . . . in which we may have a mutual Interest. . . . You have large estates to make & we some influence over people." He thought that the people whom he and two other gentlemen had brought over "will adhere to us if Sir William gives the encouragement their Sobriety & Industry will Merit." Macdonell and Johnson tended to think in the same terms, and there are strong suggestions that Macdonell hoped to retain the familiar Highland position of tacksman (Graham 1956: 81–82).

The American Revolution soon disrupted the peaceful spread of Johnson's domains and of Highland-style tenancy in New York. Johnson died in 1774, passing on his position and power to his strongly loyalist son John who, justifiably suspected of pro-British sympathies, left for Montreal in 1776 with about 250 followers. In the next few years, a large number of other loyalist New Yorkers also fled to Canada. Numerous Highlanders, some from Johnson's lands, founded a new Glengarry, now Glengarry County in eastern Ontario; and loyalist Scots from New York did military service for the British during the Revolution.

Among the loyalists were many individuals who sooner or later found livelihoods in the Canadian fur trade. Several of these had traceable connections with Sir William Johnson or with his son or came from Johnson's area of New York, if not from his lands. The four Dease brothers, grandnephews of Sir William, were perhaps the only Johnson kin to enter the fur trade; but several other links may be traced between the Johnsons and Montreal traders. The family of the noted North West explorer, Sir Alexander Mackenzie, for example, had come to New York in 1774. After the Revolution began, Mackenzie's father and uncle received commissions in Sir John Johnson's regiment, while he himself was sent north to Montreal. After finishing school there, he began his fur trade career as a clerk in one of the British fur trade businesses later absorbed into the North West Company.

Among the Scottish loyalists who moved to Canada from the Schoharie area south of the Mohawk where Johnson held several thousand acres were the parents of North Wester John Macdonell, fur trader from about 1793 to 1812. This family had come from Scotland to Schoharie in 1773. In March, 1780, John's father heard that his family had reached Montreal "naked and starving" from New York. Subsequently the family re-established itself in Glengarry, Canada, near the St. Lawrence and about fifty miles west of Montreal (PAO, Macdonell file, John Macdonell to Captain Matthews, 20 March 1780). Also from Schoharie to Glengarry came the loyalist family of Alexander Campbell, two of whose sons served the North West Company for about twenty-two and forty-nine years respectively.

The Scots who left the Johnson lands for Canada were joined by others from nearby Albany and Schenectady and other points to the east. From Schenectady to Williamstown, Glengarry, came the family of Alexander and Margaret McDonell Cameron; their son, Duncan, was a North Wester from 1784 to 1816. From Bennington on the New York–Vermont border just east of Albany came the Simon Fraser family to settle near Cornwall, Glengarry. Simon Fraser, Sr., fought for the British and died in prison at Albany, New York; Simon Fraser, Jr., was educated in Montreal where his father's brother was a judge, then served the North West Company from 1792 until nearly 1820, being best known for his discovery and exploration of the Fraser River.

Schenectady also lost one of its important early fur trade-connected businesses during the Revolutionary period. For some time the Scottish-dominated firm of Phyn, Ellice, and Company had been engaged in the Detroit and Michilimackinac fur trade. James Phyn, son of an Aberdeenshire laird, had come to New York before 1763, and in about 1765, he was joined in partnership by another Scot, Alexander Ellice. In 1774, the firm shifted its operations to London and Montreal. Between 1798 and 1804, its Montreal subsidiary, Forsyth, Richardson, and Company, combined with other Scots-dominated partnerships, first to offer organized opposition to the equally Scottish North West Company under various names (New North West Company, XY Company, and Sir Alexander Mackenzie and Company)— and finally to merge with it in 1804, inaugurating the North Westers' most successful period of growth and expansion. The extent to which these partnerships might coincide with kinship ties is demonstrated by the family connections between James Phyn, and Ellice, Forsyth, and Richardson, each of whom became related to Phyn through marriage. The overlapping of ties continued for another two generations; nine Forsyth, Richardson, and Ellice sons and grandsons were active in the Montreal fur business.

Such connections were equally prominent among the early North Westers themselves. Numerous of their relationships centred on Simon McTavish of Inverness-shire. McTavish emigrated to New York at age thirteen as an apprentice, then engaged in the fur trade in Albany. In 1775 he changed his headquarters to Montreal. Although he himself never travelled beyond the rendezvous point on Lake Superior, McTavish became actively involved in partnerships that included winterers in the Indian country as well as other Montreal merchants. He began his activities by helping to outfit a Connecticut trader, Peter Pond, to compete against other Montreal interests such as the Frobisher brothers from Yorkshire and the McGill brothers from Glasgow; these parties had begun their Montreal operations by the late 1760s (Campbell 1957: 7, 19). Once McTavish had established his own position, however, he began not only to broaden his Montreal alliances, but also to bring into the fur trade a string of relatives from Scotland. Their spreading kinship ties, along with his own, formed an extensive network of fur trade families (Brown 1975: fig. 3).

In 1779, McTavish and a new partner, the Scottish-born Patrick Small, joined the Frobishers, McGills, and others in a co-partnership of eight Montreal firms—the North West Company in its earliest form (Campbell 1957: 19), and the first of various reorganizations and coalitions with rivals. As his fortunes improved, McTavish undertook to pay for the education of three nephews in Scotland, the sons of his sister Anne and of Donald McGillivray, who was a small tenant of the Lovat estate in Inverness-shire. The eldest of these, William McGillivray, entered the North West Company by 1784, became a partner in 1790, and in 1804, on his uncle's death, was made its chief director. The second, Duncan, joined the company by 1793 and served it almost until his death in 1808. Simon, the youngest, was prevented by lameness from becoming a wintering partner like his brothers and instead became a partner in the fur trade-connected firms of McTavish, Fraser, and Company in London, and McTavish, McGillivrays, and Company in Montreal; he took an active part in the negotiations for the coalition of the North West and Hudson's Bay Companies in 1821. In the same general period two of McTavish's cousins, the Scottish-born Simon Fraser and his son of the same name (not to be confused with the more famous Fraser of Bennington, New York), were also associated with the North West Company. Another cousin, John Fraser, was by the early 1790s in charge of the London firm of McTavish, Fraser, and Company, providing McTavish with essential London business connections (ibid., 56, 70).

In 1793, at the age of forty-three, Simon McTavish made a marriage that crossed ethnic, religious (Scottish Presbyterian/French Catholic), and generational lines and linked him firmly with one of Montreal's old French fur-trading families. The father and grandfather of his young wife, Marie Marguerite Chaboillez, were both fur traders; and her marriage to McTavish surely facilitated the entry of her brother Charles into the North West Company as a clerk in 1794 and his rise to partnership status by 1799.

On a trip to Britain with his new wife in 1794, McTavish revitalized old clan ties by paying a visit to the chief of the Clan Tavish and affirming his kinship with him. The chief's record of this visit suggests that he was impressed with his new relative from Canada:

> A kinsman of mine who has lately made his appearance in England with an immense Fortune, acquired in the wilds of North America, has put upon me to take out Arms—To entitle me, however, to supporters, to which as Chief I certainly have Right, it will be necessary to trace myself up to the Root (ibid., 78).

Once the chief secured armorial bearings, Simon McTavish too was granted the right to use them. For his part, McTavish arranged to take the chief's young son, John George, into the company as a clerk in 1798. John George became a partner in 1813 and a chief factor when the North West and Hudson's Bay Companies united, and he brought three of his own nephews into the fur trade (Wallace 1934: 485–86; MacLeod 1947: xx). After the chief died in 1796, leaving his family in financial difficulties, McTavish gave them generous assistance (Campbell 1957: 117).

When McTavish died, he was owner of the ancestral clan seat of Dunardry in Argyllshire, which he had purchased when it came on the market in 1800. The terms of his will of 2 July 1804 reflected the importance he attached to clan and familial ties; elaborate provisions were made to keep Dunardry in the family and under the McTavish name, a long list of relatives received legacies, and the annual interest of one thousand pounds was to be used for "assisting such of my poor relations in Scotland as I may have neglected to provide for by this my last will and testament." The Chaboillez family, his in-laws as well as his wife, also benefited from the estate, but McTavish made it clear that his four children were not to be brought up by French relatives. At a "proper age" all were "to be removed to England for their education, with which determination my said wife must acquiesce" (Wallace 1934: 134–43).

By the end of his life, McTavish had organized an impressive and successful fur trade concern in which his kin, with his assistance, were increasingly dominant figures. Between 1799 and 1804, however, his favouring of them played an important role in his break with another influential Scot, Alexander Mackenzie. After his enterprising journey to the Pacific in 1793, Mackenzie continued to make valuable contributions to the North West Company and the related firm of McTavish, Frobisher. But in 1796, on Frobisher's retirement, McTavish chose his nephew, William McGillivray, as a replacement; and this and other slights led to Mackenzie's withdrawal from the concern, despite the strong support he received from the North West wintering partners. A colleague, Alexander Henry, commented that as a result, the North West Company was now "all in the hands of McTavish":

> Frobisher and McKensey is out, the latter went off in a pet, the cause as far as I can learn was who should be first—McTavish or McK—and as there could not be two Caesars in Rome one must remove (Campbell 1957: 117–24).

Mackenzie departed for London where, after publishing his account of his transcontinental explorations, he was knighted in 1802. He subsequently returned to Montreal to lend his support and influence to the North West Company's rival, the XY Company (built partly upon the Forsyth-Richardson partnership). The death of the other "Caesar in Rome" soon allowed the damaging rivalry to be ended by a merger, however, and the North West Company assumed control of the Montreal fur trade. Meanwhile, the familial networks continued to ramify. In 1803 McTavish's sister-in-law married Roderick McKenzie, first cousin of Alexander Mackenzie and an active North Wester until his semi-retirement in 1801.

Clan and kinship ties remained important to Highland North Westers long after they ceased to centre on Simon McTavish (whose children all died young), and even after the North Westers had supposedly merged their identity with the Hudson's Bay men. James Hargrave, a Lowland Scottish clerk who joined the North West Company in 1820, was told by William Cockran in 1832 that his lack of a clan name might have contributed to his failure to be promoted: "I begin to think that your name will have to be changed, into Mc-argrave. If you had had a Mc- before it, I have little doubt, but that it would have done you real service" (Hargrave Papers, 9 August 1832). Hargrave's marriage some years later to the young Scottish niece of Chief Factor John George McTavish (son of the clan chief and close friend of company governor Simpson), remedied this deficiency to some extent and enhanced his social position in a company in which the Scottish North Westers still carried much influence.

NORTH WESTERS AND HUDSON'S BAY MEN: SOME SOCIAL CONTRASTS

There were a number of striking differences between the Montreal North Westers and the Hudson's Bay Company men whose trade monopoly they challenged. Because they often had extensive involvement in North American colonial society, the North Westers were in the process of becoming Canadians, while the Hudson's Bay men continued to be hired directly from Britain and, before 1821, typically returned there after their years of service (Davies 1966: 168). Most North Westers were emigrants who were already enmeshed in networks of kin and friends who had either emigrated with them or had preceded them to America. While these men went on to make careers in the fur trade, their relatives were making new homes in such centres as Montreal and Glengarry County, where winterers in the Indian country could find congenial communities when they retired.

These Scots in Canada also commonly entered the fur trade as employees or business partners of their relatives or of fellow Scots with whom they had other ties. Although he does not mention the multiplicity of kin links among North Westers, K.G. Davies noted that their company benefited importantly from the ease of interaction between its Montreal agents and its wintering partners. Its resultant flexibility gave it a strong advantage over its London opponent;

> There was, above all, a close relationship between policy decisions and executive action, which the Hudson's Bay Company could not match. The annual meetings of the partners and agents at Fort William [Lake Superior] could produce a single plan for the whole region based on recent first-hand intelligence, whereas the decisions taken at Fenchurch Street were those of men who had never seen a portage and whose information was often out-of-date. The presence in the field of the North West wintering partners gave their concern such flexibility that the general plan could be responsibly modified to meet contingencies, while the Hudson's Bay men were inclined to work to rule (ibid., 169).

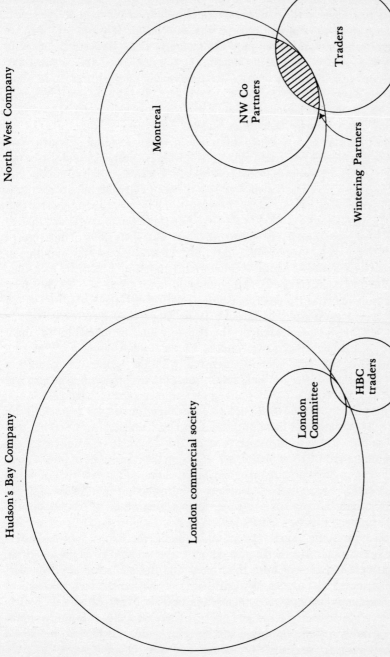

North West Company

Hudson's Bay Company

Montreal

NW Co
Partners

Traders

Wintering Partners

London commercial society

London
Committee

HBC
traders

Figure 1. The relative positions of the Hudson's Bay and North West Companies and their traders in their home cities and business communities.

The personal ties of the British North Westers in combination with the company's open partnership structure whereby clerks (usually themselves kinsmen or friends of the partners) might be admitted as shareholders served to foster a spirit of common interest and enterprise. Hudson's Bay men, in contrast, were the salaried employees of geographically remote and socially distant stockholders. Not until 1806 did the London committee begin, in the face of strong and unified North West Company competition, to develop tentatively new incentive schemes for its traders. By 1821 the North Westers' lesson had been well learned; the chief factors and chief traders of the new Hudson's Bay Company were also made shareholders.

A contrast may also be drawn between the social standing of North West wintering partners in Montreal and Hudson's Bay officers in London (see fig. 1). The latter were subordinate members of a relatively small company in a great European city. The North Westers, on the other hand, were carrying on a business that was the mainstay of Montreal, and they had a strong social and economic impact upon that community. Fur trade fortunes such as that of Simon McTavish purchased seigneuries and built mansions. Those North Westers who were protestants subscribed generously to the building of Montreal's St. Gabriel Street Presbyterian Church in 1792, in which they maintained two official pews (Morton 1929: lxxii). And in 1787, nineteen men, mainly Scots with a few Englishmen and French Canadians, founded an exclusive and prestigious social club from which even merchants such as Simon McTavish were excluded—the Beaver Club's membership was open only to gentlemen who had wintered in the Indian country. Wintering partners, wearing gold medals engraved with the motto, "Fortitude in Distress," gathered here for banquets of roast beaver, sturgeon, wild rice and other delicacies. Here too they smoked the calumet, sang old voyageur songs, and entertained distinguished guests—John Jacob Astor, Sir John Johnson (son of Sir William and head of the Indian Department), Lord Selkirk, and other notable visitors to Montreal (Campbell 1957: 57, 164). Aside from such conviviality, the club took on the task of easing the transitions of long-absent winterers from fur trade life into their home community: "Another object of this Institution was, to afford a means of introduction into Society to such Traders as might from time to time, after a long absence, retire from the Indian Country" (Beaver Club 1819: 3).

In their fur trade organization and methods, the British North Westers most closely resembled the French whom they displaced after the conquest. The business activities of both the French and British Canadian fur traders were dominated by coteries of wealthy interconnected families, numbers of whose members distinguished themselves both in Montreal society and in their service at posts in the Indian country. There were also continuities in fur trade methods and in employee categories, for all of which a specialized French vocabulary persisted. Canoemen and men who contracted for fixed terms of inland service continued to be known as *voyageurs* and *engagés.* They travelled in canoes whose designs the French had adapted to suit fur trade purposes—*canôts de maitre* and the smaller *canôts du nord.* A literate North West Company clerk (*commis*) who "invested his skill, his courage, and (if he had any) his money" in the fur trade, might rise to the rank of *bourgeois,* assuming the responsibility for the returns of the district to which he was assigned and gaining partnership in the concern (Morton 1966: 162). Inland *hivernants* or winterers who spent whole years in the fur trade country were distinguished from the mere *mangeurs du lard,* "porkeaters," who travelled the familiar and established supply route between Montreal and Grand Portage (or later Fort William) in Lake Superior, the *rendezvous* point to which the winterers brought their fur returns for transport to Canada. The Britishers also maintained the French custom of doing much of their fur trading from small temporary posts, and built up few large permanent establishments. From their various wintering headquarters, traders would travel out, *en derouine,* to various Indian groups to barter and collect debts directly—a custom that allowed flexibility and contact with a variety of dispersed Indian communities, in contrast with the more exclusive and permanent attachments that developed between the Hudson's Bay posts and their Home Indians. French fur trade methods, experience, and expertise, then, were important to the Britishers' success. The Montreal British commonly learned French, and some, like Simon McTavish and Roderick McKenzie, intermarried with the older French fur-trading families.

Certain strong social distinctions developed, however, between the British and the French. Even in cases of intermarriage, the newcomers might preserve a distance between themselves and their French relatives, as Simon McTavish's will shows. And in the fur trade, social and status differences were expressed in the division of labour. The French continued to dominate the trade numerically, but they were largely confined to the lower ranks; few advanced beyond the ranks of voyageur, guide, interpreter, or clerk. Correspondingly, few Scottish or English names were ever listed below the ranks of bourgeois or clerk.

Table 1 suggests that the North West Company's recruiting and promotion practices showed marked contrasts with those of the Hudson's Bay Company. Most employees were in effect pre-selected for either high or low-ranked positions at the time they entered the company, on the basis of their prior ethnic, social, and kinship affiliations. These positions predicted their subsequent careers; voyageurs might become guides or interpreters, but company bourgeois were drawn from the ranks of the clerks. And, at least in 1804, British dominance of these higher ranks was even greater than it appears; the two French names among the bourgeois were those of Charles Chaboillez, Simon McTavish's brother-in-law, and Pierre Rastel de Rocheblave, son of a former British governor of the Illinois country. The twenty-four seemingly

TABLE 1: ETHNIC ORIGINS, BY SURNAMES, OF TRADERS LISTED IN THE NORTH WEST
COMPANY IN 1804, FOLLOWING ITS MERGER WITH THE XY COMPANY.

	British	French	Indian or other	Total
Bourgeois	43	2	—	45
Clerks	44	32	—	76
Interpreters	2	43	—	45
Guides	—	16	—	16
Voyageurs and others	24	625	8	657
Total	113	718	8	839

British names scattered in the voyageurs' lists account for under 4 per cent of
the total; and numbers of Iroquois Indians from the Montreal area also
became canoemen and trappers from 1794 on (T. Nicks 1979). But the great
majority were French Canadians with scant prospects for advancement.

Figure 2 sketches the divergent origins and career paths of the men of the

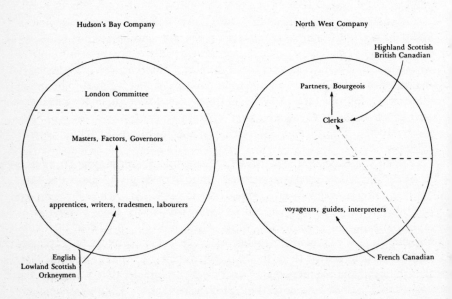

Figure 2. Typical origins and possible career paths of Hudson's Bay men and North Westers
before the coalition of 1821.

two companies. In certain respects, the Hudson's Bay Orkneymen and the French voyageurs were comparable; by the later eighteenth century, each group dominated its company numerically, providing inexpensive labour in lower ranks. But, whereas the North West Company fur trade was conducted by two sharply demarcated classes of employees, the Orkneymen entered an organization in which greater upward mobility and occupational diversity were possible. While they might occasionally combine against their masters, their opportunities for advancement exceeded those of the voyageurs and might increase their attentiveness to their company's interests. By the early nineteenth century, the behaviour of the two was often being compared, usually to the disparagement of the more homogeneous and caste-like voyageur group. William Auld, writing in 1811 at York Factory, stated these contrasts in terms that recur, more or less strongly, in the comments of others:

> Orkney-men and Scotchmen are by nature cautious and careful the lower classes of them prudent in the management of their own property are some time in learning to be utterly indifferent about anothers. . . . Not so the volatile thoughtless Canadian he is equally indifferent about himself as his Master he is by nature more strong and more wicked than the Savages and as ignorant (HBCA, A. 11/118, f. 23).

Hudson's Bay and North West Company men have often been treated as if they constituted a unified social type (Saum 1965; Hickerson 1966; O'Meara 1968). But in fact, they varied widely. The concept of frame—the binding of heterogeneous individuals into one institution seems helpful in the analysis of Hudson's Bay Company social relations and personnel practices. The concept of attribute, referring to the classification of individuals into horizontally extended occupational, status, or kin groups (Nakane 1970: 5-6) seems relevant for analysis of the North Westers. In the Hudson's Bay Company's records, recurrent categories such as master, servant, and apprentice, suggest the primacy of dyadic relations connecting men of senior and junior rank. In eighteenth-century Hudson Bay, these relationships were localized in widely separated houses or factories where each occupational category had few members.

The hierarchy of the North West Company consisted of fewer groups characterized more by internal horizontal homogeneity than by vertical integration. Broad ethnic and occupational divisions generally coincided to split company personnel into two main classes—the largely British leadership of bourgeois and of clerks destined to become bourgeois and the mainly French-Canadian voyageurs who might, at best, become guides or interpreters. The voyageurs had their own distinctive ethnic identity and social and cultural attributes—distinctive values, lifestyle, tastes, music, and so forth, which are still romanticized in Canada today. But these men and the bourgeois and clerks whose persons, furs, and trade goods they transported on the waterways of the Northwest showed little unity as a social group. The partners were colleagues and friends whose interconnections originated not only with marriage alliances but also with sibling ties and their extensions to cousins, uncles, and nephews and enmeshed them in far-reaching social networks.

These contrasts carried over into the recruiting and promotion practices of the two concerns and strongly influenced the selection of the "company men" who rose to prominence. Hudson's Bay Company men usually entered the fur trade fortuitously with few prior links to aid their advancement. Within the fur trade posts, some would later acquire the patronage and support of senior officers that would enable them to gain their own seniority.

Among the North Westers, patronage was also common; but it was of a rather different sort. Because North West traders could also be partners and directors, they were able to influence the hiring process directly and to foster the recruitment and advancement of young relatives or friends. When, for example, North Wester Aeneas Cameron brought his nephew Angus into the company, he assured his brother of his continued future support: "Rely upon it that what weight I have in the NWC will always continue to lean in his favor" (Mitchell 1973: 12).

Such favouritism to relatives might seem as dysfunctional to North West Company interests as internal patronage bonds could be for the Hudson's Bay Company; and certainly it could work to the disadvantage of well-qualified men who lacked the proper "connexions." One such case was that of North West clerk Willard F. Wentzell, of Scandinavian descent, who never attained partnership despite being known as "an active and enterprising trader, a man of great integrity" (Masson 1960, I: 70). Fellow North Wester Ross Cox observed that Wentzell, because he had

> no family connexions to place his claims in the prominent point of view which they ought to occupy, and being moreover of an honest unbending disposition, his name was struck out of the house-list of favourite clerks intended for proprietors, and he had the vexation to see many young men promoted over his head, several of whom had never slept a night with a hungry stomach (Cox 1832: 283).

And Wentzell himself wrote in 1815 that he was "convinced that some have been advanced whose claims were not superior to my own. No doubt they had the means to 'turn the wheel' which I had not" (Masson 1960, I: 114).

On the other hand, the high visibility of the leading North Westers' kinsmen and friends as their personal recruitment and promotion choices placed strong informal pressures on both the choosers and the men chosen to demonstrate their merits; failure or misbehaviour would reflect badly on the patrons as well as on the recruits. Such patrons accordingly tried to assure that their young kinsmen or friends entered the company with the necessary qualifications and often contributed to their prior education, since the paucity of permanent posts in the North Westers' fur trade sphere made on-the-job education, Hudson's Bay style, difficult or impossible (except in regard to trading or country skills). If all went well, these young men might deservedly rise to partnership status, like the McGillivray nephews of Simon McTavish. But if a clerkly recruit was a failure, he and his relatives might face (and exchange) blame for the outcome, as Finan McDonald's case demonstrates. Finan, younger brother of John McDonald, a senior North Wester, was scheduled to enter the company after finishing his schooling. But he joined it prematurely, to the great annoyance of John. Criticizing his brother James in eastern Canada for allowing this to happen, John complained to him,

> Notwithstanding that I was sending down money with every exhortation to keep him in school as I was willing to be at the expense and wished him to have a liberal education, I was cruelly deceived by being told that he was constantly in school when it was quite the contrary, and he by his deception came to this country without education and what is the consequence? Why: that he cannot rise higher than the charge of a single post for the want of education . . . no one in this country strove harder to assist his relations than I did (John McDonald "Le borgne" letters, 27 August 1825).

It was no credit to the McDonalds to have Finan abandon the fur trade as a still lowly and semi-literate clerk, a few years after the 1821 coalition. Prospective partners were expected to begin their careers as literate clerks, with some formal education behind them. This meant that they entered the trade somewhat older than most Hudson's Bay men, but at a correspondingly higher rank and with greater responsibilities and higher expectations.

The networks that bridged the gaps between the fur trade country, eastern Canada, and Britain subjected the North Westers to informal pressures and constraints in various domains of their conduct. The character of their semi-autonomy in the fur trade country accordingly differed from that of the Hudson's Bay men. They were more bound by home involvements than their London-based rivals and less remote socially and geographically from their employers, but their freedom of action within the Indian country was still considerable. While most Hudson's Bay men resided for long periods in posts that offered little privacy or independence to any but senior officers, North Westers had relatively greater flexibility. The personal relations of Hudson's Bay men and North Westers accordingly followed distinctive paths within their companies' separate fur trade settings.

3

Company Men and Native Women in Hudson Bay

By 1821, when the companies merged, practically all officers of the Hudson's Bay and North West Companies, and many lower-ranked employees as well, were allied with women born in the Indian country. Such alliances were by then, in fact, normal adjuncts of fur trade social life, and their general acceptance is reflected in the widespread use of a standard descriptive phrase—marriage "according to the custom of the country"—in records of the early to mid-1800s. When for example, the Methodist missionary George Barnley formally married the native-born Emma Good to George Moore in December, 1841, at Moose Factory, he noted that they had already "been united according to the custom of the Country since June 1816" (Moose Factory register).

Before 1821, two traits were common to all these unions. None had been formally sanctioned or recorded by a white clergyman or missionary, for neither company had made a practice of bringing churchmen into the fur trade country. And except for a few alliances with women among the first Red River settlers and the instances of the Orkney girl mentioned earlier, Marie-Anne Gaboury, who married voyageur Jean-Baptiste Lagimodière in 1806, and Jane Barnes, English barmaid and companion of a North Wester (Porter 1930), they all involved women of Indian descent and generated mixed-blood offspring whose parentage and legal standing might be subject to question by European-based civil or religious authorities.

The growth of these customary unions and the multiplication of their progeny over a period of many decades gave a distinctive social character to the fur trade and provided a basis for its development as an ongoing and to some extent self-perpetuating semi-autonomous community. New social and racial sub-groups appeared in the fur trade country as results of the first Indian-fur trader unions, producing new alliance possibilities among traders, mixed-bloods, and Indians as related and interconnected groups. Some important contrasts also developed in the kinds of relationship that the Hudson's Bay and North West Company men established with their Indian and, later, their mixed-blood wives, as might be expected in two such different concerns.

HBC MEN AND INDIAN WOMEN

Early alliances between Hudson's Bay Company men and Indian women cannot be traced in any detail for obvious reasons. Company rules forbade traders to "converse" with women in the Bay and provided for punishment of those who permitted such relationships. In 1683, for example, "strict Commands" were given to the chief of each post "upon forfiture of Wages not to Suffer any woman to come within any of our Factories" (Rich 1948: 40–41). With such penalties, it may be assumed that this rule was at least partially enforced; relationships that did exist were unlikely to be mentioned in the post records kept for the perusal of the London committee. And for the first several decades of the company's occupation of the Bay, very few other records are available.

Nevertheless, it is possible to document at least fifteen instances of Hudson's Bay men (typically officers) taking Indian women as mates before 1770. None of these women was apparently ever designated by her trader companion as a "wife" in the European sense (the Kelsey case, cited below, is unreliable on this detail), and at least five of the men involved eventually married British women whose claims as legitimate wives went unquestioned. But these early alliances are tokens of the London committee's failure to achieve complete control of its men's personal lives and of social changes to come in later decades as the taking of native mates became institutionalized as a "custom of the country." In this first century, too, Indian interests and values also helped to shape the course of these relationships.

Only one of the seven cases discussed here involved a company man of the period before 1700; and it is the least documented. In the 1680s, the London committee was seeking men to travel inland to explore and to contact more distant Indians. Their attention was drawn to one of their earliest apprentices, "the Boy Henry Kelsey" who, they were told, was "a very active Lad, delighting much in Indians Company, being never better pleased than when he is travelling amongst them." Kelsey was accordingly asked to conduct explorations on the company's behalf, sometimes for lengthy periods, in the late 1680s and early 1690s (Doughty and Martin 1929: XIII).

That information is a matter of company record; the following is not. In 1752, Joseph Robson published his account of six years as a Hudson's Bay employee in the 1730s. He therein recorded a story which had, he said, been told to him by "the servants in the Bay" about Kelsey's return from one of his trips after a long absence. Kelsey arrived with a party of Indians, dressed as one of them, "and attended by a wife, who wanted to follow him into the factory." The governor at first failed to recognize him and opposed their entry; "but upon Kelsey's telling him in English, that he would not go in himself if his wife was not suffered to go in, he knew him, and let them both enter" (ibid., XV).

There is no other record of this relationship, although Kelsey's later career is amply documented. He went on to become governor of York Fort; and in 1698 (having reached the rank of "Second" at York), he was married to one Elizabeth Dix in England. He retired in 1722 after almost continuous Bay service from 1684. Robson's account of Kelsey's Indian "wife" is unsubstantiated elsewhere, but it is plausible, since it would have been consistent with his "delighting much in Indians Company" and with his evidently extensive knowledge of "ye Indian Language" (Davies 1965: 386–89, 394).

The next Hudson's Bay Company man to leave some record of an alliance with an Indian woman was Joseph Adams, another apprentice who rose to officer's status. His will of 1737 named, besides a sister, a daughter, Mary, described as "an infant about three years and five months old born in Albany Fort." Mary, who was to receive most of her father's estate in trust, came to England with him shortly before he died in 1737 (Davies 1965: 33n, 233n). Her mother, however, remained in the Bay and was evidently still living in the vicinity of Moose or Albany Fort in James Bay in 1744 (Van Kirk 1974a: 4). Adams apparently never married in England.

A third man to form attachments in Hudson Bay was Robert Pilgrim, who entered in 1730 as a ship's steward. After serving at Prince of Wales Fort under Richard Norton and James Isham, taking charge there from 1745 to 1748, and holding the command at Moose from 1748 to 1750, Pilgrim retired to England in ill health. Like Joseph Adams, he apparently never had a British wife, and like him, he died soon after retirement. With him when he left the Bay in 1750 were two dependents, a son and an Indian woman named Ruehegan (Thu a higon). His will instructed that after his death his son was to be placed under a guardian in England and that Ruehegan was to be permitted to return to her relatives, which she later did. The fact that her kin resided at Churchill suggests that the beginning of her association with Pilgrim predated 1748, when he left for Moose. But his attachment to her was apparently not monogamous; a communication of the London committee to Pilgrim in May, 1747, indicates that he had been keeping two Indian women with their children in his Churchill apartments. Perhaps this behaviour, besides a record of apparently poor management of his commands, was one factor leading a colleague of his to tell the London committee in 1751 that "Mr Pilgrim being dead having very little to say of his general good Character We beg to be excus'd entring into his bad one" (Van Kirk 1974*a*: 4; Craig 1974: 520–21).

Richard Norton, who first arrived in the Bay as a thirteen-year-old apprentice in 1714, eventually married his patron's daughter, Elizabeth McCliesh. But in the course of becoming, like Kelsey, a seasoned traveller and good linguist, friendly with his Indian trading partners, he also developed attachments within the Indian country. There is some evidence that he took a Cree woman as a companion not many years after his arrival (Giraud 1945: 415). And despite his English marriage, he evidently continued such alliances almost until his retirement and death in 1741. In May 1739, the London committee admonished him on the subject in response to a now lost private letter: "As to your own Concience in Relation to the Indian Woman and Family, we agree with you that we have no power over that but Certainly the Company ought not to be put to any Charge, or their affairs be Damaged thereby" (Davies 1965: 292n).

Perhaps because Norton, unlike Adams and Pilgrim, had a British wife and senior company father-in-law, he omitted any mention of Indian family connections in his will of 1734. This fact complicates identification of the birthplace and race of his apparently illegitimate son Moses, who later rose through the ranks to the command of Churchill. Because of Richard Norton's known Indian connections, Moses has typically been described as born of an Indian woman—an assumption reinforced by Hudson's Bay man Samuel Hearne's description of him in 1770 as "Indian" (Tyrrell 1911: 107). Moses himself, however, designated his mother by a European name in his will, and historian Sylvia Van Kirk (personal communication) has suggested that Moses may have been born of an extramarital liaison of his father in England. Whatever his mother's origins, Moses himself, according to Samuel Hearne, surpassed his father (and other Hudson's Bay officers on record) in the multiplicity of his female companions.

Aside from having a white wife in England, he was said by Hearne (who knew Moses late in his career but had little good to say of him) to keep "for his own use five or six of the finest Indian girls which he could select," while going "to the most ridiculous length" to keep the traders under his command away from "the women of the country." Hearne further claimed that Moses had poisoned two of his women "because he thought them partial to other objects more suitable to their ages" and that he was not above poisoning those Indians "who refused him their wives or daughters" (ibid.). These allegations are difficult to evaluate. Moses certainly had a native family; one of his daughters, who died in 1782, was described by Hearne in most laudatory terms (ibid., 159–60), and other apparent descendants turn up later. But he also, unlike Robert Pilgrim, handled his command and responsibilities in such a way as to retain the confidence of the London committee. "Private animosities" probably coloured Hearne's portrait and complicate the problems of tracing and analyzing Norton's attachments.

The evidence on the final two instances outlined here, those of James Isham and Humphrey Marten, is by no means complete, but it is less ambiguous than that on Moses Norton. Isham entered the company in 1732 as writer and bookkeeper and early rose to high positions, being placed in charge of York Fort in 1737 and of Churchill from 1741 to 1745. Thereafter, except for sojourns in England in 1745–46, 1748–50, and 1758–59, Isham remained in charge at York, where he died in April 1761.

Like the Nortons, Isham acquired both Indian family connections and a British wife; and there is some suggestion that he may have maintained more than one female companion at a time in Hudson Bay. In 1746–47, Isham's domestic arrangements were noticed by some unwelcome visitors when an expedition sent to the Bay by Arthur Dobbs, company critic and seeker after a Northwest Passage, wintered there. After months of friction with their unwilling hosts, Dobbs's men sailed home and launched public attacks upon the company and its officers, taking a critical view of, among other things, the "Governor's woman" (Rich 1961, I: 605). In these years the company was facing strong hostility from Dobbs and other proponents of free trade, Bay colonization, and exploration for a northern sea route to the west—hostility that culminated in the 1749 parliamentary inquiry into its operations. Possibly its vulnerability to public criticism was urgently relayed to Isham; only a few days after his return to London in October 1748 to testify on the company's behalf, he was married to an Englishwoman. And in 1751, when he was reconfirmed as chief at York, the London committee warned in his paper of appointment that:

> as in this we have granted your Request do expect in return that you do not harbour or Entertain any Indian Woman or Women in our Factory or permit others under you so to do, and that you be an Example to your people of Sobriety, diligence, and whatever else is commendable and praiseworthy (Rich 1949: 322).

Isham apparently continued to be permissive about allowing Indian women into York Fort. Ferdinand Jacobs, his successor, claimed that Isham remained lax and informed the London committee that "the worst Brothel House in London is Not So Common a Stew as the men's House in this Factory." While Jacobs himself had an Indian family, he claimed to have changed Isham's standards, refusing to allow Indian women to be with their mates in the post, to the great discontent of all involved (Van Kirk 1974*a*: 6; Tyrrell 1911: 160; HBCA, A. 11/117, f. 60).

In 1758, Isham secured leave to return to England on family business; his English wife and daughter had been moving from place to place putting him "to a great Deal of unnecessary charges," and, he wrote, "My child and goods are at stake, for the want of a Husband and fatherly Assistance." In 1760 there were signs that Isham's marriage had ended; his request that £40 be paid "Quarterly to the Late Cathern. Isham" was met by the company secretary's answer that part of it had been paid "for your late Wifes use which was all that was required." Isham's will of 1760 made no mention of his British family and bequeathed all his "money goods and Chattels" to his son Charles, born in Hudson Bay about 1754. After his death in 1761, the London governor and committee instructed the new chief at York to "send home Charles . . . an Indian Lad said to be the Natural Son of Mr. James Isham Deceased," and they later ordered that Charles, still under age, be delivered to Isham's brother, Thomas (Rich 1949: 325). Charles remained with his uncle in England from 1763 to 1766, then returned as an apprentice to Rupert's Land where he served the company until 1814. In this case, as in many later ones, a fur trade child was placed with a collateral relative at home who assumed responsibility for his education and care; and the company became involved in his affairs first as administrator and later as employer.

One final case, that of Humphrey Marten, offers some interesting contrasts. Marten entered the company as a writer (apprentice clerk) in 1750, later was chief at York and Albany Forts, and ended his career in 1786 in charge of York. Like numerous other Hudson's Bay officers, he apparently formed his closest social ties within the fur trade. He served first under Isham and on the latter's death, he mourned his superior's loss both as a friend and as "the Idol of the Indians . . . whose name will be dear to them as long as one is alive that knew him." Marten in turn became the object of a similar attachment; the young Joseph Colen wrote in 1786 that "Mr. Marten hath given me great assistance ever since my arrival and with fatherly affection" (HBC Library, Winnipeg, typed biography of Marten, p. 8).

Like his predecessors Joseph Adams and Robert Pilgrim, Marten acquired a native family and apparently did not have a British wife. But one striking novelty sets Marten's case apart from all those cited above and is vividly expressed in his official Albany journal, dated January 1771:

> at 10 minutes before 3 O Clock this morning departed this life, the Indian woman called Pawpitch, Daughter to the Captain of the Goose Hunters, by whose Death my poor Child becomes Motherless, and should Your Honours not Consent to his going to England (which O my God forbid) he will be a poor helpless Orphan indeed his Grandfather being deep in Years and having a numerous family, cannot provide for him hard if the Son is debarr'd from reaping the fruits of the Father honest industry (ibid., pp. 2–3).

The company writings of Kelsey, the Nortons, Isham, and the others show no similar subjective expressions of personal familial bonds in Hudson Bay nor even the use of "my" for their women and children. In his lengthy *Observations in Hudson's Bay,* for example, which he wrote in an informal and personal style in the 1740s, James Isham never mentioned his own Bay attachments, although he went so far as to describe Indian girls as "very frisky when Young . . . well shap'd . . . very Bewitchen" and their children by Englishmen as "streight Lim'd, Lively active, and Indeed fair exceeds the true born Indians in all things . . . and . . . pretty Numerious" (Rich 1949: 78–79). The documentation of these early cases lies not in those company records left by the individuals involved, but in the accounts of others (Robson on Kelsey, Dobbs's men wintering at York on Isham, Samuel Hearne on Moses Norton), in wills where final personal loyalties had to be stated (Adams, Pilgrim, Isham), or in disciplinary strictures sent from London to the Bay as the committee responded to reports of its officers' disobedience of its rules. For a century, then, the company maintained its sternly monastic stance and regulations, while its officers maintained a close reserve about the sexual and familial relationships that numbers of them founded in the Bay.

But by the time of Pawpitch's death, there were cracks in the walls of this monasticism and reserve. Company ships had openly carried the native-born Mary Adams, Ruehegan and her son, Charles Isham, and probably other natives, home to England. After Robert Pilgrim's death, the directors had felt it necessary to require that no ship's captain bring any native-born adult or child to England without express written consent from London (Van Kirk 1974a: 11; Williams 1969: 145). And even before Pawpitch died, Marten was asking the company to grant his son, John America Marten, a passage to England to be educated (typed biography, p. 2). Officers' native families were becoming a matter of record; and officers themselves began to grow more open and assertive about their welfare from the 1770s on. It is interesting that while he inserted his family concerns into the Albany journal in 1771, Marten still refrained from describing Pawpitch as his. But by 1781, he was using the possessive adjective in referring to his new Indian mate in the York journal. As part of the preparations for his trip to England in that year he noted, "An old Man and family arrived from Albany . . . he coming to take charge of my woman who is his daughter, and to conduct her, and her two children back to Albany" (ibid., p. 6). There is still circumspection here and an absence of the term "wife," which the Hudson's Bay traders did not use freely before the mid-1790s. But Marten's case suggests that it was becoming possible for company men to be increasingly frank about their "connections" without suffering censure.

Despite the apparent "monogamy" of Marten's Bay ties, there is some indication, as there is for Pilgrim, Moses Norton, and Isham, that he may sometimes have had more than one mate. In 1786, the final year of Marten's command at York, his surgeon, Alfred Robinson, complained to the London committee about his chief's behaviour. Among other things, he was "called a thief" only because,

> I gave to a young Girl (who he had allowed me to take care of) a mouthful of Victuals from the 2nd Table . . . her friends that were able to procure food were gone to their winter quarters, I could not see her starve . . . especially when certain that ye allowance for Victuals for 1 man would nearly suffice us both; But in order to show his tyrannical authority ye more . . . nothing less would do but she must be turned out of Doors to be exposed to hunger and every insult, when at the same time he was keeping 2 or 3 day and night gorging in the midst of plenty (HBCA, A. 11/116, f. 180).

As in the cases of Norton and Isham, the testimony came from a hostile witness; but such recurring examples suggest that some Hudson's Bay commanding officers indeed used their high positions not only to claim continuous female companionship as Andrew Graham, who himself had two Hudson Bay children, noted (Williams 1969: 248, 344, 349) but also to practise a polygyny that did not find approval among their colleagues or outside observers. One further case, at York Factory in 1812, reinforces this impression. While Miles Macdonell, leader of a group of Red River colonists, was wintering there, he observed that York's chief officer, William Hemmings Cook, "appeared anxious to keep all the men away from the Factory" and added,

> It may be easily supposed that a chief who occupied himself the Mess Room with a squaw occupying an appartment on each side opening into it, would not be very desirous of having his family arrangements deranged by visitors (PAC, Miles Macdonell Papers, Macdonell to Selkirk, 31 May 1812).

FAMILY CONNECTIONS IN HUDSON BAY: INDIAN AND BRITISH VIEWS, MOTIVES, AND OPTIONS

The foregoing cases indicate the patterns that alliances between Hudson's Bay men and Indian women followed in the period before such unions were accepted as normal or proper and before mixed-blood women were available as mates in any number. It now remains to examine the traders' and Indians' conceptions of these unions, their respective motives in entering them, and the options available to them in pursuing these relationships.

The Hudson's Bay traders' side is fairly clear. The two outstanding elements of their Bay life were their lengthy periods of isolation from Britain and even from other posts and their subjection to strongly monastic regulations laid down by the London committee. Not surprisingly, the very isolation which gave them freedom from observation also enabled them to offset their loneliness by taking Indian female companions, risking committee censure and damage to company interests in their pursuit of personal gratification.

These relationships were largely the prerogatives of officers, and their unions, if monogamous, came to be tolerated both by their colleagues and, eventually, by a resigned London committee. Taking multiple mates, however, was unacceptable; polygyny was too much of a violation of British values to find approval. The practice of allowing lower-ranked servants general access to women was equally deplored by the committee and by some company men. From their use of terms such as "whoring" and "brothel," it seems clear that such licence was equated by both traders and their employers with the urban prostitution in European centres such as London and was seen to exemplify the worst of British immorality. Monogamous masters of houses were at least implicitly following an accepted British model, although they could not legitimize their unions. But those traders who found that they could gain access to Indian women in exchange for payment, notably in brandy, were unlikely to consider their activities as anything other than whoring as they knew it at home. The damaging linkage between brandy and "lewdness" was acknowledged by James Isham in his 1743 *Observations:*

> I think, as others has, itts a pitty they was allow'd to taste of that Bewitching spirit calld. Brandy, or any other Spiritious Liquor's,— which has been the Ruing of a Great many Indians, and the Cheif Cause of their Ludness and bad way's they are now given to, their being some few that Drinks none—what may be Calld. Virtious women (Rich 1949: 95).

The problem, however, went beyond matters of brandy and "ludness." The fact was that the early Britishers were also encountering among Hudson Bay Indians a widespread, morally sanctioned, and controlled pattern of wife-lending that was quite unfamiliar to them. Understandably, they were slow to grasp the important contrasts between London prostitution and this novel custom or to recognize that these two practices, despite some formal resemblances, were very different in meaning. Later company men became well aware that many northern Indian groups customarily established friendship bonds with strangers not by means of impersonal diplomatic contracts and trappings such as the early London committee had proposed to use, but by lending or exchanging wives or daughters. During his sojourn in the Cree and Chipewyan Athabaska country in 1820-21, for example, George Simpson, later the governor of the new Hudson's Bay Company, informed the London committee that among the Indian groups he knew, "the offer of their Wives and Daughters is the first token of their Friendship and hospitality" (Rich 1938: 392). Such patterns were apparently so widespread that Marcel Giraud in his comprehensive study of *métissage* in Canada discovered only one Indian society that consistently shunned sexual contacts between themselves and whites—the Athapascan-speaking Beaver Indians were, or by the late 1700s had become, strongly averse to such relationships (Giraud 1945: 111; Mackenzie 1911, II: 26).

The Cree or Homeguard Indians of the coastal areas of Hudson Bay were the first to introduce traders to a complex pattern that they later found in many Indian societies—visible, but in British terms immoral, freedom in sexual behaviour, combined with less visible and thus less readily understood social controls. Strangers to Indian ways recorded this freedom long before they came to comprehend the controls that went with it. It was easy, then, for early Britishers to misrepresent Indian views, as did former company employee Richard White when called as a witness during the 1749 parliamentary inquiry. When asked "if the Europeans were allowed to converse with the Women it would not drive away the Indians?" White answered simply, "He believed not; for the Indians were a sensible People, and agree their Women should be made use of" (Great Britain 1749: 219).

Other observers saw that such "use" was hedged about with social forms that Europeans disregarded at their peril. In 1743 James Isham reported the consequences of a case of neglect of Cree expectations and forms which probably took place during the French occupation of the York Fort area from 1697 to 1714:

Jelioussey . . . is Likewise very much amongst these Natives . . . and often will be the Death of such that has offended them, as I have Known both English and french by these offences,—a sample of which—the French had formerly a setlemt. up ———— River where the Natives (women) was forc'd into the fort against their will which aggravated them to that Degree, that they fixd. upon Revenge,—they therefore unperceivd. informd. their husbands to be Ready upon a Signal they wou'd make, accordingly the women took an oppertunity to wett all the french fuzes with their 'urine, and then gave the Signal, when their husbands Gott in under cover of the Night, and put their Enemies to the rout, when the french run to their arm's and found how they was betrayd, and was Kill'd for their perfidiousness, being 8 in Number,—some of which Indians are now alive and have told me the same (Rich 1949: 95).

Later writers recognized, further, that Cree "jealousy" was provoked particularly in situations where wives were "borrowed" without having been lent and would doubtless have seen the episode recorded by Isham as a case in point. Andrew Graham, the arctic explorer Sir John Richardson, and the Montreal-based explorers and traders, Alexander Mackenzie and Alexander Henry the Younger, all agreed that the lending or exchanging of wives was a generally accepted custom among the Cree, contingent, however, upon the approval of the husbands. Women, and European men, engaging in unapproved and clandestine affairs risked severe retaliation. In his *Observations,* Andrew Graham gave a concise summary of Cree wife-lending, recording also the Cree means of handling the children born during lending periods:

> If the woman commits adultery without the knowledge and permission of her husband, he makes no scruple of turning her off; and very often knocks out her brains with a hatchet. . . . But they frequently lend their wives to other men for a night, week, month, or year; and will sometimes make an exchange for several years. And afterwards the women return to their former husbands, taking with them all the children they have born by the other man (Williams 1969: 158).

Such children, Graham went on to note, were readily adopted by these women's husbands and were in fact seen as gains, at least in cases involving children of British fathers: "when any of the married women has a child by an Englishman the husband is not angry with her but proud of his present. Indeed the affair rivets her firmly in his favor" (Giraud 1945: 410n).

In summary, in any post where the chief officer permitted contacts between his men and Indian women, the traders' desires for female companionship were readily fulfilled because the Indians were eager to cement social ties with their new European trading partners. But Indian and white perceptions of these relationships could vary widely, leaving much room for misunderstanding. If the London committee in its early decades had not required its traders to be circumspect in their dealings with Indians, Indian-white relations in the Bay might have been far less peaceful. The vertical social organization of the posts also facilitated the control of trader-Indian relations; although officers might abuse their power, their subordinates' behaviour was quite closely regulated. As a result, only one serious clash over "too much freedom given on account of the Indian Women" occurred during the company's first century in Hudson Bay. In 1755, Henley House was attacked by Indians angry because their women were kept in the post while their own access was denied, in violation of what they saw as a social compact involving the exchanging of women for post rights (Bishop 1976*b*: 41).

While the traders in general were subject to fairly stern controls, chief officers and masters of houses had a special position both in their posts and in the Indians' view. Being highly placed, they were able simultaneously to require their subordinates to obey company rules and to claim personal privileges regarding access to women. Samuel Hearne accused Moses Norton of following this practice to extremes:

> no man took more pains to inculcate virtue, morality, and continence on others. . . . Lectures of this kind from a man of established virtue might have had some effect; but when they came from one who was known to live in open defiance of every law, human and divine, they were always heard with indignation, and considered as the hypocritical cant of a selfish debauchee, who wished to engross every woman in the country to himself (Tyrrell 1911: 107–8).

Alfred Robinson's charges against Humphrey Marten, cited above, were similar.

At the same time, these officers faced social pressures from Indian groups. When Indian traders discovered who was the most important man at a particular post, they sought his favour and friendship by offering him gifts, especially of women. In 1779, surveyor Philip Turnor told the London committee that their bachelor officers inland were continually pressed to accept such gifts; "were they not to keep a Woman . . . above half the Indians that came to the House would offer the Master their Wife though he was to make the Indian a present for his offer the Woman would think herself slighted." If the master already had a woman, he was subjected to fewer offers; "very few Indians make that offer when they know the Master keeps a woman" (Tyrrell 1934: 274–75).

If officers refused to become involved in wife-borrowing, with its suggestions of whoremongering, they were all the likelier to receive offers of their Indian associates' daughters in marriage. Being more congruent with British values, these proposals might meet with greater success. A trader interested in taking a bride could readily go through the simple formalities of Cree marriage, easing his way with presents of trade goods. Andrew Graham and James Isham, two men who may themselves have taken part in the procedure, have described it. When a young man wished to marry, he applied for the consent of the girl's father, brother, or other family head, making him a "present of furs or European articles" (Williams 1969: 175–76).

That being granted,

> When a Young man has a mind for a wife, they do not make Long tedious Ceremony's, nor yet use much formality's . . . the man goes out of his tent, to the woman's tent door, where he Looks in and Lays before her as much Cloth as will make her a smock, Sleeves, and Stockings, no words Spoke, he then Return's to his own tent, and waits for the womans Comming,—in the mean time, if the woman takes this Cloth up the match is made, that she will be his wife, when she gett's up and goes and Sitts by him in his tent; as man and wife and all is over; But if the woman [refuses] to take the Cloth, some one in the tent Carry's itt and lays itt by the man, which Denotes she will not be his wife, when he Looks out for another (Rich 1949: 101).

Women acquired in this way regarded themselves as married, and husband and wife were expected to remain loyal to each other. As they came to understand Indian custom, traders who went through such ceremonies began to take their fur trade unions seriously, recognizing their native families in wills and in other contexts. By the 1770s, company men had learned that the Cree, except in cases of excessive addiction to brandy, were not promiscuous libertines and that wife-lending did not vitiate the seriousness of the marriage relationship. William Falconer, an officer at Severn on the Bay coast in the 1760s and 1770s, wrote that while the informality of Cree marriage rites might "seem frivolous," both man and wife "performs their dutys, and are more chaste to each other than the more civilized Nations who are instructed with the Dutys of Christianity" (PAC, MG19, D2, Falconer, "Remarks on the Natives": 55).

But even if chief officers acquired women by accepting wives or marrying Crees, they still remained somewhat subject to further offers of women. Although Cree marriage customs forbade promiscuity, they permitted the taking of more than one mate; and indeed the Cree, like the Chipewyans and other groups, expected leading men to show their importance by practising polygyny. As Andrew Graham wrote of the Cree, "When an Indian's abilities as a hunter are sufficient to provide for a larger family, it is usual for him to take another wife, or perhaps two. I have known some leaders have seven wives" (Williams 1969: 176). William Falconer wrote that polygynists came under both internal and external pressures to take still more wives. Perhaps because "the youngest married Wife does the most labour," women often urged "their Husbands to take more Wives, when they find, they are able to procure a living for them." And men capable of maintaining several wives were "so much esteemed by the other Natives, that they are as desirous to have their Daughters marryed to such, as poor People in Great Britain are of having their's to Men of fortune" ("Remarks on the Natives": 55).

In such a social context, chiefs of posts, with their high standing and superior access to provisions and trade goods, would sometimes be pressed by Indians to take more than one mate, and they were in a position to take advantage of these offers if they chose. The cases of Pilgrim, Isham, Moses Norton, and Cook suggest that some officers did so, at least between the 1740s and 1812. Turnor and Falconer agreed, however, that Cree wives had some say in the extent of their husbands' polygyny. While Falconer mentioned that a wife might urge a man to take an additional mate, Turnor also noted that a wife's feelings against polygyny could also carry weight; if a trader already had a companion, he could refuse further offers by saying that he had "a Women of his own and she would be offended" (Tyrrell 1934: 274-75).

Fairly early in the company's history, economic motives also began to lead Hudson's Bay traders into further involvement in these alliances, as they discovered that Indian women, because of their socio-economic roles in Indian society, could make substantial contributions to the trade. One of the earliest women to prove of great value to company interests was Thanadelthur, a Chipewyan or "Northern" Indian. The British called her the "Slave Woman" since she had been a captive of some Cree Indians until she escaped and reached York Fort in 1714, "Allmost Starv'd." At York, Governor James Knight had been seeking ways to establish trade contacts with the Chipewyans, who were on hostile terms with the Cree and had not ventured to the Bay posts. With her knowledge of Cree and Chipewyan, and of her people and their country, Thanadelthur provided the opportunity he had hoped for. In 1715-16 she travelled inland with William Stuart and some Crees, located a large band of Chipewyans, brought the two groups together, and by dint of "perpetuall talking" and scolding and pushing, "forced them to ye peace." The following winter, she and some other Chipewyans stayed at York, and she taught her associates which furs were most valued by the British and how to prepare them. But in early 1717, to the deep regret of Governor Knight, she became ill and died. So great had been her contributions that Knight made special efforts, at the cost of "above 60 skins value in goods," to secure the services of another Chipewyan woman, who travelled inland with Richard Norton the following summer and renewed contact with her countrymen (Van Kirk 1974b).

There is no evidence that these Chipewyans became sexual partners of Hudson's Bay men. But they certainly demonstrated to the Britishers the contributions that Indian women could make to the profits and expansion of the fur trade as guides, interpreters, and intermediaries, and to trade-related activities such as preparing pelts (traditionally women's work in Indian society). The aid of such women was more explicitly recognized in company records as time went on.

In 1754, Anthony Henday made a long journey inland from York to the Blackfoot country. One version of his journal of that trip, polished for transmittal to the London committee, makes no reference to female assistance; but another copy frequently notes that his Indian "bedfellow" was invaluable to him as interpreter, helper, and source of information (Williams 1978: 46). When Henday's journal came into the hands of his superior, James Isham, at York, one passage also prompted Isham to comment explicitly on the potential usefulness of marital alliances with strategically placed Indian women:

I can but own if I had been in Captn Henday's place, when the King of the Earchithinues [Blackfeet] offerred him his Daughter in Marriage ... would have Embraced ye proposal, which would have Created a firm friendship and would have been A great help in Engageing them to trade (ibid., 54).

Later eighteenth-century records emphasized with increasing openness the importance of Indian women's contributions both on journeys and at the posts. At Churchill in the 1770s, Samuel Hearne's first journey inland to explore and trade failed; and his Indian guide Matonabee, who directed his second and successful effort, attributed the failure to Hearne's lack of female assistants, who had been forbidden him by the authoritarian Moses Norton. Matonabee, who himself had six strong wives to aid the progress of the second journey, expressed his opinion in the following terms:

the very plan we pursued by the desire of the Governor, in not taking any women with us on the journey, was, he said, the principal thing that occasioned all our wants: "for," said he, "when all the men are heavy laden, they can neither hunt nor travel to any considerable distance; and in case they meet with success in hunting, who is to carry the produce of their labour? . . . one [woman] can carry, or haul, as much as two men can do. They also pitch our tents, make and mend our clothing, keep us warm at night; and in fact there is no such thing as travelling any considerable distance, or for any length of time, in this country without their assistance" (Tyrrell 1911: 101–2).

Certain passages in the York Factory journal for the fall of 1800 demonstrate that by then women were also making substantial economic contributions at the posts. On 7 October, chief officer John Ballenden recorded that he had "Employed the Invalid Natives now on the Plantation to cut up Deer skins for netting Snow Shoes for the Men." On 19 October, when the "poor Natives now on the Plantation" were granted refuge from sudden snow and cold within the factory, Ballenden identified them further: "15 in number; the whole is Women one poor old man excepted which is employed in making Snow Shoe frames and the Women nets them." By 10 November, they had made "650 pairs of Leather Shoes" for the traders. Ballenden "Gave them some triffles as an encouragement for their trouble," having earlier given them "supplies of Oatmeal &c according to custom, also some firewood," and set them again to netting snowshoes ("delivered them out 55 pairs of fframes for that purpose"). In December, some of the women served as emergency emissaries from the post, doubtless using some of the snowshoes they had made. Word came that a large family of Indians was in great distress a few days' journey distant; and Ballenden was at first uncertain what to do because he had no Indian men to send and no Englishmen who could walk in snowshoes were available. But the following day, he despatched three of the strongest of the Indian women to the rescue, promising them a reward. Four days later, they returned from their mission with five starving Indians (HBCA, B. 239/a/105, ff. 5, 7-8, 11, 15-16).

Two years later, the officers at York summarized to the London committee a variety of important tasks that native women were now performing in the posts:

> they clean and put into a state of preservation all Beavr. and Otter skins brought by the Indians undried and in bad Condition. They prepare Line for Snow shoes and knit them also without which your Honors servants could not give efficient opposition to the Canadian traders they make Leather shoes for the men who are obliged to travel about in search of Indians and furs and are usefull in a variety of other instances (Van Kirk 1972: 4).

Economic considerations, then, as well as social and sexual motives, encouraged the Hudson's Bay men to accept offers of Indian women and to permit them in the posts. The Indian families involved also expected economic rewards: gifts, favours in trade, and support for relatives in time of need, as well as, perhaps, the gaining of children as productive family members with useful company contacts were among the benefits that might accrue.

Hudson's Bay Company men who acquired Indian wives and families might find their "connections" personally, socially, and economically beneficial during their Bay service, but they had relatively few options to choose from in pursuing these relationships as their careers drew to a close. Before the founding of the Red River Colony, the fur trade country offered no centre to which a trader and his family could retire. Settlement at the posts was not possible; the company could not afford to allow its retired servants and their families to accumulate at its establishments. And the London committee was firmly set against transporting native dependents to England, perhaps fortunately in some ways, since the adjustment and health problems of Indians taken to Europe were generally considerable. A few late eighteenth- and early nineteenth-century Hudson's Bay men retired with their families to Canada (Tyrrell 1934: 98n; Rich 1939: 219–20, 1954: 370); but most had no ties there. Fewer still left the company to live with their families in Indian society; most were evidently not eager to exchange their relatively secure sedentary life for the precarious nomadism of Indian life in northern Canada. Nor did the company favour the idea of its retired servants settling among the Indians as potential free traders challenging their former employer's monopoly.

The major remaining option was therefore the dissolution of the alliance. These separations sometimes meant that native families were abandoned. But numerous officers' wills attest the continuing strength of their fur trade bonds. In his will of 1784, for example, John Favell left annuities for his Indian wife and their four children, appointing as executor Thomas Hutchins, a colleague with whom he had served at Albany. Hutchins's own will, proved in 1790, was also largely concerned with the money he had held in trust for Favell's family in the Bay (Williams 1969: 365; Van Kirk 1974a: 13). William Bolland of Eastmain Factory, in his will of 1804, left annuities for his seven children and their mother, "my Helpmate Penachequay," to be administered by the Hudson's Bay Company secretary in London, and to be used "yearly to find them clothes and necessaries" (HBCA, A. 36/3, ff. 155–56). And other examples of like solicitude are plentiful.

On the Indians' side, established custom allowed traders' wives and children to return to the band; Cree divorce procedures provided a model for handling the placement of traders' native families. In the 1770s, Andrew Graham described Cree customs on these matters as follows:

> Should the husband conceive a dislike for his wife for misbehaviour, or any other cause, he will part with her at once, and she returns to her own relations with her children. The friends never offer to mediate between them, but marry her to another. The woman will also leave the man upon maltreatment, or inability to provide for her. The children being always esteemed the maternal property, is the principal reason why men seldom put away the women by whom they have issue, because it would be depriving themselves of their support in their old age (Williams 1969: 176).

Cree views of the mother-child relationship allowed traders' children to be reintegrated without stigma, along with their mothers, despite the general patrilineal and patrilocal tendencies of the society (Honigmann 1953: 811; Skinner 1911: 56–57).

The relative ease of Cree divorce also allowed traders' Indian wives, as well as the Britishers, to terminate the alliances if they saw reason to. When an officer returned home on leave or furlough, he might make arrangements for his family to be provided for at his post only to find that his mate was little disposed to remain loyal during his enforced absence of a year or more. On 2 December 1798, for example, the chief officer replacing Joseph Colen at York recorded that some Indians had just left that place accompanied by

> Mr. Colens Girl and Children who was desirous to follow them—she having soon after the Ships departure engaged a Male Companion who had long since been in the habits of her attention and Affection,—She and her Children has received every civility from me since Mr. Colen's departure that one Brother officer could expect from another—so no Blame can be attached to me of her not residing near the Factory should he again visit this Country—which I know it was his wish when he went Home (HBCA, B. 239/a/101, f. 62).

In sum, it was apparently not difficult for a trader's Indian mate to return to her own people if she chose, or was obliged, to do so.

In the late 1700s and early 1800s, then, increasing numbers of Home Indians were in fact widows, former wives, or descendants of earlier traders, who had re-entered Indian social life yet had strong attachments to particular posts. Joseph Adams's Indian mate continued to live in the vicinity of the post at which he had served. And at York in May 1800, John Ballenden recorded the illness and death of "a very old Indian Woman who has long been ailing on the Plantation" who was the former mate of a company factor many years before:

> She certainly must be upwards of one hundred years old. Her voice is still strong, and speaks as well at present as ever I knew her. This woman was for many years a wife to Mr. Isbester formerly a Chief Factor in your Honours Service (HBCA, B. 239/a/104, ff. 38–39).

The regular provision of annuities by some later traders also encouraged their native families to remain in the vicinity of the post at which they received them. Ferdinand Jacob's daughter, Thu'cotch, was by 1790 married to a York Home Indian, and she and her children received ten pounds annually there from his estate for many years (HBCA, A. 11/117, f. 60; Giraud 1945: 437–38).

Such was the domestic cycle that eighteenth-century Hudson's Bay men and their Indian mates might typically follow. There was as yet no separately classified intermediate social, racial, or co-residential group of traders' families or descendants. A few individuals found placement in Britain, when their domestic units were dissolved. But for most, an eventual return to Indian life was the expected norm. This pattern, along with the absence from the company territories of civilizing agents such as missionaries, meant that Indian wives and children (except for the few who travelled to England) were not subjected to strong pressure to assimilate to European ways. One symptom of this is that most Indian wives of Hudson's Bay men, and numerous of their children, kept their Indian names. Thu a higon, Pawpitch, Penachequay, and Thu'cotch are a few of many examples.

Despite the fact that these families could retain a place in Indian society, however, and despite the Hudson's Bay men's lack of a name for the mixed-bloods as a separate group, it was becoming evident in the late 1700s that the native-born children of traders were likely to maintain supplementary identities and affiliations distinctive from their mothers and other Indians. Their physical appearance set them apart to some degree; William Falconer described them as "a breed of People easily distinguished from the real Indians by their lighter coloured hair a few of whom there are at each of their Hon.[rs] Settlements" ("Remarks on the Natives": 27–28). Hudson's Bay traders with whom they had contact remembered their British fathers and supplemented their generic identification of these people as Indian with a specific identification of them as children of a particular trader. Their mothers might remarry and be re-assimilated or die within a few years after a trader's departure. But the children, although described as "Indians," were often distinguished from their peers as individuals. A case in point was the "Indian Lad" who came to John Ballenden at York in the severe winter of 1801, with messages from a party of Indians in great distress. In his journal for 7 February, Ballenden recorded that he

> Examind the Indian Lad that came yesterday (and who is the Son of an Officer that holds a very high Station in Yr Honours Service) He informs me that the Indians he has been residing with ever since the Fall, has all along experienced great want, and finding little probability of their soon experiencing better, he by the consent of those that took care of him, set off toward the Factory (HBCA, B. 239/a/105, f. 28).

Ballenden categorized this youth as Indian, but he also recognized his British paternity, probably knew his father personally, and may accordingly have treated him with extra consideration. It is also likely that the Indians believed this lad would receive preferential treatment given his origins and thought him the most effective messenger of their distress and also of the fact that, because of their hardships, Ballenden "need not expect any ffurs from them on their arrival at the Factory, if they should be fortunate enough to see it again, which they much despaired of."

From the late 1700s on, company men increasingly tended to find their fur trade mates among the mixed-blood daughters of their senior colleagues. These daughters might be broadly classed as Indian, yet they also had a specific paternally derived identity. As their numbers grew, their unions with traders initiated a new pattern of fur trade endogamy that was to change the character of Hudson's Bay social life in some important respects.

HUDSON'S BAY COMPANY MEN AND MIXED-BLOOD WOMEN, 1770-1821

Probably a few company men took daughters of senior colleagues as mates before 1770; there were certainly some such women available by then. Writing in the 1740s, James Isham described the native children of "Englishmen" (as all servants were known) as "pretty Numerous." But before 1770 the London committee still actively entertained hopes of suppressing or at least discouraging traders' sexual alliances. Early relationships between company men and mixed-blood women (whose identity would in any case have been obscured by their classification as "Indian") were therefore as unlikely to be reported in the records as alliances with Indians.

From the 1770s on, specific references to unions between traders and native daughters of company men begin to appear. Sometime in the 1770s, Edward Jarvis, surgeon at Albany and Moose, apparently took as his fur trade wife "the daughter of an Englishman" (unnamed) whom he described as having "few or no Indian friends." Their son Edward was allowed to travel to England in 1784 since he too lacked Indian contacts (Rich 1954: 350–53). Another trader, James Spence, took as his wife a woman whom he described in his will of 1795 as "my Indian Wife Nostishio [Nestitio?] daughter of the deceased Isaac Batt," a company trader who died at an inland post in 1791. Since Spence and Nostishio had four children by 1795, it is likely that their marriage had begun at least as early as the 1780s (HBCA, A. 36/12, f. 224).

Two officers of the later eighteenth century, Matthew Cocking and Moses Norton, each had several daughters, some of whom became allied with later company men. Cocking, who entered as a writer in 1765, left three daughters in Hudson Bay upon his retirement for health reasons in 1782. Thereafter, he provided his family with annuities that for many years were paid to them at York Factory. Two of the daughters, who all went by Indian names, became country wives of company officers (HBCA, A. 11/117, ff. 36, 60, 119, 160; ibid., A. 36/1A/11; Spry in press).

As far as they are known the daughters of Moses Norton probably made similar alliances. Samuel Hearne's description of Mary Norton implies an attachment between them before her death in 1782. She was, he affirmed, "directly the reverse" of other "Southern" (Cree) Indian women, who were too much addicted to liquor and debauchery. Although lacking education or "the assistance of religion," she possessed "virtue and virtuous principles" and "every other good and amiable quality, in a most eminent degree." This "most innocent and virtuous woman" perished in her twenty-second year "by the most excruciating of all deaths," from cold and hunger in the winter after the French had struck a final blow against the British after the American Revolution by destroying the company's establishment at Churchill. Hearne's "epitaph" for Mary was a passage from a poem by Edmund Waller that suggests his affection for her:

> Stranger alike to envy and to pride,
> Good sense her light, and Nature all her guide;
> But now removed from all the ills of life,
> Here rests the pleasing friend and faithful wife.
> (Tyrrell 1911: 158–60)

Hearne mentions that Mary died "amidst her own relations" (her father having died in 1773). According to a strong tradition still preserved in Selkirk, Manitoba, in the early 1970s, one of those relations was Margaret (Nahoway), a younger blue-eyed sister who, sometime in the 1790s, became the wife of William Sinclair I, an officer from the Orkneys, and mother of their ten children (interview with Ruby and Barbara Johnstone, 8 July 1972). Although company records do not confirm that Margaret was Norton's daughter, these family recollections are all plausible or in accord with known history. They also allude to a Hudson's Bay officer named Holden who assisted the family. No Holden occurs in company records of the time, and it is a reasonable linguistic possibility that this is an allusion to Hearne. Another woman named Norton, who turned up in Red River in the 1830s, may have been a sister to Mary and Margaret. The Anglican Red River register for 1834 records the baptisms of "Charlotte Norton an Adult Half Breed" and her five children "by a deceased Indian" (nos. 658–63).

The above cases have some common elements. These early mixed-blood women were generally close to Indian society and relatives (except in the

Jarvis case) and most went by Indian names. They were perhaps as likely to marry Indians (as did Thu'cotch Jacobs) as to be allied with "Englishmen." There is no particular evidence that their fathers arranged or intervened in their marriages; indeed Cocking, Norton, and Jarvis's wife's father were all either absent or deceased when their daughters married. And there is little sign of sentiment on the traders' part that native company daughters should be allied with traders rather than Indians or that they were preferred to Indian women as mates. It is possible, in fact, that numerous eighteenth-century officers would have preferred Indian women as partners, since their value in forming trade alliances with their Indian relatives and communities was considerable.

Accompanying their general assumption that native-born children would pass into Indian society, some company men held the logical corollary belief that they should be actively prepared for an Indian life. Although he admired Mary Norton's distinctiveness from Indian women, Samuel Hearne felt that her father was "very blamable from bringing her up in the tender manner which he did," for she therefore lacked resistance to fatigue and hardship, and lacked the skills to provide for herself. He went on to state his point in more general terms:

> This is, indeed, too frequent a practice among Europeans in that country, who bring up their children in so indulgent a manner, that when they retire, and leave their offspring behind, they find themselves so helpless, as to be unable to provide for the few wants to which they are subject. The late Mr. Ferdinand Jacobs . . . was the only person whom I ever knew that acted in a different manner; though no man could possibly be fonder of his children . . . as there were some that he could not bring to England, he had them brought up entirely among the natives; so that when he left the country, they scarcely ever felt the loss, though they regretted the absence of a fond and indulgent parent (Tyrrell 1911: 160).

By the late 1790s, however, company men were no longer advocating Hearne's or Jacobs's approach. With growing openness, officers and even some lower-ranked men were fathering children who began to play their own parts in the social and economic life of the posts. It is doubtful whether the small local Indian groups with their often precarious subsistence base could have absorbed all these offspring, even if they were willing. And as traders grew more visibly committed to their native families, they became more reluctant to see these children slip away into Indian life and sought to find them new roles within the company's establishments.

In time, then, traders' native-born daughters became increasingly conspicuous in the social order of the fur trade. There were perhaps four main reasons why they were preferred over Indian women from the late 1700s on, aside from the fact that there were more of them. Two of these reasons relate to declining fur trade needs for Indian women; and two reflect the increasing advantages that company daughters could offer their husbands and children in the changing fur trade social context of the early 1800s.

In the first place, by the 1790s the company had been established in a broad region west and south of Hudson Bay for many decades; and in areas where trade contacts were already made, alliances with Indian women for trade purposes were less important. In the far west, as traders reached new Indian groups, some such alliances were still being made in the 1820s; and in his 1821 report to the London committee, George Simpson told his employers that "Connubial alliances are the best security we can have of the goodwill of the Natives, I have therefore recommended the Gentlemen to form connections with the principal Families immediately on their arrival" (Rich 1938: 392). But in older trading areas, such alliances were declining.

Additionally, many traders' daughters could make the same contributions as Indian women; probably few were as indulgently protected as Mary Norton was said to have been. As company journal-keepers became more frank about the existence of native families, they often made clear how the mixed-blood women helped at the posts. By the 1800s, their contributions to the food supply were considerable, for example at Moose Factory, in the vicinity of which they gathered quantities of country provisions. On 18 December 1806, it was recorded that "Mr Browns Wife [Anne, daughter of George Humble; see HBCA, A. 1/44, f. 147] came home with 63 W[hite] fish yesterday and returned to her tent today." In 1807–8, while chief officer John Thomas was on furlough in England, his wife and their daughters were of great assistance in provisioning the post. On 28 November 1807, for example, they brought in 28 pounds of fish and 25 rabbits; on 5 December, the daughters brought 16 rabbits, and on 27 February 1808, they supplied 35 pounds of fish. On 8 July, the Thomases contributed 28 pounds of fish and "Mrs Mannall," another officer's wife, brought 40 pounds. On another occasion, 70 pounds of fish came from the women (HBCA, B. 135/a/94, f. 15; B. 135/a/95, ff. 5, 10, 18, 20). Most of these women were of mixed descent.

Indian women, then, had no monopoly on country skills, and indeed taught them to their mixed-blood daughters in many cases. When daughters married company men, they and their mothers often continued to work together as co-providers for themselves and their post. On 25 June 1809, for example, Moose Factory received 88 pounds of fish "from Mrs Good and Mother" (HBCA, B. 135/a/97, f. 22). These daughters also acquired language skills useful to their trader relatives, Indian and white.

Along with the advantages derived from their Indian backgrounds, mixed-blood women might increasingly offer useful connections to prospective husbands, particularly as senior traders began to show more open concern for their daughters. As Hearne remarked, the more indulgent among them were tempted to keep them in or near the post with regular access to its provisions and minor luxuries. Naturally, they began to try to ensure that their adult daughters could continue this mode of life. And the best means of doing so was to find them husbands among rising junior traders to whom they were already linked by vertical ties of patronage.

Although the specific roles of company fathers in arranging their daughters' alliances are often unknown, there is evidence in several cases of their influence and of their other ties with the sons-in-law whom they acquired. In about 1810, John Thomas, chief at Moose, began to keep a "Register of Births Christenings Deaths and other occurrences at Moose Factory" and recorded at its beginning the marriages of four of his daughters, whose choices he had doubtless influenced. One daughter, Elizabeth, was the widow of one company man and had since married another; a second, Charlotte, was the wife of Orkneyman Peter Spence, who had joined the company in 1800. When Thomas left Moose and the company's service for Canada in 1814, the Spence family and several other relatives travelled with him. The other two daughters, Eleanor and Ann, took the other marriage option open to girls who remained within the orbit of post life and married the native-born sons or grandsons of older officers, who were themselves just beginning careers as company employees (Moose Factory register; Rich and Johnson 1954: 370; HBC Library, biography of Peter Spence).

The sometimes unfortunate influence of a father over his daughter's marriage was made clear in the case of the young Harriet Vincent's alliance with David Ramsay Stewart. Over twenty years later, when Harriet was more happily married to Chief Trader George Gladman, Jr., she told Letitia Hargrave at York Factory the story of this early marriage:

> Mr. Stewart a man who had established steam mills for sawing timber at Moose and who was employed by the Coy asked her father for her when she was 12 years old. She was dragged out of her mothers room and sent away with him. She declares that she never hated man as she did him, and he beat and maltreated her till life was a burden.... After living with him 9 years he left her and the children and went to Canada.... She waited 4 years and then "I went with Mr. Gladman." She always says "When I *was sent* with Mr. Stewart" and "When I *went* with Mr. Gladman" (MacLeod 1947: 82).

Other marriages arranged between senior men and prospective sons-in-law

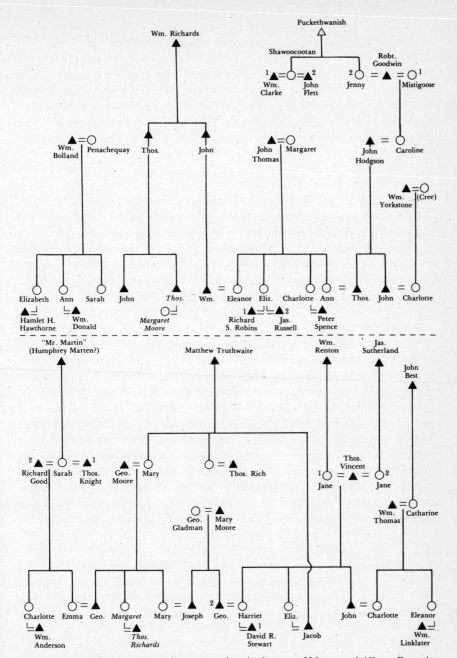

Figure 3. Some kinship and marriage connections in the area of Moose and Albany Factories between the 1760s and 1820s. Black triangles represent Hudson's Bay Company employees. Women known to be Indians include Penachequay, the daughters of Puckethwanish, and Mistigoose. The two charts intersect with the couple whose names are italicized. Sources: Moose Factory registers; HBCA wills and records.

were more satisfactory; and this alliance pattern became sufficiently well established that it came to be what Hudson's Bay men had in mind when they referred to or defined marriage in the "custom of the country." John Edward Harriott, an Englishman who entered the company in 1809, defined the "custom" as consisting primarily of an agreement between father-in-law and son-in-law when he testified in the Connolly court case of the 1860s and described his own marriage to the daughter of Chief Trader John Peter Pruden:

> When I say married, I mean according to the custom of the country, which was by an agreement between the father of the girl and the person who was going to take the girl for wife. We lived as married people, when married this way. . . . I was married after the custom of the country myself. . . . When I took a wife as above mentioned, I made a solemn promise to her father to live with her and treat her as my wife as long as we both lived (Johnstone et al. v. Connolly 1869: 285–86).

This particular kind of customary marriage, centring on arrangements made by the two men, apparently persisted locally among company families and descendants for some time after the coalition of 1821 and after the first clergymen had entered the areas around Hudson Bay. When James Harper married Charlet Turner at the Hudson Bay outpost of Martins Falls on 21 June 1841, Charlet's father, a native employee and descendant of a late eighteenth-century trader, made a record of the agreement to be filed at Moose Factory. From his phrasing it is clear that he regarded the tie being established between himself and the junior employee who was marrying his daughter as being as important as the uniting of the couple. Further, like company fathers before him, he reserved the right to approve or perhaps even to arrange the marriage and officiated at it himself as the key party involved:

> James harper I this day consent to be your father in law and by the blessings of the ald mite god join you to my beloved Daughter Charlet Turner hoping that you will consider your self as well married to her as if you were joined by a minester (Moose Factory register).

In the early nineteenth century, the London Committee finally lost hope of trying to suppress its servants' marriages. It also began to confront the problems raised by the growing numbers of native families around the posts. In its new efforts to make the best of the situation, it gained the broad support of traders who were increasingly concerned about the fates of their native dependents.

Two solutions soon began to be discussed. One which was implemented to a degree was the founding of schools at the major posts and the providing of apprenticeships so that native children could acquire a basic education and useful skills. In 1806, the London committee explicitly stated its new goals in this area. Not only should these children learn "the first rudiments of Religion," but they should also be taught "from their Youth reading, writing, arithmetic accounts, which we should hope would attach them to our Service & in a short time become a Colony of very useful Hands" (HBCA, A. 6/17, f. 69). The other major solution proposed was the establishment of a new colony, Red River, where retired servants and their families might acquire land, housing, and educational and religious facilities beyond anything provided at the posts. The traders were as interested in and supportive of this proposal as the first. As Thomas Thomas at Albany wrote to George Gladman, Sr., on 3 March 1813, "I lament the want of an asylum in this part of the country to which a parent might retire with a prospect of supporting his family and which would prevent the miseries of a separation and check the burden of the factories" (Giraud 1945: 435).

These developments made marriage to company daughters more attractive. The setting-up of modest educational facilities and the plan for a colony (even though it faced many practical difficulties and great insecurity in its early stages) dramatically raised traders' aspirations for their children as they suddenly saw prospects for them to enter British occupations. More broadly, the introduction of British education, even on a minor scale, seemed to open the door to the civilization of these children and of the fur trade itself; and new value was placed upon alliances with women of some British background, culture, and connections, even if native-born. In the earliest period of the existence of Red River, this sentiment was explicitly expressed by William Hemmings Cook, chief at York Factory, in the following policy recommendation to a fellow officer:

As the colony is at length set on foot and there is a prospect of civilization diffusing itself among us in a few years, I would not advise you for the sake of the rising generation to consent to either officers or men contracting matrimonial connections unless with the daughters of Englishmen, and then only with the previous concurrence of the superintendant (ibid., 416).

Traders were encouraged to marry company daughters who would more readily adapt to white civilized society than would Indians; and lest the informality of these marriages shock incoming clergy and brand these children as illegitimate, the highest available company official was to be asked to sanction all new alliances.

With traders' new aspirations for their sons and daughters, their mothers also began to be viewed and treated as lawful "wives." From about 1800 on a native fur trade mate was more likely to be described as wife or as "Mrs." rather than by older terms such as "my woman," "mother of my children," "bedfellow," or "helpmate." This change is evident both in post journals and in certain other records dating from the first decade of the 1800s. In 1808, the London committee asked that for school purposes "a Register should be kept at the Factory in which the Birth of the Children will be enter'd . . . the Ages of the Children will be ascertained by this Register" (HBCA, A. 6/17, f. 119). In the register at Moose, John Thomas recorded far more information than required on his own and other families. Besides reporting the birthdates of his nine children and his older daughters' marriages, he also initiated the practice of recording deaths. The following entry describes the passing of Thomas's wife in the same terms that might be used of a white wife:

> 31 December 1813 Died of the Gout in her Stomach Mrs. Margaret Thomas at this Factory leaving a disconsolate Husband and a large family of Children and grand Children to lament her loss, Viz. Three sons and Five Daughters and Six grandsons and six grand daughters, *in this Country,* besides her Daughter, Margaret, in England.—Short before her departure she express'd strong hopes of Immortality, the 3 January she was buried with every respect to her remains (Moose Factory register).

At Eastmain Factory, a similar register more narrowly confined to children's birth records affirmed with equal clarity the recognition now given to fur trade wives. Noting the birth of his son Robert on 20 April 1811, George Gladman, Sr., listed the parents as "George Gladman and Mary Moore but my lawful wife" (HBCA, B. 59/z/1, f. 95). Company men were thus declaring the validity of their marriages and the legitimacy of their children in statements that were much more explicit than any preserved from eighteenth-century Hudson Bay.

CONCLUSIONS

By the early 1800s, communities resembling the one at Moose had grown up around all the major Hudson's Bay Company posts. Organizationally, vertical integration and linkages continued and were evident in marital patterns as well as in other domains. But marital and sexual privileges were becoming less the prerogatives of the highest officers than they had been before, as old company rules continued to weaken. High-ranked officers themselves hastened this trend as they looked for young men who would marry their daughters and maintain them within the posts.

The taking of fur trade wives from within the posts in turn led the members of these communities to become increasingly interrelated. The rise and consequences of fur trade endogamy appear clearly in figure 3. Within three generations, dozens of company men, British and native-born, became part of a ramifying network that is the more striking because most of the Britishers involved entered the fur trade country without prior ties to their colleagues.

Other social changes accompanied fur trade endogamy. Daughters and sons who married and worked within the posts were unlikely to keep Indian names, and their Indian contacts were usually reduced. They grew up in clearly bounded communities, filling the roles of junior servants, apprentices, and children that were familiar adjuncts of older British household organization. And when they married, in the case of daughters and perhaps even of native-born sons, their fathers, acting as patron and master, helped to give marriage "according to the custom of the country" whatever formality it had.

The importance of Indian marriage practices as models for these customary unions is difficult to assess. Certainly Cree fathers played a role in offering their daughters to prospective bridegrooms and influenced their daughters' choices. But English models, according to which fathers and masters controlled the marriage choices of their offspring and servants, would also have carried influence. As for the relative informality of "the custom of the country," some men might have drawn on Scottish models as well as on Indian to justify unions of this kind, as one later Hudson's Bay man in fact did (Van Kirk 1974*a*: 27). In England, the Marriage Act of 1753 "for the better preventing of clandestine marriages" had declared that all marriages must "be solemnized in the parish church or public chapel . . . of one of the parties, and that all marriages celebrated without publication of banns, or licence duly granted, should be absolutely null and void" and that they must be registered with a minister and witnesses. But Scotland's marriage law was strikingly permissive:

> consent to be husband and wife interchanged between a man and woman competent to contract, makes marriage between them without a compliance with any statutory forms or a religious ceremony (Hammick 1887: 12–13, 20, 222).

Whatever precedents may have influenced the "custom of the country," Hudson's Bay Company style, its institutionalization at the Bay posts was significant to the ordering of social relations in the years leading up to 1821. These communities acquired distinct populations of company servants and native families whose British ancestry might reach back several decades. To a degree they absorbed the successive contingents of young British employees who came to the Bay and married their locally born daughters; but, particularly with the advent of Bay schooling opportunities and proposals for colonization, they were increasingly sensitive to British culture and values. These changes led them to make efforts to affirm the legitimacy and respectability of their native "connections" and fur trade domesticity.

4

North West Company Men and Native Women

The North Westers of the period between the 1770s and 1821 frequently allied themselves with Indian women for the same trade-related reasons as did the Hudson's Bay Company men. Like them, the wintering North Westers soon learned that Indian women could be important both in building alliances and in helping traders survive. In late 1786, Alexander Mackenzie arrived in the northern Saskatchewan country to spend the winter and found himself opposed by trade rivals who had a great advantage over him because of their established Indian relationships:

> There are about ten men of the Cree nation at the other fort, all connexions, and I cannot see one of them. I have no one at the fort that can make raquettes [snowshoes]; I do not know what to do without those articles. See what it is to have no wives: . . . I find none of my men speak Cree (Masson 1960, I: 16).

Other North Westers, fortunate enough to have the aid of native women, left ample records of the contributions that these women made to subsistence. Donald McKay's life at his wintering spot in the Timiskaming district was eased by the assistance of his "girl," who regularly snared rabbits, helped with net fishing, trapped martens, and probably secured waterfowl and other small game as well (PAO, Journal of Donald McKay, 1799, 1800–1801, 1805–6, passim).

Because the backgrounds and traditions of North Westers differed widely from those of the Hudson's Bay men, their response to the pressure to take Indian mates was also distinctive. The first Montreal British to enter the Canadian fur trade and acquire native families found themselves among whites and Indians already accustomed to social patterns that had become established during the French régime. Many French trading posts were temporary headquarters from which traders would travel to various Indian groups to barter furs and collect debts directly. After the British conquest of New France, Montreal traders continued to trade *en derouine* and built, besides a few major posts, mainly informal structures from which each man could trade with relative independence. Hudson's Bay men encountering the French and early British "Pedlars" on their trips inland during those years were impressed, sometimes negatively, by the contrasts between Canadian trade structures, physical and social, and their own. In his journal for 19 March 1779, Philip Turnor described the building activities of the Canadians at one inland trading point:

> 3 trading Houses within 200 yards . . . likewise about 10 small Houses inhabitet by their men, which in fact are trading Houses every one of their men being a trader, being so many houses built upon the spot they had used all the timber which is proper for building being nothing but very large Poplar left (Rich and Johnson 1951, I: 312n).

And during his 1772–73 journey inland from York Fort, Turnor's colleague Matthew Cocking found the organization of one Pedlar, "Franceways" (François Le Blanc), whom he met on the route, all too informal:

> As to Command I do not find he keeps any the Common Fellows coming into his apartment and talking with him almost like one of themselves. The Natives I observed had free liberty to come in when they liked (Tyrrell 1934: 120; see also Giraud 1945: 346n).

The informality, flexibility, and intimacy of the French and British Canadians' trade dealings with the Indians carried over to their relationships with Indian women; and the contrasts between Montreal and Hudson's Bay Company traders in this respect are conspicuous. Although their influence was remote, the London committee interested themselves in the discipline and morality of their employees; and since their men were generally less mobile than the North Westers, standard rules of behaviour could be drawn up and applied to all. Hudson's Bay men, then, accustomed to the more regulated life of their Bayside posts and to rules that (although imperfectly enforced) urged that social relations with Indians be circumspect, recorded with displeasure some of their Canadian rivals' conduct.

In the late 1700s, for example, the Hudson's Bay men competing with Montrealers for the trade with the Athapascan-speaking Chipewyan Indians, found the Canadians abusing the Indians and their women. Like the Cree, the Chipewyans were willing to offer their women to traders, and they also had the custom of wife exchange, their version of which was sympathetically recorded by Samuel Hearne in 1771. Such exchanges established "the strongest ties of friendship" between the families involved, and each husband thereby committed himself to the support of the other's family if the need arose; they were "far from viewing this engagement as a mere ceremony" (Tyrrell 1911: 160). The Canadians' behaviour therefore stirred complaints as Hudson's Bay man Malchom Ross recorded on 28 April 1792:

> The Jepowyan Indians complains very much of the injustice done them by the Canadians in taking their women from them by force, some of the Canadians keeps no less than 3 women and several 2.—an instance happened this day of the injustice of the Canadians in the traffic of the Fair Sex.—A Canadian that had 2 women before, went to their tents and took a young woman away by force, which was the only support of her aged Parents: The old Indian her Father, interfered, he was knocked down and dragged some distance by the hair of his head, altho so infirm with age that he is obliged to walk with a stick to support himself—such is the goings on in this Quarter, all this is encouraged by their masters, who often stand as Pimps to procure women for their men, all to get the mens wages from them (Tyrrell 1934: 446n).

And on 2 May of that year, after noting that his rivals had just come close to provoking violent retaliation by the Indians, Philip Turnor (ibid., 449) added some further ethnographic details on their ways.

> Capt[n] Mis-ta-poose a leading Indian who went to the North Sea with Alex. Mackenzie and 18 men with him passed by our House with Guns and a Woman with a hatchet vowing vengeance against the Canadians on account of their fetching some Women from them which had run

away with them from the Canadians but they left their Guns in the woods and went to the Canadian House without them they disputed a little but did not get the Women . . . the method by which they [Canadians] get most of the Che-pa-wy-an Women is by the Masters seizin them for their Husbands or Fathers debts and then selling them to their men from 500 to 2000 Livres and if the Father or Husband or any of them resist the only satisfaction they get is a beating and they are frequently not satisfied with taking the Woman but their Gun and Tent likewise.

These accounts of the 1790s draw attention to a feature of the Montrealers' dealings with native women that is too common in their own records to be dismissed as the biased story-telling of their opponents. Although North Westers often formed stable domestic ties in the Indian country, many of them also became involved in what Malchom Ross aptly called a "traffic of the Fair Sex." Women might be economically productive interpreters, alliance-builders, and companions; but they could also become items of trade and sometimes turbulent bargaining between North Westers and Indians and between the bourgeois or wintering partners and their own engagés. These employees, generally of French-Canadian backgrounds, were accustomed to female companionship and often placed an explicit economic value on that privilege, particularly if they were in debt. On 26 November 1802, Alexander Henry the Younger recorded that one of his men offered to serve him as long as he was able in return only for his clothes and permission to keep his woman. Henry added that he had "seen several people as foolish as he is, who would not hesitate to sign an agreement of perpetual bondage on condition of being permitted to have a woman who struck their fancy" (Coues 1897, I: 206).

Some North Westers became involved in more complex transactions, in which women were traded off as commodities for wages or debts. On 9 April 1800, while he was at Fort Chipewyan in the Athabaska district, James McKenzie recorded the arrival of an Indian with furs and added the following:

This Indian brought his daughter, who deserted in the course of the winter from Morin, at Slave Lake, in order to be returned to her husband (Morin). Mr. Porter wrote me, by Morin's orders, to sell her to the highest bidder and debit [*sic:* credit] Morin for the amount.

Two advantages may be reaped from this affair; the first is that it will assist to discharge the debts of a man unable to do it by any other means, for he is neither good middleman, foreman, steersman [canoe positions], interpreter or carpenter; the second is that it may be the means to thickling some lecherous miser to part with some of his hoard. I therefore kept the woman to be disposed of in the season when the Peace River bucks look out for women, in the month of May (Masson 1960, II: 384–85).

Sometimes North West bourgeois engaged in such transactions not just to settle debts but also for profit. Archibald Norman McLeod, in charge of the district between Lake Winnipeg and the Red and Assiniboine rivers, wrote on 8 May 1801, that he had given "the Chef de Canard's widow to the Amt of 28 Plus, & took the Slave Woman, whom next Fall I shall sell for a good price to one of the men. She was wife to the Deceased old man" (Gates 1965: 179). According to Edward Umfreville, the Canadians' trafficking in female "slaves" or captives was also a source of gain to some western Indian groups. In their war expeditions against Indians on the western side of the Rocky Mountains, he wrote in 1790, they took female slaves whom they would have killed had there been no chance of selling them to the traders (Wallace 1954: 91–92). How many captives ended up in Canada is problematic; numbers of these women probably shared the fate of McLeod's "Slave Woman" and became fur trade mates of voyageurs.

Bargaining over women might also occur between bourgeois and engagé when the terms of an engagé's contract were uncertain and when his superior found it necessary to require unusual duties of him. Unlike Hudson's Bay Company apprentices, voyageurs were not generally bound by long contracts; one to three years was the usual term of service (Nute 1931: 36). North Westers pursuing long journeys and explorations were sometimes obliged to renegotiate work agreements with their men, and the voyageur as well as his bourgeois might use women as counters. In his journal of his journey across the Rocky Mountains in 1806, Simon Fraser described his difficulties with one La Malice in this respect:

[May 17] La Malice . . . debauched the woman Blais had and afterwards prevailed on Mr. McDougall to sell her . . . and she accompanied him here but [neither] Mr. McDougall nor any other had any such power from me, and I intend that La Malice will not keep her at least at such a cheap rate. This does not please La Malice and he refuses to accompany us across the Mountains, alledging that by his agreement that he is not obliged to go there or even to winter in any part of the Peace River, and as I had not his engagement I was obliged to take him on his word, and told him that though much in want of him that I would not oblige him to go since he said it was contrary to his agreement, but that he was answerable for the consequences. . . .

[May 19] I spoke again to La Malice and told him that I was particularly in want of him, and told him to tell [me] in [a] few words what he intended to do . . . but if he expected the woman he had would accompany him, whether he went up or down [to Montreal], that he would be mistaken, to which he replied that the woman was sold him and that he considered her as his property, that he was not obliged by his engagement to come to any part of the Peace River; and much less to go farther, but if allowed to keep the woman that he was willing to follow where ever I would lead. I told him that however [much] I might be in want of him that I would not embark the best man in Athabasca on such conditions, that however I might acceed it as a favor . . . and that he had only one choice of two to make either to accompany me or to go to Montreal.

La Malice finally agreed to go with Fraser, who, pleased with his compliance, granted him permission to take the woman "but not as his property" and "provided she was willing to remain with him" (Lamb 1966: 183–85).

Fraser's difficulties with La Malice highlight the relative independence of the voyageurs and their ability to bargain, particularly in circumstances where their superiors were at a disadvantage. But the bourgeois' control over their men was also continually limited by the latters' willingness to choose the option of remaining in the country as freemen instead of either returning to Montreal or pursuing their fur trade duties. Equipped with wilderness skills and often unwilling to return to the more constrained life of their home society, a considerable but undetermined number left their employers to settle with their native families in the Northwest, where they subsisted partially independently and partially by income gained from work as guides, suppliers or hunters for fur trade company men in their area. In 1803, Alexander Henry the Younger reported that one J.M. Bouché, a "petty trader" on the Kaministiquia River west of Lake Superior, was "really a nuisance" on that route (Coues 1897, I: 219). And in 1814, Gabriel Franchère described the life of Antoine Desjarlais, who had left the North West Company's service in 1805 in the Saskatchewan country:

This man was married to an Indian woman, and lived with his family on the produce of his chase; he appeared quite contented with his lot. Nobody, at least, disputed with him the sovereignty of Red Deer Lake, of which he had, as it were, taken possession (Quaife 1968: 241).

Sometimes several freemen settled in the same vicinity and formed a small community. Alexander Mackenzie reported that ten or twelve of them were living at Sault Ste. Marie with their families in 1789; and others formed the first nuclei of settlement or joined older French and mixed-blood groups at points such as Green Bay and Prairie du Chien, Wisconsin; St. Paul, Minnesota; and Red River Settlement (Grignon 1857: 242; Peterson 1977).

If they did not acquire mates through purchase from their bourgeois or by bargaining with him or threatening to leave his service, engagés might make their own arrangements among themselves for women or attempt sometimes risky dealings with Indians. At Cumberland House in 1819, Dr. John Richardson of the first Franklin expedition recorded some of their practices:

> It is not very uncommon, amongst the Canadian voyageurs, for one woman to be common to and maintained at the joint expense of two men; nor for a voyageur to sell his wife, either for a season or altogether, for a sum of money proportional to her beauty and other good qualities, but always inferior to the price of a team of dogs (Franklin 1823: 80).

Some of their efforts to trade for women from Indians are described in John Macdonell's Red River journal for 5 January 1795. When some of his men returned from trading furs, Macdonell found that one Gareau had "staid behind at the *Foutreau's* lodge" for other trade purposes:

> He gave them a keg of one gallon rum he had of his own, and that not sufficing to get the *Foutreau's* daughter, as he expected, he pierced the keg of high-wines he had in charge and gave it to the Indians, pure; in short, there are six quarts missing off the keg and six large knives wanting in his load.
>
> The whole keg would have been taken from him by the *Foutreau* and his band, who got enraged with drinking pure highwines, had it not been for the *Gendre* [son-in-law] *du Foutreau,* a good Indian, who hurried Gareau and Alain . . . off in the night, *en fuyards,* leaving the girl, as well as the rum and knives in the quiet possession of the Indians (Masson 1960, I: 292–93).

Several factors might have induced the Montrealers who recorded such dealings to tolerate this "traffic of the Fair Sex" with resignation or cynicism, despite the troubles it could cause. But their relative lack of control was doubtless important in many cases. For the British bourgeois and clerks, there was no London committee laying down standard rules of conduct to which the more scrupulous might turn as bases for governing their men's behaviour.

And discipline was not easy to maintain among men trading *en derouine* or on long journeys on which their support and assistance were urgently required.

Another organizational factor may also have reduced the amount of informal control that higher-ranked North Westers could exert. Not only were they much outnumbered by the French Canadians of the voyageur class; they also generally lacked the vertical social integration that helped to hold the Hudson's Bay men together. Differences of status, without the mitigating prospect of promotion, and of ethnic background meant that relations between the two groups were often characterized more by opposition, bargaining, and counter-bargaining, than by solidarity. In addition, the French Canadians could draw on a long tradition of independent behaviour, social and sexual, in the Indian country. It is not surprising, therefore, that the voyageurs (little constrained and occasionally encouraged by their superiors) should have behaved as they did.

Another factor, Indian in origin, would have influenced the British North Westers to accept traffic in women as an adjunct of the fur trade. The Cree and Chipewyans urged both North Westers and Hudson's Bay men to accept women in the interests of friendship and alliance; but farther to the west among various Plains Indian groups, the North Westers frequently encountered societies that had for some time actively engaged in trafficking in women for profit. The pattern of selling female slaves to the Canadians, noted by Umfreville in 1790, went back at least to the 1730s and 1740s, in which period up to sixty Indian slaves a year had been sent to Montreal (Eccles 1969: 140).

In the 1700s and early 1800s the most important group trading captives to the Canadians and other Indians were the Blackfoot, who also adopted or married many of these women into their own families. In historic Blackfoot culture women were a form of and a means to riches. Polygyny was associated with wealth, and a man with numerous wives gained from both their productive and reproductive capacities. The resulting emphasis on the acquisition of women, along with a high male casualty rate from their increasingly wealth-oriented warfare, made a three to one ratio of women to men "normal" among the Blackfoot for much of the nineteenth century (Lewis 1970: 186-87).

A census taken by a North Wester, Alexander Henry the Younger, in 1805-6, suggests that similarly unbalanced sex ratios were also more broadly typical of Plains groups. Henry's figures, covering all the "Departments" in which his company operated except Athabaska, and of course omitting the Hudson Bay Cree, listed a total of 16,995 Indian women and only 7,502 men. By far the greatest imbalances were on the Plains, particularly in the upper Saskatchewan region where there were 13,632 women to 4,823 men (Coues 1897, I: 282). North Westers of all ranks trading with such groups as these may well have received many offers of women not just for alliance purposes, but also because they were a plentiful, profitable, and even a surplus commodity.

Efforts to traffic in women continued on the Plains after the 1821 founding of the new Hudson's Bay Company, to the concern of the new as well as the old Hudson's Bay men. A report from the 1823–24 trading season noted that the Plains Indians still sought to cultivate "an intimacy between their wives and our men."

> And when their property which they bring for trade is insufficient to purchase the articles of which they immediately stand in need, then they are most officious and have recourse to this most shameful kind of traffic. We however use our endeavors to prevent such dealings by punishing our people (Giraud 1945: 120n).

These circumstances encouraged some North Westers to take considerable freedom in the alliances that they themselves formed with Indian women. Since many of the western Indians, as well as their own voyageurs, treated such alliances as transient affairs that could be included among other fur trade transactions, some British clerks and bourgeois were influenced to do likewise. But others formed more permanent attachments and gave their Indian families as much recognition as some Hudson's Bay families received, even retiring with them to Canada. Because of the multiple options open to them, there was thus considerable variability in British North Westers' relationships with Indian women.

The Indian mates of James Finlay, Cuthbert Grant, and Aeneas Cameron are among the numerous female companions of North Westers who left no trace in the records except through their children. The "Sauteur" or Ojibwa mate of Finlay is on record only because of the documentation available on the career of her son Jacco (Jacques). Finlay himself was one of the earliest Scots to enter the Montreal fur trade, first wintering in the Indian country in 1766. Jacco Finlay was apparently born about 1768 and spent his life as a company trader, clerk for a time in the early 1800s, free trader, and guide. But his mother never became James Finlay's wife; Finlay married a white woman in Montreal in about 1765 and had a legitimate family of four children there (Myers 1919: 163–67).

Although Montreal Scots Cuthbert Grant and Aeneas Cameron never had white wives to claim ascendancy, their Indian mates still remained unrecognized and unknown except through their children. Cameron had a daughter by an Indian in the Timiskaming area of northern Ontario, who later became the fur trade wife of Chief Factor Allan McDonell (Mitchell 1977: 234). Grant had no acknowledged wife, but the baptisms of two sons born in the Indian country in the 1790s are on record in Montreal. Both boys received some education, and one, Cuthbert, was later important in the affairs of Red River

Settlement. Their mother was probably a Plains Indian, since they were born at a company post on the upper Assiniboine River (MacLeod and Morton 1974: 3–5).

The identity of William McGillivray's fur trade mate is better known. In the late 1780s and 1790s McGillivray was allied with Susan, a Cree woman, who bore him several children (including Simon and Joseph McGillivray who were made chief traders in the coalition of 1821). Susan spent her last years at the company post of Fort William on Lake Superior, where she died in 1819 (Fort William *Times-Journal* 1965). But in the meantime, William McGillivray had been married to Magdeleine McDonald, sister of his colleague John McDonald of Garth, from 1800 until her death in 1810. Although Susan was the acknowledged mother of McGillivray's native-born children, McGillivray gave precedence to making a marriage with a Scotswoman chosen from among his company connections.

A few North Westers chose to bring their Indian companions home to Canada. Among these were William Morrison, James Hughes, Alexander Fraser, and William Connolly. Morrison lived with his Indian wife near Berthier, Lower Canada, for many years after retirement. Hughes's name was the subject of remark in the Connolly court case in the late 1860s as an example of a company "gentleman" who had brought his Indian wife home but continued to live with her "without remarrying her according to the form practiced in Canada" (Connolly v. Woolrich and Johnson et al. 1867: 239). In both cases, a stable familial relationship formed in the Indian country was apparently continued and the formal legal status of these "wives" was unchallenged.

The cases of Alexander Fraser and William Connolly are rather different. Both men's actions led to controversy between white and native relatives over their Indian wives' legal standing in Canada and over their legacies. By bringing their Indian mates home, both Fraser and Connolly made these relationships subject to Canadian domestic and inheritance law, yet they subsequently allied themselves with white women in Canada. As the court records show, Fraser's case in particular was complicated by his lack of concern (likely reflective of his own family background) with questions of legitimacy.

Fraser's personal life can be reconstructed from the plentiful testimony of court witnesses who had known him and his family. His father was Malcolm Fraser who, after serving the British in the conquest of New France, received the seigneury of Murray Bay in 1761. In about that year Alexander was born, his mother being Marie Allaire. According to the evidence Alexander was illegitimate; and a "tradition at Murray Bay" stated that Malcolm had also fathered several other illegitimate children who, however, took their mothers' names (Wallace 1933: 267–71; Fraser v. Pouliot et al., et Jones 1885).

By the late 1780s, Alexander Fraser had become a clerk in the North West Company, possibly through the assistance of his father's financial agent,

Simon Fraser, cousin of Simon McTavish. By 1799 he was a partner in the concern. Some time before 1789, Fraser took an Indian companion known in the records as Angélique Meadows, remained with her throughout his fur trade career, and in 1806, retired with her and their children to the seigneury of Rivière-du-Loup-en-Bas which he had purchased in 1802. In 1801, when Fraser was on leave in Canada, he and his father presented three of his and Angélique's children, born in 1789, 1791, and 1796 respectively, for baptism at St. Andrew's Church in Quebec. Angélique was absent, presumably still in the Indian country with their two youngest children; but Fraser's father signed as a witness with him, and the baptisms were recorded "in accord with all the formalities required by the laws then in force" with no reference to illegitimacy. In contrast, William Fraser, born in the early 1830s of Alexander Fraser and a servant girl, Pauline Michaud, with whom he cohabited in the 1820s and 1830s, was designated as *enfant naturel* in his baptismal certificate, and Fraser was not present at the ceremony (Fraser v. Pouliot et al. 1884: 2; 1885: 541–43).

Fraser never formally married Angélique, and when she died at Rivière du Loup in 1833 (four years before Fraser), her burial certificate described her simply as "Angélique, sauvage native du pays du Nord-Ouest." But neither did he ever marry either of the two house servants with whom he also became connected at Rivière du Loup, one of whom (Pauline Michaud) bore him six children. (Of the illegitimacy of these children, wrote Justice Meredith of the Quebec Superior Court in 1881, "there can be no doubt, and indeed there is no question.") Fraser "treated all his children alike, and brought them up, and educated them, so as to fit them for the sphere of society in which he himself lived" (ibid., 1885: 539, 544, 551; 1881: 150). His will of 1833 was equally balanced in its terms; the two survivors among Angélique's five children, Pauline Michaud's children, and his grandchildren were all included as heirs, and Angélique and Pauline were each to receive £30 a year. While Pauline's four sons received the bulk of the estate, her two daughters and Angélique's were placed "on a footing of exact equality in the distribution of his property" (ibid., 1881: 151, 158).

Because the will made no statement about the legitimacy of either set of children or about the standing of their mothers, the litigation over the estate in the 1870s and 1880s was prolonged. While the baptismal records tended to support the claim of Angélique's children to legitimacy, the evidence on the nature of Fraser's marriage with her was less conclusive. As in the Connolly case, there was considerable discussion of what constituted marriage "according to the custom of the country" in areas lying beyond the jurisdiction of European legal and religious authorities. Connolly had taken "to live with him, as his squaw or Indian wife, an Indian girl, the daughter of an Indian Chief, with the consent of her father, and cohabited with her . . . according to the usages and customs of the Cree nation to which she belonged," her father being "a chief who had great interest among the Indians" (Connolly v. Woolrich and Johnson et al. 1867: 197, 234). In the absence of other jurisdictions in that region, the judges in that case were willing to consider Indian custom, upon which basis Connolly had founded his alliance with Susanne Pas-de-nom, as valid and binding.

But in Fraser's case, no evidence was produced that he and Angélique had been united by a rite or serious agreement involving senior relatives or a sanctioned customary procedure. Witnesses quoted various disparate accounts of Fraser's Indian "marriage," some doubtless embellished, but all having the same "blanket" theme. According to one account:

> they [Fraser and others?] made all the Indian women pass by, and then it was decided amongst them that he would take as wife the Indian woman who would throw him her blanket.

Other versions combined the blanket theme with a Pocahontas story. Angélique had told one witness that she married Fraser "according to the custom of the savages, with the blanket . . . that she had saved his life." Another witness told of hearing Fraser elaborate upon this version as follows:

> I was fastened by the savages to a tree, and the wood cut to burn me.... My Indian woman [*sauvagesse*], *my wife* [*femme*] that I have at present, took her blanket and came to cover me, saying to me: if you want to marry me, I will save your life . . . it is there that I took her for my wife, I have always taken care of her until now; I will take care of her for my whole life (Fraser v. Pouliot et al. 1884: 24–25, 27, 29).

Struck by the inconsistencies of these accounts, Canadian judges probably became more sceptical about Angélique's legitimacy when they heard the details of Fraser's domestic life and conduct at Rivière du Loup. Although he continually supported Angélique, Fraser had one lengthy involvement and one of lesser importance with female house servants. His will awarded Angélique an income and implicit status exactly equal to Pauline Michaud's; and at her death she was buried under her own name, not as Mme. Fraser. Additionally, although several witnesses asserted that Angélique was known and accepted as Fraser's wife (meeting the legal criteria of *nomen, tractatus, et fama* or name, treatment, and repute), conflicting accounts and pieces of evidence were presented. On one side of the issue, it was said that "according to general reputation and public rumor . . . Fraser was married to the first woman . . . *la femme sauvagesse* . . . The other woman was considered to be adopted [*adoptée*] by M. Fraser." And again, "The Indian woman was considered as very respectable [*très honnête*] and the other, Pauline Michaud, as the servant of the house. The children born of the Indian woman with M. Fraser were considered *legitimate,* and those of Pauline, *illegitimate"* (ibid., 24, 25). Also cited was Angélique's acceptance by the family of Fraser's sister (mother of John McLoughlin, one of the best known North Westers in the Hudson's Bay Company after 1821).

> The family of J. McLaughlin, brother-in-law of M. Alex. Fraser, visited this woman, and considered her as among their relatives; on arriving from the North-West at Rivière du Loup, she went to the McLaughlins' house. Her reputation as a respectable woman was maintained without interruption, in spite of the disorderly life of Alex. Fraser, in spite of his liaisons.

And again, "At the McLaughlins', she was regarded as madame Fraser" (ibid., 1885: 544, 549). On the other hand, one witness who claimed to have known Fraser well asserted that he "always understood that the children that he had were also all illegitimate . . . from the reputation he generally had of having never been married." And another testified that Angélique had also had an alliance with a French-Canadian trader who was still alive in the Indian country (ibid., 538).

Conflicting testimonies and interpretations were also given with regard to Fraser's and Angélique's cohabitation at Rivière du Loup. It was generally agreed that after his retirement, they inhabited the same house for at least a short time. But then Fraser built Angélique a separate house nearby. One witness recalled Fraser's explanation of this change; "M. Fraser told us that the Indian woman *preferred,* in the daytime, to stay in the little house, given the *cabat* [commotion?] of the world. Fraser visited her there, and some recalled seeing her "in her house, smoking her pipe and seated on the hearth." There were of course differing interpretations of this separate residency, as the Court of Queen's Bench noted in 1885:

> [Fraser] was a *seigneur,* who saw many people, important people, a society of *gentlemen.* The Indian woman, who came from the North-West, where she had lived in a very different manner, would not have been anxious to live in the midst of all this company. . . . It is possible that M. Fraser assigned her a house apart to withdraw her from all this commotion. . . . But there is also another reason that would explain

these facts: Alex. Fraser lived maritally with servants: Victoire Asselin and Pauline Michaud (ibid., 1884: 30; 1885: 544, 551).

On the basis of doubts raised by this and other features of the case, the Court of Queen's Bench in 1885 and the Supreme Court in 1886 reversed an earlier Superior Court decision upholding Angélique's legitimacy as Fraser's wife. The judges' opinions were surely influenced by the evidence on Fraser's background, character, and intentions. Illegitimacy, it appeared, ran unchecked in both his father's family and his own. While it was granted that in the eighteenth-century fur trade country, Fraser had no means of undergoing a Christian marriage ceremony, the accounts of his "blanket marriage" were unlikely to reassure the courts about his seriousness.

The judges were also influenced in their decisions by some of the versions of "the custom of the country" that had been placed on record in the Connolly case. Witnesses such as John Edward Harriott who testified for the plaintiff, Connolly's half-Cree son, indeed produced considerable evidence that fur trade marriages were often seriously undertaken and followed customary forms, either Indian or based on established company practice or precedent. But defence witnesses emphasized the prevalence of the assumption, on the part of North West Company men in particular, that country alliances were not necessarily binding in the Indian country or valid in Canada without proper consecration. Joseph Larocque, a former North Wester, claimed that "according to reputation" Connolly was not married to Susanne (although the engagés called her Mme Connolly out of politeness) and went on to summarize the variability of North Westers' marital practices in the Indian country:

> that is, he was married according to the custom of the country there— that is taking a woman and sending her off when he pleased. When I say the custom of the country, I mean that the people did that as a common practice in those days. There was not a legal binding marriage, there could not be. . . . Some of the servants of the company brought wives or women with them to Canada and married them there according to the legal forms of Canada. On the contrary, some lived with women in the interior and did not marry them and abandoned them, and others lived with them and abandoned them to marry white women in the civilized world (Connolly v. Woolrich and Johnson et al. 1867: 237).

Another former North Wester, Pierre Marois, told of his own marriage *sous la couverte* ("blanket marriage"), accomplished by asking the girl's parents and his bourgeois if he might be permitted to take her. Although he regarded this as a proper marriage in the fur trade country, he felt it necessary to have it consecrated when he and his family came down to Canada from the *pays d'en haut.* Fanny Boucher, widow of Chief Trader Joseph McGillivray (son of William and his Cree wife) and herself of Indian and French descent, testified that she herself had been married in the Northwest, and portrayed the proceedings as still more informal: "the custom is that one sleeps with men. I do not know if one is obliged to give presents in order to marry." It was accordingly easy for the first clergymen in the Northwest to see fur trade marriages as consisting of conspicuously casual relationships; and one of these churchmen, a Roman Catholic priest named Boucher, told the Connolly judges that he knew of "no custom there relating to marriage: the dominant vice in the North-West was concubinage" (Johnstone et al. v. Connolly 1869: 285, 287, 289).

Such depositions as these, when combined with the evidence about Fraser's behaviour, led in that case to the failure of efforts to declare Angélique and her children legitimate. In the Connolly case, on the other hand, the accounts of his marriage according to the custom of the country and of his regular cohabitation with Susanne for twenty-nine years gave weight to testimonies favouring the other side of the issue and led the majority of judges to uphold the validity of his Indian marriage. Taken together, the two cases demonstrate the variable character of North Westers' relationships with Indian women and the problems that could result when these relationships were carried over into their home communities in Canada—particularly if the traders involved left sizable estates and had white relatives strongly interested in asserting their own rights. For the Indian relatives of these North Westers, validating their legitimacy was an uphill battle against these kin and against traditional Canadian public opinion that had long viewed casual liaisons between traders and Indians as normal but quite distinct from marriage. A dissenting judge in the Connolly case painted a clear picture of the established Montreal attitudes that sanctioned a church marriage between Connolly and his cousin Julia Woolrich (with proper *dispense de parenté*) in 1832, despite his known connection with Susanne:

> As to her [Julia's] good faith it is clear. She was not unaware of the liaison of Connolly and Suzanne; but sharing the belief of public opinion which considered so-called Indian marriages to be null, she contracted with him a marriage ratified by religious and civil authority and under the protection of public law. How could she be removed from her place, deprived of her station and see her children disgraced as bastards and replaced by those who had always been considered illegitimate, and see her own place occupied by the Indian woman, it is this that appears unjustifiable to me (ibid., 1869: 313).

Canadian values, then, encouraged a casualness in fur trade marriages that, while unattractive to some company men, was accepted by others. And even in cases such as Connolly's, in which a North Wester remained many years in the Indian country with one mate and recognized his children by her, it was still permissible for him to set her aside without opprobrium, particularly if he contributed to her support thereafter as Connolly did. In the last decades before the 1821 coalition, however, some important changes appeared in fur trade marriage practices and attitudes among the British North Westers, as increasing numbers of them found mixed-blood wives.

BRITISH NORTH WESTERS AND MIXED-BLOOD WOMEN

By the end of the 1770s, North Westers were at least as likely as Hudson's Bay Company men to form alliances with mixed-blood women. Several decades of contact between Canadian traders and Indians had produced a considerable mixed-blood population in the areas bordering the southern and western fringes of the Cree territories near Hudson Bay, and women bearing the surnames of French trading families and voyageurs began to turn up as the fur trade wives of British clerks and bourgeois. Indian alliances still occurred in new trade areas in the far west—for example in the 1814 alliance of Duncan McDougall with a Chinook girl to whose father, the chief Concomly, he paid "15 guns and 15 blankets, besides a great deal of other property" (Coues, 1897, II: 901). But in older trading areas, many North Westers chose mixed-bloods, particularly as they became assured of the Indians' trade even without marital alliances. Some were also motivated by a desire to avoid becoming involved in "trafficking" in Indian women and because of their concern for the welfare of these offspring of former traders.

The trend toward choosing women of mixed descent was much accelerated in the early 1800s by demographic developments and associated changes in North West Company rules and policy. Before 1806, the company partners made no special effort to control the numbers of dependents at their posts; and as a result the complement of women and children attached to their employees of all ranks grew rapidly. The 1805 census figures of Alexander Henry the Younger provide the best indication of the size of the population the company was supporting. In his "Report of Northwest Population" for the company's fifteen districts or "Departments" in the Indian country, Henry enumerated a total "white" fur trade population of 1,090 men, 368 women, and 569 children (there being no white women in the country, the latter groups were all of Indian or mixed descent). And when he took a census of his own post, Fort Vermilion in the western Cree-Assiniboine country in 1809, he found that in that restricted context, the proportions of women and children to traders were even higher. In ten houses and two tents there were wintering 36 men and their families. The engagés and their families were living 4 or 5 men to a house in seven of the houses; each of these buildings contained between 10 and 18 persons. All but 6 of these men had wives and/or children. Including the families of their 3 superiors, each of whom had a house to himself, Henry counted a total of 130 persons settled to winter at the post: 36 men, 27 women, and 67 children (ibid., 553–55).

In 1806, this unchecked growth of fur trade domesticity was recognized as the cause of great expense to the company and led to an attempt to control the permissiveness that had created the situation. On 14 July of that year, the partners meeting at Kaministiquia (Lake Superior) set their hands to a resolution forbidding their men to take Indian women. But the partners had no unrealistic hopes for a new celibacy; nor did they wish to make it impossible for traders' native-born daughters to find husbands compatible with their mixed backgrounds and upbringing. The resolution concluded: "It is however understood that taken the Daughter of a white Man after the fashion of the Country, should be considered no violation of this resolve" (Wallace 1934: 211).

The new rule was of course not likely to be strictly or universally enforced. Simon Fraser, for example, recorded and regretted a violation of it soon after its enactment, but he responded only with admonishments. Writing to clerk James McDougall on 31 January 1807, he observed,

> Regarding what you say about the woman that Bugni has, I am noways apprehensive that the Company can put their resolve in execution. But then it was wrong of you to have given him leave to take her, you Knew full well that she was taken from St. Pierre last spring, merely to give up the Custom of taking any more women from the Indians, and that he was promised that no other Frenchman would get her (Lamb 1966: 246).

Another instance of the rule being ignored was experienced by George Nelson, clerk to partner Duncan Cameron. In September 1808, Cameron decided to find a new home for an orphan girl, a cousin of his Indian wife, who had been living in his family. Nelson attempted to avoid being chosen to provide for her and to communicate "how very averse I was to connexions of that sort." But Cameron derided his scruples and organized a ball at the post to celebrate their union. Nelson "gave way, & went as the ox to the Slaughter," admitting that "the Sex had charms for me as it had for others" and probably also appreciating the fact that his respected bourgeois did take a sincere interest in the welfare of his Indian relatives (Metropolitan Toronto Library, Nelson Papers, 206–7).

On 18 July 1809, at Fort William on Lake Superior, it was recorded that two parties had been fined for transgressing the rule: "The Agents for apparently countenancing or giving leave to Mr. Logan at St. Mary's, to take a Woman from the Indians; And Mr. Daniel Mackenzie from Lower Red River for having permitted one of his Men to do the same" (Wallace 1934: 262). In at least one of these cases the Indian alliance was allowed to continue. Robert Logan, a clerk at Sault Ste. Marie, later became a "Principal Settler" in Red River with his Indian wife and large family (Red River Anglican register, baptisms 31–38, marriage no. 8, 1821). And in 1814 Duncan McDougall's alliance with the Chinook chief's daughter met no objections.

If the prohibition against Indian women was not strictly enforced, it nonetheless probably still encouraged increasing numbers of traders to ally themselves with "daughters of white Men." Marriage according to the custom of the country (*en façon du pays*) accordingly changed in character among North Westers as well as among Hudson's Bay men. The company's "heavy burthen" of dependents was doubtless little reduced by its traders' shifting marriage patterns, but at least after 1806 fathers concerned about their offspring could hope that their native daughters might find company husbands and remain in the posts rather than be lost to them by rejoining Indian societies.

North Westers' alliances with mixed-bloods, however, occurred in a context different from those in the Hudson's Bay Company. Because Highland Scottish North Westers in particular were likely to belong to strong kinship, clan, and friendship networks, their prior attachments to white relatives and friends in some cases weakened or even superseded their ties to mixed-blood women in the fur trade country, just as sometimes happened with Indian mates. Even in instances where North Westers asserted in their wills that their final loyalties lay with their mixed-blood women and families, white relatives sometimes challenged the legitimacy of these heirs. The mixed-blood families of Samuel Black, Hugh Faries, Peter Skene Ogden, and John Stuart all faced court challenges regarding their inheritances, despite the recognition that these men had given them (PAC, James Keith Papers, B.6, C.4; Connolly v. Woolrich and Johnson et al. 1867: 249–50; Cline 1974: 215–16). By the early 1800s, of course, senior North Westers themselves had numbers of native daughters, some of whom became fur trade wives to some of their colleagues. A degree of company endogamy thus developed among senior and junior men, somewhat along Hudson's Bay Company lines. But these white and fur trade sets of kin ties sometimes both complemented and competed with each other.

The British, Canadian, and fur trade linkages among the Small, McDonald, and other families illustrate the complexities that could develop (figure 4). John McDonald of Garth was doubly connected to the Smalls through his mother and his wife, the half-Cree daughter of Patrick Small, and to the

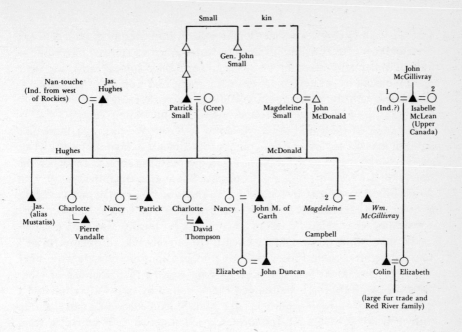

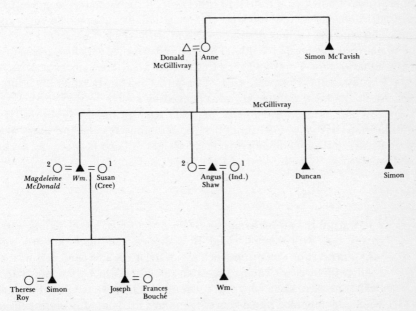

Figure 4. Some fur trade kin connections of Patrick Small, John McDonald of Garth, and other Montreal British traders between the 1760s and 1820s. Black triangles represent men in the fur trade. Magdeleine Small and the second wives of William McGillivray, John McGillivray, and Angus Shaw were white; the other women are mixed-blood unless otherwise designated. The charts intersect in the marriage of William McGillivray and Magdeleine McDonald (italics).

McGillivrays through his sister's marriage. Ramifications of this network stretched from Great Britain to western North America and involved white as well as Indian and mixed-blood women. Their geographical range and their reinforcement by white ties in both fur trade and non-fur trade contexts contrasted with the contemporary Hudson Bay pattern of localized kinship networks based on mixed marriages within the fur trade country.

But some of these and other examples of North Westers' marriages also indicate that the setting aside of country attachments in favour of white wives was a recurring pattern when the home ties were strong enough and when the country ties were with Indians (Connolly, Shaw, the McGillivrays) or with mixed-blood women of low standing. In the long run, Indian and voyageur fathers could exercise few controls over Britishers who became their fur trade sons-in-law and could offer them few rewards for loyalty. The traders themselves, then, while they might have reason not to set aside a British superior's native daughter, could follow individual inclinations more freely with other mates. Some ended their alliances, perhaps leaving their families in other traders' care. But others maintained them, bound by ties of affection and a sense of personal responsibility, as did John Macdonell and Daniel Harmon with their wives of French-Indian descent. These two cases convey a vivid impression of how two serious and observant North Westers, one a Scottish Catholic and one a New England Congregationalist, adapted to fur trade social life and the various domestic options with which it presented them.

Macdonell was born in Scotland in 1768 and travelled with his parents first to Schoharie, New York, and then to Canada, where they settled at Rivière aux Raisins in the Cornwall area of eastern Ontario. In May 1793, after serving in the local militia, he was engaged as a clerk in the North West Company and went inland to the fur trade country for the first time. His journal for 11 August 1793 describes the ceremony that he and other new winterers went through upon crossing the Height of Land between the Arctic and Atlantic watersheds, west of Lake Superior:

I was instituted a *North man* by *Batême* performed by sprinkling water in my face with a small cedar Bow dipped in a ditch of water and accepting certain conditions such as not to let any new hand pass by that road without experiencing the same ceremony which stipulates particularly never to kiss a voyageur's wife against her own free will the whole being accompanied by a dozen of Gun shots fired one after another in an Indian manner. The intention of the Batême being only to claim a glass . . . I complied with the custom and gave the men . . . a two gallon keg as my worthy Bourgeois Mr Cuthbert Grant directed me (Gates 1965: 63; 99–100).

In early October, Macdonell arrived at his wintering place, Fort Esperance on the Qu'appelle River, a western tributary of the Red and Assiniboine Rivers. On 2 December he made his first reference to the family with which he was later connected by marriage; "Poitra's wife made me nine pairs of shoes." On 26 March 1795, he was the unwilling object of Indian pressure to accept the loan of a wife from an important trading Indian, after exchanging presents with him:

> *Le Grand Diable* went away after making me a tender of his wife's fancy and seemed surprised and chagrined at my refusal, but the Lady much more so, and I thought it prudent to make her some trifling presents to pacify her (Masson 1960, I: 283, 285, 293).

By this date, according to Macdonell's own later testimony, he was already allied with Magdeleine, a young daughter of the Poitras family. She remained with him not only during his fur trade years in the Northwest, but for the rest of his life at Point Fortune, his place of retirement on the Ottawa River. In a letter to his brother, Miles, dated 27 June 1812, Macdonell summarized the history of his fur trade family and listed his plans for them, now that he was a North West partner on the verge of retiring:

> I take down my NW wife and two Boys and a Girl in addition to the two boys and girl I have already below—The Children I propose giving common education to that they may work their way thro' life in some honest calling—The mother has been my constant companion these eighteen years and under my protection since her twelfth year I find it cruel to turn her off in this country and to tear her Children from her— My intentions are to settle Something upon her to enable her to live in a comfortable obscure mediocrity but upon this I mean to take the advice of my worthy friend Mr. Lesaulnier; Indeed he and the deceased Mr. Roderick advised me to take down upon my consulting them (Miles Macdonell Papers).

From this passage and other sources, it is clear that Macdonell's wife was very young when he first took her under his "protection" in 1794; her age at death in 1870 was eighty-seven, which confirms that she was born in 1783. Taking such a young wife was apparently not unusual among North Westers, as other examples attest. Michel Curot, trading among the Chippewa of northern Wisconsin in 1803, recorded in November of that year that one of his men, David, "took a Young girl 9 or 10 years old for his wife," although he then decided she was a little too young ("he sent her back to take another one, who was Larger" [Thwaites 1911: 418]). Similar ages were noted by John Richardson of the Franklin Expedition at Cumberland House in 1819:

> The girls at the forts, particularly the daughters of the Canadians, are given in marriage very young; they are frequently wives at 12 years of age and mothers at 14. Nay, more than once, instance has come under our observation of the master of a post having permitted a voyageur to take to wife a poor child that had scarcely attained the age of 10 years (Franklin 1823: 80).

Although Richardson saw this pattern as one of "criminal indulgence," guardianship ("protection" of a parental quality) and marriage may often have been successive phases in the same relationship, at least in cases such as Macdonell's where girls were allied with men almost old enough to be their fathers. Significantly, Macdonell did not describe Magdeleine Poitras as his "wife" of eighteen years, but noted instead that she had been "under my protection since her twelfth year." And their first child, Aeneas Daniel, was not born until four years after Magdeleine became Macdonell's "companion," on 12 December 1798; five others followed in 1801, 1804, 1807, 1809, and 1812 (Gates 1965: 65).

It is also evident in Macdonell's letter that he had been uncertain about "taking down" his wife to Canada (although not about taking the children): he had probably considered the alternative of leaving her under another's protection in the Indian country. His strong religious affiliations may have influenced his decision. Macdonell's father was helping in the project of building a stone church at Rivière aux Raisins in 1801; and its priest was Roderick Macdonell, John's "Grand Uncle" and perhaps the "Mr. Roderick" who had advised him to take her with him (Morice 1929a: 230–31). And in the fur trade country, Macdonell himself had been nicknamed "Le Prêtre," owing, said one who met him in 1817,

> to the rigid manner in which he made his men adhere to the various feasts of the Catholic church; a proof of orthodoxy with which the great majority of them would have gladly dispensed. From this circumstance, joined to his general character among the voyageurs, I was led to expect . . . a second St. Francis; but in lieu of the austere monk, we saw in the retired trader a cheerful, healthy, and contented old man (Morice 1929b: 322–23).

After Macdonell settled at Point Fortune, where for many years he ran a store and a boat service to Montreal, he raised a calvary in front of his house and was said to take his neighbours to church on Sundays. Yet it does not appear that he formally married Magdeleine during the thirty-eight years that they lived in Canada between 1812 and his death in 1850. If he had, it surely would not have been necessary for Magdeleine to go through an "act of remarriage for legal ends" after his death. Yet she apparently went through this posthumous marriage on 24 April 1853, to make it possible for herself and her children to be Macdonell's legal heirs (Gates 1965: 65; Morice 1929*b*: 322–23).

A final sidelight on John Macdonell and his family may be gleaned from descriptions of his large stone house at Point Fortune. It was built on a scale to allow all Macdonell's sons to remain as residents in it with their families when they reached adulthood and contained distinct suites of rooms for the domestic units that were thus to be held together. The early deaths of several of the children kept Macdonell's patriarchal hopes from being fulfilled; and by the 1890s only the house remained to serve as the basis for a fictionalized account of its occupants, in a short story by E.W. Thomson (1895) who was familiar with its history.

Macdonell's colleague Daniel Williams Harmon was born in Bennington, Vermont, in 1778, entered the North West Company as a clerk in 1800, and served on the Saskatchewan, in Athabaska, and in New Caledonia. He was appointed a chief trader when the North West and Hudson's Bay Companies combined, but since he retired without taking up his appointment, he in fact never joined the new concern, and, like Fraser and Macdonell, spent all of his fur trade years in the North West Company. After retiring to Burlington, Vermont, Harmon prepared his journal for publication. Much edited by a local minister, it was first printed in 1820. An unedited copy covering the years 1800–1816 survived separately, however, and most of the citations that follow are drawn from this more authentic and unpolished text. As a social and historical document, the diary is a valuable account of a Protestant New Englander's initiation into the fur trade. And because Harmon entered as an outsider rather than as a member of a family to whom its life was already commonplace, he was sensitive to its novel social order.

As Harmon travelled inland from Montreal in 1800, his impressions of his new colleagues and life were at first negative. On 12 May, he found a fellow clerk with whom he was travelling in a state of intoxication and extracted from him a promise that such conduct would not recur. But, Harmon added, "as his Mother was a *Squaw* (and it is in the blood of the Savages to be fond of Spirituous Liquor) I can place but little confidence . . . in his promises or resolutions." By 3 September, Harmon was speculating on the effects of his new life upon himself; "I have past the Day in reading the Bible and in meditating on my present way of living, which appears to me to resemble too much that of a savage." On 16 November, he recorded an unsuccessful effort to stop his fellow-travellers from playing cards on the Sabbath; they responded that there was "no Sabbath in this Country." Their attitudes disturbed him: "It is a lamentable fact that the most of those who are in this wild part of the World, lay aside the most of Christian and Civilized regulations and behave but little better than the savages themselves" (Lamb 1957: 14, 32, 37–38).

In the same months, however, Harmon was beginning to observe that fur traders, even if too closely resembling "savages," had their own social patterns that gave some order, even if unchristian, to their lives. On 8 August 1800, he described a fur trade marriage ceremony near Lake Winnipeg, although he was unwilling to admit that the woman might have wifely status:

> in the evening Monsr. Mayotte [Malhiot] took a Woman of this country for a Wife or rather Concubine, and all the ceremonies (as I am informed) attending such a circumstance is, when a person is desirous of having one of the Natives Daughters to live with him, he makes a present to the Parents of the Damsel, of such articles as he may suppose that will best please them, but Rum always forms a principal part of the donation . . . and should they accept the articles offered, the Girl remains at the Fort with her lover, and is clothed after the fashion of the Canadians . . . and the most of them I am told are better pleased to remain with the White People than with their own Relations. But should the newly joined couple not agree, they are at full liberty to separate whenever either chooses—however no part of the property that was given to the Girls Parents will be refunded (ibid., 28–29).

During the next year, Harmon found himself favourably impressed with at least some "women of the country," and even, on occasion, with the children of "squaws." At the Hudson's Bay post near his wintering place he met on 24 December 1800, the wife of the man in charge, John Sutherland, and was pleased that, unlike many of his North West Company Canadians, she could speak English "tolerably well," as well as read and write. She could also speak Cree and Ojibwa and appeared to be "a sensible Woman." In July, 1801, Harmon met Alexander, the son of partner Archibald Norman McLeod and a Rapid Indian woman, and while teaching him some English, he found that the boy spoke Sauteux and Cree "fluently, for a child" and could make himself understood in Assiniboine and French. "In short," Harmon concluded, "He is like most of the Children of this Country blessed with a retentive memory and apt to learn" (ibid., 40, 50).

When Payet, one of Harmon's interpreters, took "one of the Natives daughters for a Wife" in December, 1801, Harmon's description of the occasion reflected his increasing appreciation that such unions were a flexible form of wedlock rather than simply concubinage:

> to her Parents he gave in Rum & dry Goods &c. to the value of two hundred Dollars, and all the cerimonies attending such circumstances are that when it becomes time to retire, the Husband or rather Bridegroom (for as yet they are not joined by any *bonds*) shews his Bride where his Bed is, and then they, of course, both go to rest together, and so they continue to do as long as they can agree among themselves, but when either is displeased with their choice, he or she will seek another Partner, and thus the Hymenial Bond, without any more ado is broke asunder—which is *law* here & I think reasonable also, for I cannot conceive it to be right for a Man & Woman to cohabit when they cannot agree, but to live in discontent, if not downright hatered to each other, as many do (ibid., 52–53).

In August, 1802, while in charge of the post of Alexandria, Harmon received his own first marriage proposal from a Cree chief who "wished to have his Daughter with the white people and he almost persuaded me to accept of her, for I was sure that while I had the Daughter I should not only have the Fathers hunts but those of his relations also" (ibid., 62–63). While now willing to accept the idea of such matches for others, he was not willing to participate in them.

Harmon did, however, agree in June, 1803, to assume the guardianship of the half-Ojibwa son of another company man (ibid., 67). And on 10 October 1805, he finally accepted the "offer" of a daughter of a Canadian and a "Snare" (Interior Salish) Indian woman, "a Girl of about fourteen years of age":

> after mature consideration concerning the step I ought to take I finally concluded it would be best to accept of her, as it is customary for all the Gentlemen who come in this Country to remain any length of time to have a *fair* Partner with whom they can pass away their time at least more sociably if not more agreeably than to live a lonely, solitary life, as they must do if single. In case we can live in harmony together, my intentions now are to keep her as long as I remain in this uncivilized part of the world, but when I return to my native land shall endeavour to place her into the hands of some good honest Man, with whom she can pass the remainder of her Days much more agreeably, than it would be possible for her to do, were she to be taken down into the civilized world,

where she would be a stranger to the People, their manners, customs & Language. . . . The Girl is said to be of a mild disposition & even tempered, which are qualities very necessary to make an agreeable Woman and an affectionate Partner (ibid., 98).

In July, 1807, Harmon completed his seven-year term with the company. Although anxious to return home, he observed that he could not leave for such a visit "with the least degree of propriety . . . I must try to make the best I can of it." An event five months later may be linked to his reluctance to depart; on 4 December 1807, he recorded, "The Woman who remains with me was brought to bed of a Boy, whom I name George Harmon" (ibid., 105, 108).

For the rest of his years in the Indian country, Harmon remained with his fur trade wife and their family, although he never designated her his "wife" or mentioned her name. On 15 February 1810, "my Woman" gave premature birth to twin boys who survived only a few days. In April 1811, "my Woman" had a daughter, "whom I name Polly Harmon." The next month, Harmon parted from his "beloved son" George, whom he was sending to Vermont and "the arms of my kind Relations, who will have it more in their power to bring him up in the paths of virtue . . . than it could be possible for me to do in this Savage Country." In December, 1813, Harmon and his "Son's Mother" were deeply saddened to receive word of George's death the preceding March. And in February, 1817, another daughter was born to "the mother of my children" (ibid., 125, 138, 190).

Two years later Harmon decided he would leave the fur trade country the next summer and take his children home to "be educated in a civilized and christian manner." Along with them he also planned to take their mother rather than "place her under the protection of some honest man" as he had proposed fourteen years before.

if she shall be satisfied to remain in that part of the world, I design to make her regularly my wife by a formal marriage . . . as my conduct in this respect is different from that which has generally been pursued by the gentlemen of the North West Company, it will be proper to state some of the reasons which have governed my decision, in regard to this weighty affair. . . . Having lived with this woman as my wife, though we were never formally contracted to each other, . . . and having children by her, I consider that I am under moral obligation not to dissolve the connexion, if she is willing to continue it.

Harmon goes on to speak of their "long and mutual performance of kind offices" and of the instruction he had given her in "the great doctrines and duties of christianity" as binding them together. The fate of their children if they should separate also concerned him:

> How could I spend my days in the civilized world, and leave my beloved children in the wilderness? The thought has in it the bitterness of death. How could I tear them from a mother's love, and leave her to mourn over their absence, to the day of her death? (ibid., 194–95).

Accordingly the family travelled to Vermont, to live first in Burlington and then in Coventry as active Congregationalists. After living for about two decades in Coventry (where Harmon and two of his brothers were among the earliest settlers, and where several more children were born to the family), the Harmons moved to Sault au Recollet near Montreal, an area possibly more hospitable to former fur traders and their part-Indian wives. Harmon died there not long after, and his wife (whose name according to other sources was Elizabeth Duval), died some years later at a son's house in Brooklyn, New York (O'Meara 1950; Quaife 1944: 6).

CONCLUSIONS

The Macdonell and Harmon cases demonstrate that by the early 1800s, some North Westers were taking their fur trade alliances as seriously as their Hudson's Bay contemporaries, even when no father-in-law was visible to influence their behaviour or offer incentives for maintaining the relationship. Early British North Westers had often taken advantage of a social sphere characterized by a considerable trafficking in women and casualness in domestic relationships. But later clerks and bourgeois left increasing evidence of the institutionalization of procedures for the continuing support of their fur trade wives and dependents. Although Harmon and others made it clear that simple repudiation and divorce were among the options, they also increasingly referred to the possibilities of placing their families "under protection" or taking them down to Canada and the "civilized world."

Although bringing home native families avoided painful separations, it was not necessarily easy for family members born and brought up entirely in the Indian country, aside from the difficulties and strains it could cause to the traders themselves and to their white relatives at home. In 1829, Chief Factor Alexander Stewart brought Susan Spence, his mixed-blood fur trade wife of long standing to Montreal, where she died within a few months. North Wester

John Siveright commented to James Hargrave on her death, and on the general problems of "taking down" as follows:

> Mr. Stewart's Old Lady did not live long to enjoy the sweets of civilized life. Taking of any age down from the Interior is not, I think of much benefit in any respect to them. To those advanced in years tis to render them miserable if climate or change of living does not soon release them from their misery altogether (Glazebrook 1938: 66).

The other major option open to those North Westers who decided against "taking down" was, as Harmon put it, to place their native mates "into the hands of some good honest man," combining separation and "divorce" with an arranged "remarriage" that would assure their continued support. While this arrangement broke up the family unit, fur trade wives who were so "placed" could maintain a social position similar to that they had known, rather than face readjustment to Indian societies to which they might no longer have strong affiliations. The bonds of these women to their Indian kin were commonly weakened by the mobility of the North Westers to whom they were attached; a woman who had followed her trader spouse from, for example, Red River to Athabaska or the Rocky Mountains might lose her Indian ties and have a place only in fur trade life. Placing helped resolve such difficulties.

As well as securing the welfare of the women, placing also had the broader function of maintaining order at the posts. Unattached women were potential sources of disorder among the men, and officers often attempted either to return them to their Indian relatives or to establish them in a regularized relationship. Placing was also a means by which traders could find positions for their dependent native children, male and female. Harmon's assumption of responsibility for another trader's young son has already been noted. And he may have taken Elizabeth Duval on the same terms, just as John Macdonell had taken Magdeleine Poitras under his "protection."

For the North Westers before 1821, placing and protection patterns were particularly important, since these men were not participants in the founding of Red River Colony, did not view it as an "asylum" for themselves and their native families, and indeed viewed their rival's settlement venture as a threat to the fur trade. Accordingly, for those Montreal Britishers who decided against "taking down," placing their native wives with another party was an important option. Still a third possibility, that of settling with their families in the Indian country, as numerous French Canadians did, did not appear to be seriously considered by these largely Scottish clerks and bourgeois; strong familial and associational ties in Canada or Britain usually drew them back to the "civilized world," with or without their native wives.

In certain respects, the British North Westers of the early 1800s developed domestic patterns similar to those of their Hudson's Bay contemporaries. Both groups increasingly moved toward fur trade endogamy, and both tended to accord their alliances with native women an increasing degree of recognition, formality, and permanence. The standard sets of practices and procedures that resulted were eventually described by both as marriage "according to the custom of the country."

Nevertheless, use of the same phrase obscures the contrasts between them in the years before 1821. The differing backgrounds of the men and the distinctive structures of the companies meant that their attitudes and the kinds of social and domestic relationships that they built up in the Indian country diverged accordingly.

The permanent residential posts on Hudson Bay formed fairly stable social units, providing homes for traders and their dependents and for the latter if their husbands and fathers retired to Britain or died. And for the last decade before 1821, Hudson's Bay men increasingly looked to Red River as a retirement settlement. Many therefore affirmed the validity of their fur trade marriages, expecting to maintain these connections for life. Such moves were made easier because these company men generally did not have strong white kin connections to compete with or challenge the legitimacy of their native familial ties. Whatever British kin they had might in fact prove supportive. The sister of Hudson's Bay officer William Hemmings Cook, for example, left a bequest in her will of 1827, to be divided among his eight Hudson Bay children if he should die before her (HBCA, A. 36/10, f. 5).

The British North Westers' situation was rather different. Their posts were generally less permanent, and their relations with Indians were often marked by greater transience than those of their rivals. Their company was less formally organized and seldom tried to legislate its employees' behaviour. Until 1806, no rules restricted traders from acquiring native mates and families; but there were also no means of making provision for native dependents beyond their *de facto* support at the posts. Any educational, religious, or other non-trade activities were carried forth solely on a personal basis by individuals.

Accordingly, while Hudson's Bay men began to anticipate and support the organized diffusion of "civilization" into the fur trade country, the North Westers envisaged no such prospect and followed their personal inclinations with regard to their families. Their version of the custom of the country might follow accepted forms; the accounts of Harmon and others certainly indicate that it did. But there was much less institutional control and ordering of social relations than Hudson's Bay men usually experienced. When the two companies merged in 1821, then, two groups of officers and gentlemen, distinct in their backgrounds, attitudes and fur trade ways despite their shared Britishness, were suddenly brought into a close and sometimes uneasy association.

5

Gentlemen of 1821: New Directions
in Fur Trade Social Life

HUDSON'S BAY AND NORTH WEST OFFICERS OF THE COALITION

In 1821, the coalition of the Hudson's Bay and North West Companies made old opponents into colleagues and removed the main structural basis of their social separation and distinctiveness. Traders of diverse backgrounds found themselves obliged to cope with new circumstances and new associates in a unified concern that was itself subject to new external pressures for change from settlers and missionaries.

Gentlemen of the new company were placed in three ranks, according to their seniority, qualifications, and visibility to the London and Montreal directors who arranged the terms of their reorganization. A deed poll was drawn up, granting shares to the two highest-ranked groups, the twenty-five chief factors and twenty-eight chief traders. Younger or less fortunate officers were placed on the list of clerks, at salaries that varied from twenty to over a hundred pounds annually (HBCA, A. 34/1-2; Fleming 1940: 304-5, 345-6). Their numbers were more subject to change; since they were in surplus once the companies combined, attrition in the clerks' list was actively encouraged.

Of the twenty-five chief factors appointed in 1821, ten were Hudson's Bay men and fifteen were North Westers. This disparity in numbers, present in the other ranks as well, reflected the fact that at least since the end of the eighteenth century, the North Westers had employed more men (Rich and Johnson 1951, II: xxxvi; Mackenzie 1911, I: liii–liv), and had correspondingly more aspirants for high positions. The Hudson's Bay Company was compensated in some degree when the two governorships in the Indian country were given to men from its own employ; George Simpson and William Williams.

The origins of the chief factors are consistent with the backgrounds of the two companies. All fifteen of the North Westers were of Scottish descent, and at least nine were actually born in Scotland, mostly in Highland counties such as Inverness-shire, Ross-shire, and Aberdeenshire. Three others are known to have been born in Canada; and the three whose birthplaces were not discovered were doubtless born in either Scotland or Canada, to judge by other biographical data. Of the ten Hudson's Bay chief factors, on the other hand, five were English-born, as most Hudson's Bay officers had been before them. One, John Clarke, who had served the North West and Pacific Fur Companies until 1814, was born in Montreal. The other four were Scottish-born but lacked the Highland clan associations of their North West colleagues (HBCA, A. 36/1B, ff. 12, 29; A. 34/2, f. 1; Bowsfield 1974*a*: 167–68).

The prior fur trade kinship connections of these chief factors also differed along company lines. For the most part, the Hudson's Bay men did not possess significant affiliations that would have aided their entry into the fur trade. Only one Hudson's Bay chief factor of 1821 had an earlier fur trader relative; John Charles's older brother George was apprenticed from the Grey Coat Hospital in 1784, or about the time that John was born, and died in Hudson Bay in 1807, without having gained any major company position (HBCA, A. 44/1, f. 83; A. 36/4, ff. 102–4; John Charles to London Committee, 14 May 1851 [copy in HBC Library, Winnipeg]). It is unlikely that he played much part in advancing his younger brother's fortunes.

In contrast, several North West chief factors had important connections who contributed to their success. John George McTavish was brought into the fur trade by his prominent kinsman, Simon McTavish. Angus Bethune was doubtless encouraged to enter the company by the example of his mother's father, a Swiss Protestant named Jean Etienne Wadin, who was one of the partners in the original North West Company in 1779. (Bethune's mother's sister's son, William Morrison, was also in the fur trade for many years, and his sister married North Wester Robert Henry.) John McLoughlin, later a relative of Bethune through marriage, was the nephew of Alexander Fraser. Chief Factor Donald McKenzie had three brothers, Roderick, Henry, and James, who were prominent members of the North West Company; additionally he could claim the explorer, Sir Alexander Mackenzie, as a first cousin. James Leith and John Thomson also appear to have had personal affiliations with the Montreal fur trade; their backgrounds and connections are, however, less fully documented (Wallace 1933; Burpee 1919; Massicotte 1933).

Of the twenty-eight chief traders appointed to the new company, seventeen were North Westers and eleven Hudson's Bay men, a distribution approximating the 60 to 40 per cent ratio of North West to Hudson's Bay chief factors. Their origins were much the same as the factors', differing along traditional company lines. Three Hudson's Bay traders were English, and seven were Scots. Of the latter, two came from the Orkneys, two from the Glasgow area, two from the Hebrides, and one was a Highlander from Ross-shire—the only known Highland Scot among the Hudson's Bay commissioned officers of 1821. The birthplace of one Hudson's Bay chief trader, Alexander McDonald, is not known; it was probably Scotland.

In contrast, at least eight North West chief traders were Canadians, mostly from the Montreal area. Among them appear one French Canadian, Joseph Larocque, and three of Irish ancestry, the two Dease brothers and William Connolly. At least two (Angus Cameron and James McMillan) were Highland Scots; so, possibly, were three others with Scottish names whose birthplaces are not known. Daniel Harmon was an American from Vermont. And two chief traders, the brothers Simon and Joseph McGillivray, were the sons of William McGillivray.

Like the chief factors, the links of the chief traders differed along old company lines. None of the Hudson's Bay men seem to have had kin or friendship ties to aid them. The sole Highlander, Roderick McKenzie, may have had connections with the Canadian North West Company McKenzies since in his will of 1829 he named James McKenzie of Quebec as an executor; but he worked in opposition to the North Westers for ten years before the coalition (HBCA, A.34/1, f. 65). Robert McVicar had a fur trader brother, but not in his early years and not in the Hudson's Bay Company; Walter McVicar entered the North West Company as a clerk in 1820 and left the fur trade two years after coalition, having been "merely engaged for temporary purposes" in the new concern (Rich 1938: 457; HBCA, A. 34/1, f. 65). Several Hudson's Bay chief traders appear to have been hired impersonally by company agents in various centres. Some of the Scots had been hired in 1811 and 1812 by an agent in Glasgow. And John Spencer, like several of his company predecessors, was "once a Blue Coat Boy" from Christ's Hospital (HBCA, A. 11/118, f. 32; Rich 1938: 468).

In several cases the picture for the North West chief traders is quite different. Angus Cameron was brought into the fur trade by his paternal uncle, Aeneas, a partner since 1798, who assured his brother that he would continue to advance this nephew's interests (Mitchell 1973: 12). The two Dease brothers were linked to the British fur trade in Canada through their relationship with Sir William Johnson and his son; and Joseph Larocque was the younger brother of a former North Wester, François Antoine Larocque. And the connections of Joseph and Simon McGillivray certainly aided the careers of the only two mixed-bloods to be included in the deed poll of 1821.

As a result of the coalition, noted one veteran fur trader in 1822, "The

Concern is at present incumbered with Gentlemen"—a reference to all those officers of the old companies who were not commissioned and were instead retained at the rank of clerk. In 1821–22 in the Northern Department alone (the most important of the fur trade districts), there were over 140 clerks on the rolls. The Hudson's Bay list included fourteen Englishmen, fourteen Orkneymen, twenty-two men from other parts of Scotland, sixteen Canadians, nine born in the Northwest, and six Irishmen. Among the North Westers there were twenty-six Scotsmen, twenty-five Canadians, four Irishmen, and seven natives of the Indian country. Four clerks came from other parts of Europe besides the British Isles (HBCA, B. 239/f/12, pp. 1–7; B. 239/f/13, pp. 1–6).

A large majority of clerks—sixty-one of the seventy-nine men surveyed— had had less than a decade of fur trade employment at the time of the coalition and thus had no claim to seniority. As a whole they averaged about six years less service than the chief traders, and were generally about six years younger. There were exceptions, however. Three old Hudson's Bay clerks, Henry Hallett (who had left to join the North Westers from 1810 to 1821), Richard Good, and Joseph Spence, had by the time of coalition put in a collective total of eighty-one years in the fur trade, yet, despite their seniority, they lacked the merit, vigour, or favour needed to claim commissions. North Wester James McDougall could claim a similar seniority, having first entered the fur trade in 1799. He was allowed to stay on till 1832 since he was "still useful" in the far west. But he was also the object of company charity; in 1826 it was observed that he was "Worn out" and "would have been allowed to retire had he any prospect of providing for himself in the Civilized World" (HBCA, A. 34/1, f. 114).

One of the new company's first orders of business was to reduce the number of clerks, so many of whom had been hired in the last few years of rivalry preceding coalition. These reductions were ably carried forth by the energetic George Simpson, governor of the Northern Department, who proved a harder bargainer in personnel matters than his superiors in London. When Simpson was instructed in 1822 that on account of their seniority and merits, eleven officers were to receive £175 a year, higher than a first class clerk's salary, he responded that three of them had decided to retire and that the others would be glad to accept £150. When presented with a salary schedule proposing annual compensations of £150, £120, £100, and £50–£75 to the four classes of clerks, Simpson revised the figures downward to £100, £75, £60, and £40 respectively (Fleming 1940: 304–5; 345–46). In other domains of the business Simpson also vigorously advanced the causes of efficiency and economy, leading one veteran North West clerk to observe in 1824 that, "In short, the North West is now beginning to be ruled by a rod of iron" (Masson 1960, I: 150).

In the face of these severe new measures, many clerks justifiably felt their careers threatened. Their prior ties with senior officers carried little weight with Simpson; he was not attached to the social network of either company, having been appointed from London only in 1820. Most of the clerks whose salaries and futures he was to decide had similar backgrounds to their superiors—with ties established long before Simpson assumed his governorship. Numerous North West Company clerks, for example, were linked to other traders and each other by paternal, fraternal, avuncular, and other relationships. Charles Brisbois was a cousin of clerks Henry and Alexander Fisher, and all were members of a group of Canadian families that had been established at Prairie du Chien, Wisconsin, on the Mississippi River before the War of 1812. Colin Campbell, of Loyalist background from Glengarry, Canada, followed his older brother, John Duncan, into the North West Company. Charles J.W. Dease was a younger brother of two North West chief traders. Richard Grant's father, William, was involved in the Montreal fur trade as early as 1777. William Henry, son of Alexander Henry the Elder, was one of at least five members of that family involved in the fur trade. Finan McDonald was the younger brother of John McDonald "le Borgne," a North West chief factor in the coalition (Fleming 1940: 440–41).

But Simpson devised his own standards for the retention and promotion of fur trade personnel. And those numerous clerks of both companies who, like young William McGillivray or John Edward Harriott, could claim senior officers as fathers-in-law, were not likely to receive preferential treatment. Instead, in the process of gaining control of administrative matters, Simpson himself became the focal point of new networks in the fur trade country. As his influence grew, he also became a major force for broader social changes in the new company.

SIMPSON, "CONNECTIONS," AND COMPANY PERSONNEL

For four decades George Simpson's influence upon fur trade social life was strongly felt. His conduct and attitudes need to be viewed in the context of his background and the circumstances of his unusual appointment to a high Hudson's Bay Company position in 1820.

Simpson was probably born in 1786 or in 1787 in Ross-shire, the illegitimate son of the eldest son of the Reverend Thomas Simpson. His grandmother was of the Highland Mackenzie clan. He was brought up mainly by his father's sister (the wife of Alexander Simpson, schoolmaster at Dingwall, Ross-shire) and was educated in local parish schools. In 1810 or before, George was taken as clerk into the London firm in which his uncle, Geddes Mackenzie Simpson, was a partner—Graham, Simpson, and Wedderburn, West Indian merchants (Galbraith 1976: 14–16).

The senior partner of this firm was Andrew Wedderburn (later Colvile) whose sister had married Red River's founder, Lord Selkirk, in 1807. In about 1809, along with Selkirk and John Halkett (Selkirk's sister's husband), he had begun to buy up Hudson's Bay Company stock, which was selling at low prices and paying no dividends because of North West Company competition; and Selkirk began to plan his colonization project. Colvile became a member of the London committee and interested himself greatly in improving the company's organization and fortunes. But during these years, the violent competition with the North Westers was worsening. By 1819–20, the conflict had reached the point that William Williams, Hudson's Bay Company overseas governor, was in danger of being arrested by the Canadians and sent to Montreal for trial on various charges. Colvile chose Simpson to go out to replace Williams as governor *locum tenens* if the need arose.

As it turned out, Williams was safe; but Colin Robertson, in charge of the Hudson's Bay Company's operations in the much contested fur trade region of Athabaska, had been taken by the North Westers. Simpson replaced him and was abruptly thrust into first-hand field experience (ibid., 34–35). When coalition occurred the following year, Simpson was made governor of the new Northern Department, while Williams assumed governorship of the Southern Department. After Williams retired in 1826, Simpson took over the direction of that region as well. The "Little Emperor," as he later became known, went on to govern the company's affairs in North America until his death in 1860.

Accounts of Simpson agree that he had unbounded energy and showed considerable administrative and organizational talents. He had a solid education and a substantial clerkly training in London. And his Highland Scottish and London "connections" gave him unusual opportunities for advancement. Because of his special position, Simpson was also well equipped to act as a mediator among diverse and mutually hostile groups in the delicate transitional period. During his first year in the Indian country, he was already aware that secret negotiations for union of the companies were under way in London and Montreal. Letters exchanged in 1820 betwen Andrew Colvile and his Montreal correspondent, Samuel Gale, Jr., refer to Simpson's "honor and discretion" and "his prudence and his knowledge of *certain topicks*" (Morton 1944: 36–39). In 1820–21 Colvile was confident that Simpson could be relied upon to defend Hudson's Bay Company interests, yet govern his conduct by the knowledge that his North West rivals might soon be colleagues. When coalition came, Simpson accordingly had already had some cordial contact with North Westers, notably with senior wintering partner John George McTavish, who became a close friend and associate. And when the chief factors of the new company met together for the first time at a banquet at York Factory in 1821, Simpson's social skills helped to make the affair a success, according to a later account:

The Nor-Westers in one compact body kept together & evidently had no inclination at first to mix up with their old rivals in trade. But that crafty fox Sir George Simpson coming hastily to the rescue with his usual tact & dexterity on such occasions succeeded, though partially, somewhat in dispelling that reserve in which both parties had hitherto continued to envelope themselves . . . it soon became evident that his stratagems in bows and smiles alone would eventually succeed in producing the desired effect on the exterior appearance of his haughty guests. Their previously stiffened features began to relax a little, they gradually but slowly mingled together (John Tod, quoted in ibid., 58; see also Galbraith 1976: 55, 212).

To the Hudson's Bay commissioned officers of 1821 in particular, Simpson's rapid elevation must have appeared anomalous and even disturbing; and it was fortunate that Simpson could conduct himself diplomatically. High Hudson's Bay officers had customarily risen through the ranks during the course of long service, and these men were no exception; the only other high-ranked Hudson's Bay man with such a short tenure was Governor Williams, who had taken up his position in 1818. The North Westers too could justifiably have resented Simpson's authority, since most of them had been senior wintering partners for some years (table 2). But in his council meetings with them, Simpson soon assumed leadership and won their respect, if not always their affection. His account of an 1823 council, in which former Hudson's Bay man Colin Robertson and others expressed discontent over the governors' salaries and other matters, indicates his tactics:

Robertson was one of the leading malcontents, but his blustering folly knocked the whole on the head, and in order to make himself pass for a man of weight came out with all their secrets which gave me an opportunity of bringing them to their senses; in short I found it necessary to show my power and authority and in full Council gave them a lecture which had the desired effect, made them look on each other with suspicion and restored their confidence in myself. . . . I found it necessary to act with firmness, convinced them that I could talk loud also, and made an example of Robertson to begin with . . . the lecture . . . had the desired effect, none seemed inclined to enter the Lists with me again, and on the whole we all separated on excellent terms and I believe they have now a greater respect for me than ever (MacKay 1936: 181–82).

It soon became evident that Simpson's personal fur trade friendships were to be stronger with the former North Westers than with the Hudson's Bay men. There were several reasons for this pattern. Of all the Hudson's Bay officers, Simpson had been the most briefly involved in the pre-1821 rivalries. Most of the others, including Governor Williams, had histories of bitter, sometimes violent, trade conflicts with numerous of the gentlemen whose councils they now shared. As a newcomer, Simpson was in the best position to form friendly ties with these former enemies.

Simpson's potential compatibility with the North Westers was based on other factors as well. Like most of them, he had a Highland background and helpful "connections." His prior ties may not have linked him directly to the Scottish North Westers (except perhaps through the Mackenzie clan); but his affiliations showed the same kind of relationship to his advancement as those found among his North West colleagues. There were, then, considerable social similarities between Simpson and the North West factors and traders which laid a basis for his greater compatibility with them.

Simpson's educational background was also similar. Like him, most North West Company officers had been trained as clerks before they entered the fur trade. Those who became partners maintained high positions in the company's Montreal business and in their home society even while wintering in the Northwest. Several of them proved more congenial than the isolated field officers from the old Hudson's Bay Company, as indicated in a comment Simpson made to Chief Factor John George McTavish while staying with Colin Robertson at Norway House before their relations deteriorated in 1823: "Mine host had improved much on acquaintance, he is a pleasant Gentlemanly fellow and has none of those constricted illiberal ideas which so much characterizes the Gentry of Ruperts Land" (Rich 1939: 181n).

Wills offer other evidence of his relatively greater friendship with the senior North Westers during his governorship. Five of the twelve North West chief factors' wills I have been able to consult named Simpson as an executor, whereas among nine Hudson's Bay factors' wills, he is only listed once—in John Clarke's will of 23 July 1830 (HBCA, A. 36/4, f. 182); and it is clear from Simpson's 1832 character sketch of Clarke that this chief factor was not among the governor's favourites. "A boasting ignorant low fellow," Simpson wrote of him; "rarely speaks suspected of dishonesty . . . total want of any principle or feeling . . . cruel and tyrannical disposition . . . in short a disgrace to the 'Fur Trade'" (HBCA, A. 34/2, f. 3). Among the chief traders, a partial survey suggests a similar contrast. Four of fourteen North West chief traders' wills named Simpson executor, compared to one among six Hudson's Bay chief traders' wills (that of Highlander Roderick McKenzie [HBCA, A. 36/9, f. 201]).

Personnel records suggest that early in Simpson's tenure as governor, some of his North West colleagues, doubtless benefiting from his friendship and support, rose to positions of considerable dominance, while the former Hudson's Bay men, already a minority, lost ground in numbers and importance. Table 2 illustrates some of the career patterns of the commissioned officers of 1821. Officers from the two companies did not differ greatly in their average length of service before the coalition. But North Westers tended to remain with the new company rather longer and to retire later. And the chief traders among them stood a conspicuously greater chance of becoming chief factors. By 1832, eighteen of the twenty-five chief factorships were held by North Westers and only seven by Hudson's Bay men (HBCA, A. 34/2, ff. 1–9). Even by 1828, North Wester James Hargrave was remarking upon a trend favouring men of his old company. In a letter to fellow-clerk George Barnston, he noted, "By the way the higher ranks have even yet been recruited from the NW side of the question, a circumstance that speaks the superior enterprise and efficiency of the partners in the late concern" (Hargrave Papers, 1 July 1828).

TABLE 2: CAREER LENGTHS AND PROMOTION PATTERNS AMONG HUDSON'S BAY AND NORTH WEST COMPANY COMMISSIONED OFFICERS OF 1821 (Figures in parentheses denote numbers of cases averaged)

	Av. Yrs. Served before Coalition	Av. Yrs. Served after Coalition	Total Av. Yrs. Served	No. of Ch. Traders made Ch. Factors
HBC	17.9 (21)	12.6	30.5	2(11)
NWCo	19.6+(32)	17.5	38.3+	10(17)
Diff.	1.7 (53)	4.9	7.8	8

Certainly promotions might come more readily to traders who exhibited "superior enterprise and efficiency"; and George Simpson had early in 1821 assured a correspondent that the company's opinions of "Gentlemen" were formed "solely by their Deportment in the Service" (Rich 1938: 285). But merit no more guaranteed success in the new company than it had in the old ones, and its recognition was still assured by the cultivation of patronage, kinship, and friendship ties. After 1821, North Westers dominated these chains of influence as they increasingly centred on Governor Simpson. It is true that Simpson's 1832 book of "Characters" of his commissioned officers shows that North West factors of 1821, as well as Hudson's Bay man Clarke, could be subject to his strong criticism; Angus Bethune, Donald McKenzie, John McBean, and William McIntosh suffered particularly from his sometimes vitriolic pen. But his strongest praise was still reserved mainly for the North Westers—for John George McTavish, John Dugald Cameron, Edward Smith, and James Keith, and with some reservations, for Alexander Stewart,

George Keith, and John Stuart, five of whose wills named him as executor. Of the Hudson's Bay factors of 1821, only Alexander Christie and Joseph Beioley received high marks. John Charles was a "Plain blunt Englishman . . . not well educated but regular attentive economical . . . not bright, could easily be led by a designing person"; and Colin Robertson was a "frothy trifling conceited man who would starve in any other country and is quite useless here . . . a burden to the Fur Trade" (HBCA, A. 34/2, ff. 1–9).

In 1821, of course, Simpson had not been in a position to appoint his own chief factors and chief traders; this task had been carried out by Nicholas Garry, deputy governor of the Hudson's Bay Company, one of the rare London committee men to travel to Canada, when he handled negotiations for the merger, and the North West partners William and Simon McGillivray. Although he could certainly influence his officers' roles, encourage or discourage their retirements, and determine which chief traders attained factorships according to his own judgment and preferences, he was obliged to tolerate them all until they retired, no matter what his personal inclinations toward them might be. Unlike clerks and lower-ranked servants, they were shareholders and could not be readily dismissed.

In the matter of recruiting new officers, however, Simpson could take new initiatives, and his conduct in this area began to exhibit a characteristic pattern even before he assumed a company position. In 1818, while Simpson was still employed by Andrew Colvile's sugar-broking firm, two brothers, Duncan and Nicol Finlayson, joined the Hudson's Bay Company as clerks. Duncan in particular was a lifelong friend of Simpson, married his wife's sister, and was named executor in his two wills of 1841 and 1860. Like Simpson, he became a close associate of several of the North Westers of 1821 and was sometimes named among their executors (HBCA, A. 44/2, f. 114; A. 36/10, f.1; A. 36/11, f. 286). Both Simpson and the Finlaysons had strong family ties in Ross-shire and, more particularly, to the community of Dingwall where Simpson's uncle Alexander resided. Letters from Simpson and Finlayson relatives in Dingwall to the company and from George Simpson to his uncle suggest that Simpson "helped directly or indirectly to recruit the Finlaysons for the Hudson's Bay Company" (Davies 1963: 367). If so, his actions in 1818 were the earliest examples of his later frequent tendency to recruit company officers through personal channels. From his uncle's family in Dingwall, for example, he recruited three cousins, Aemilius, Thomas, and Alexander Simpson, by the end of the 1820s; and other family members soon followed along with Finlayson relatives and their McKenzie connections (figure 5). In sum, Simpson and his close colleagues fostered recruitment patterns resembling those common in the old North West Company. Not surprisingly, the proliferation of Simpson, McKenzie, and Finlayson connections in the ranks of company gentlemen after 1821 gave rise to unfavourable comment among former Hudson's Bay men and native-born

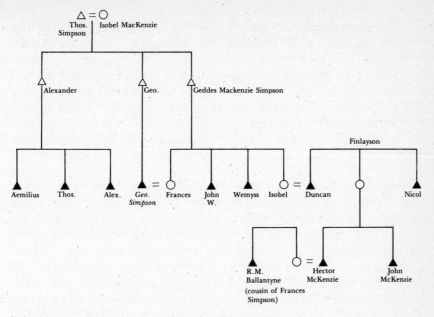

Figure 5. Simpson and Finlayson kinsmen from Scotland in the Hudson's Bay Company (Company men represented by solid triangles).

officers who resented the advantages and rapid promotions granted to these privileged newcomers. By February 1840, John Tod, who had been a Hudson's Bay clerk in the 1821 coalition, was writing to his retired colleague and contemporary, Edward Ermatinger, that "the Service is at present also lately swarming with Finlaysons Simpsons and McKenzies, so that few others, no matter what their qualifications, may be stand any chance" (PAC, Edward Ermatinger Papers). A few years later in a letter to A.C. Anderson, Chief Trader James Anderson spoke out still more vigorously against this pattern of favouritism toward the governor's kin, also detecting in it an element of racial prejudice:

> If Interest is to be the Main Channel of Promotion—let it be proclaimed abroad—and let not young men waste their best days in the Vain and delusive hope—that acknowledged Merit, Long Service and abilities are to be rewarded by promotion in due time. . . . The promotion of the two McTavishes and Hecr McKenzie has been the Subject of bitter Remark not only among the Clerks but also the Commissioned officers—I know that it was anticipated by every one in this quarter that I should have been promoted as well as Joseph Gladman—his Case is most gross—He was a district Master before the McTavishes were (perhaps) born—has

borne an excellent Character . . . now mark how he has been treated—he was succeeded in the Charge of New Brunswick by Peter McKenzie—who is (entre nous) but three Removes from a Fool—and who could no more take charge of a district than he could fly—Still Peter was promoted in /44 as soon as he could be—he owed this to being a Governors Protege—but poor Joe has some 16th part of Indian blood in his Veins and for that unpardonable *defect*—he is deprived of the Fruits of his Labours (PABC, James Anderson Papers, 24 December 1846).

Although Simpson certainly favoured his relatives and those of his close friends (such as the Mactavishes mentioned by James Anderson), he recognized that the matter was sensitive and attempted to assure himself that these kin fully merited the ranks that they attained. In writing his private character sketches of his commissioned officers in 1832, he was doubtless conscious that only one chief trader of the twenty-five listed that year had reached that rank with less than a decade's fur trade experience—his cousin, Aemilius Simpson. Somewhat defensively he wrote, "A namesake and relation of my own, whom I should not have introduced to the Fur Trade, had I not known him to be a man of high character and respectable abilities." Aemilius met premature death that year and so was not fully tested for his presumed qualities (HBCA, A. 34/2, f. 19).

Another cousin caused Simpson some tribulation, at least for a period in the 1830s. Alexander Simpson entered the company in 1828 and was described by the governor in 1832 as "well educated, attentive to business, fills situation of principal accountant at LaChine, correct in conduct and private character" (ibid., f. 49). But on 18 November 1834, James Keith, who was in charge of the Lachine office, wrote privately to Simpson that he intended to retire soon, in part because of "no longer being able to tolerate your Cousin's behavior." Alexander was prone to intoxication without any "apology or regret," showing instead only a "greater forwardness." Since he gave Keith "no handle for retaining him," Keith had sent him to Moose Factory and the wilds of Timiskaming, fearing that if he had remained, there were risks of his gaining "much greater and more unpleasant notoriety" in an office so close to Montreal. A few months later, Keith warned Simpson more broadly against placing his kin at Lachine with its proximity to "vice, profligacy, dissipation, and loose company" rather than in the interior where young men had few chances "to deviate from rectitude and propriety":

I see objections to your placing any of your Relations or namesakes in any prominent Situation at this place, exposed to the Critique and Comments of the Public, apart from those of the Company and its members, who in the event of committing themselves would naturally identify you with them—whereas if a stranger, he may stand or fall without affecting you (Keith Papers, 20 April 1835).

Thus, in his efforts to assist his relatives' careers, Simpson encountered problems familiar to senior North Westers. Like them he had high expectations of officers who were both "well educated and respectably connected." But these attributes did not guarantee good performance; and as James Keith recognized, well-connected recruits could damage the reputations of their fur trade patrons and sponsors as well as themselves by poor conduct. Several North Westers could have sympathized with their new governor's concerns over his relatives, given their own anxieties in that area.

SIMPSON AND NATIVE WOMEN

George Simpson's impact on fur trade domestic relations was even more conspicuous than his influence on the social relations of his officers. When Simpson entered the company, he was a bachelor, and remained so until he married his eighteen-year-old cousin Frances in London in 1830. Prior to that marriage, however, he had fathered at least five children by four different women. The first of these natural children was a daughter born in Britain before he joined the Hudson's Bay Company; the rest were born in the fur trade country (HBC Library, file on George Simpson).

Soon after he came to the Northwest, Simpson began to find female companionship at the company posts. By early 1821, he was associated with Betsey, daughter of Hudson's Bay factor William Sinclair (who had died in 1818) and his native wife Margaret (Nahoway) Norton; and their child, Maria, was born at York Factory in 1822, while Simpson was travelling inland (Van Kirk 1972: 11). It is clear, however, from his actions and from the record of his private correspondence with J.G. McTavish, that he did not regard this alliance as binding and did not view Betsey as his wife. His attitude went against conventions of that time and place; while the York Factory journal for 10 February 1822 recorded that Maria was born to "Mrs. Simpson" on that day, Simpson referred to her by such terms as "my article" or "my Japan helpmate." In June of 1822, he asked McTavish to send his "Damsel" from York to the care of her brother-in-law, Thomas Bunn, "as I do not wish to be troubled with a Lady during the busy Season" (Fleming 1940: 411). On 12 November 1822, he wrote from an inland post to McTavish at York that he was leaving his "Family concerns" to the latter's "kind management":

if you can dispose of the Lady it will be satisfactory as she is an unnecessary & expensive appendage, I see no fun in keeping a Woman without
enjoying her charms which my present rambling Life does not enable me
to do; but if she is unmarketable I have no wish that she should be a
general accommodation shop to all the young bucks at the Factory
(ibid., 424).

McTavish evidently attended to the matter; by 1 February 1823, Betsey had
been married according to country custom to English Hudson's Bay clerk
Robert Miles, an event marked by festivities and a dance at York (Van Kirk
1972: 11). Like many company marriages this union endured, producing ten
children; it received church consecration in 1840, and the family eventually
retired to eastern Ontario (Moose Factory register; Rich 1938: 459).

From late 1822 until his visit to England in 1825, Simpson appears not to
have been linked with any particular woman, although such matters were not
far from his mind. In his private November 1822 letter to McTavish from Isle à
la Crosse, he noted that "White Fish seems to be favorable to procreation and
had I a good pimp in my suite I might have been inclined to deposit a little of
my Spawn but have become . . . vastly tenacious of my reputation" (Fleming
1940: 423). In 1823–24 he was residing at Red River Colony where he claimed
to be remaining an "exemplary batchelor" (Van Kirk 1972: 12). By that time
Red River was a growing settlement where "exemplary" behaviour was
advisable for high company officers. It now contained representatives of both
the Church of England and the Canadian Roman Catholic Church who were
campaigning against fur trade customary marriages and general immorality.
In July 1823, Chief Factor Donald McKenzie, a former North Wester and
early a close associate of Simpson, communicated to the governor that Red
River was a place at which deliberate (if condescending) role-playing by
company leaders was tactically useful:

The Red River Settlers . . . are a distinct sort of beings, somewhere
between the half Indians and overgrown children. At times they need
caressing and not unfrequently the discipline of the birch, in other words
the iron rod of retribution. But in the present instance the latter not
being within our reach, it behooves us to attempt by stratagem what we
cannot compass by force. In the first place therefore all former scrapes
and barefaced practices should be carefully avoided by every person
holding a conspicuous station and the bottle and the girls so late the
bane must with monastic strictness be forborne. Order and religion likewise to be held in veneration; therefore with faces long and minds most
pure and delicate shall you & I regularly attend the chapel in the coldest
as well as the warmest weather (Merk 1968: 198).

During his sojourn in Red River, Simpson may have been the more inclined to such exemplary role-playing by his own hopes of finding a wife during his impending visit to England. He evidently expressed these hopes to Andrew Colvile, for Colvile wrote on 11 March 1824, recommending that Simpson postpone his plans in that direction "both on your own account & that of the Company. . . . A wife I fear would be an embarrassment to you until the business gets into more complete order" (ibid., 206). Simpson accepted the advice and returned from his 1825 voyage to England still unmarried and with continuing interest in the companionship of native-born women.

From 1826 until his second trip to England in 1829–30, Simpson's major country attachment was to another Hudson's Bay Company woman, Margaret Taylor, daughter of a former sloop master at York. Margaret was the sister of Thomas Taylor who had been Simpson's personal servant for several years. She bore Simpson two sons, George in 1827 and John McKenzie in August 1829, and during that period he showed evidence of affection and concern for her and her family (Van Kirk 1972: 13).

Margaret Taylor, however, was not to become Simpson's formal wife any more than Betsey Sinclair—although she and some others (such as North West Chief Factor John Stuart) believed for a while that the attachment was permanent. Simpson informally recognized Thomas Taylor as his brother-in-law and described Margaret as "my fair one"; but some of his other references to her were less complimentary. Nor did Margaret receive his undivided loyalty during this period. There is evidence that, at least in early 1828, Simpson was keeping a "mistress" at his Lachine headquarters; and this woman may have been the mother of another natural child born to the governor and named James Keith Simpson, after North Wester James Keith (Van Kirk n.d.: 41n52). Keith's own interest in this son (manifest in a provision of his will) suggests along with other circumstantial evidence that the "mistress" in question may have been his native-born daughter Mary. In the spring of 1830 Mary was betrothed to Thomas Taylor "by joint *act*" of Simpson and Chief Factor George Keith (brother of James); and Simpson's participation in this "act" reinforces the impression that he and Mary Keith may have had some connection (HBCA, A. 36/8, f. 58; Keith Papers, B. 2). As in Betsey Sinclair's case, he may have wanted to see a former female companion safely married.

From late 1826 until early 1830, however, fur trade officers less intimate with Simpson than McTavish and Keith accepted Margaret Taylor and her children as their governor's legitimate family, having no notion of any other attachments or of his private intentions. On 1 February 1830, Chief Factor John Stuart sent Simpson an account of his native family and their life at one of the company posts during the governor's absence in England. Clearly he had no idea that, less than two weeks later, Simpson would be marrying a British wife in London; for he praised the family and particularly Margaret's "decent and modest" comportment and reported that she appeared "as contented as it is possible for one of her sex to be in the absence of their Lord and natural protector" (PAC, Strathcona Papers, box 3). Simpson's return to the fur trade country in May, 1830, with his young cousin as his bride, was a great shock to Stuart, to the Taylor family, and to many other members of the fur trade community. Interestingly, soon after his marriage to Frances, he arranged for Margaret Taylor's marriage to a French Canadian in Red River, following a pattern he had laid down with Betsey Sinclair and perhaps with Mary Keith (Van Kirk 1972: 18).

Simpson thus showed little appreciation for many of his older colleagues' views of the binding nature of customary marriages. Indeed his early tendency was to regard fur trade wives as "mistresses" or concubines, much as did the newly arrived missionaries, the difference being that he personally exploited the informality of fur trade domestic relations while the clergy sought their reform. He also appreciated their practical value for the trade in some situations, for he soon recognized the business utility of "connubial alliances" with newly contacted Indian groups. In May of 1821 he recommended that gentlemen inland "form connections with the principal families immediately on their arrival" and deplored as "most baneful to the interests of the Company" those "restrictions which the Honble Committee have put on Matrimonial alliances" (Rich 1938: 392, 395-96). Country marriages with mixed-bloods could also serve commercial motives. On 26 January 1821 Simpson sent the following directive to the Hudson's Bay clerk in charge at Great Slave Lake:

[Cayenne Grogne's] services are now absolutely required as a Guide for the Grand River and his Wife is a good Interpreter; you will therefore have the goodness to fix him for three years . . . the old man is rather of a capricious disposition, you will therefore take him on the subject of his contract at some interval of extraordinary good humour and let the instrument be executed . . . before he has time to reflect on the value of his services; I wish you could make up a match between his Daughter and Neil MacDonald, she speaks French, Cree, and Mountainy fluently and we can depend upon her as an Interpreter while under Neil's protection: . . . the old man may talk of marriage and a settlement, you must endeavor to make these matters palatable to him by fair promises as we have no Clergymen in this country (ibid., 245).

In another case in the same trading season, Hudson's Bay clerk George Peter Andries was granted more "Flour and Luxuries" than his usual allowance on the insistence of Andries's native wife, a valued interpreter "extensively connected amongst the Chipewyan and Yellow Knife Tribes" (ibid., 136, 252). In a dispatch dated 14 November 1820, Simpson instructed Robert Miles to retain the services of this woman, even at extra cost: "she is a useful woman, and therefore must be humoured" (ibid., 109).

But if a man's attachment to his native wife threatened to interfere with his performance of duty or cause expense, Simpson's criticisms could be strong indeed. Early in the 1820–21 season, Simpson informed the London committee that John Clarke had on a journey left behind the cargo of one large canoe rather than inconvenience his wife, Sapphira Spence, daughter of an old Hudson's Bay clerk:

> Mr. Clarke converted one of the Canoes of his Brigade into a Light Canoe with 8 men *for the better accomodation of his Woman and her Servant* . . . the Committee may well be displeased when they learn that one of their Officers deliberately puts them to an expense of about £500, exclusive of the injury their business may sustain by the want of goods *merely for the accomodation of an Indian mistress* (ibid., 23).

Several days later Simpson noted that company business had not been well managed in that district and complained that "it could not be otherways, when a poor superannuated Man like Spence has the charge who can have no other claims to such an important trust than the circumstances of his being the *Father of Mr. Clarke's Mistress*" (ibid., 31–32).

In 1825, on a tour of inspection to the Columbia River region, Simpson found that fur trade domesticity frequently interfered with business and recorded his disapproval of his officers' family involvements, with particular reference to Hudson's Bay Chief Trader John McLeod and his wife (daughter of Hudson's Bay Chief Trader John Peter Pruden):

> almost every man in the District has a Family, which is productive of serious injury and inconvenience on account of the great consumption of Provisions; but by changing the men this evil will be remedied and the Women and Children sent to their Indian relatives. Mr M. . . . is really the most stupid useless inactive Commissioned Gentleman I have seen; his Woman and Family occupy his whole attention and the Compy's interests are become quite a secondary consideration with him. . . . We must really put a stop to the practise of Gentlemen bringing their Women & Children from the East to the West side of the Mountain, it is

attended with much expense and inconvenience on the Voyage, business itself must give way to domestick considerations, the Gentlemen become drones and are not disposible in short the evil is more serious than I am well able to describe (Merk 1968: 131).

Simpson also expressed concern over the influence that country wives exercised. In 1825 he found two of the three chief traders in the Columbia district so much concerned for their wives' faithfulness and "so much under the influence of their Women . . . that what they say is Law and they can not muster sufficient resolution in themselves or confidence in their Ladies to be 5 Minutes on end out of their presence." These "petty coat politicians" could even influence their husbands' business decisions, as in the instance of Hudson's Bay Chief Factor James Bird, who too frequently consulted "his Copper Cold. Mate" regarding the company's affairs at Red River (ibid., 132; Van Kirk 1972: 10).

By the mid-1820s, Simpson was agreeing with Andrew Colvile that any wife could be a distracting encumbrance and at one point even told Colvile that white wives in particular could prove burdensome: "native women are a serious incumbrance but with women from the civilized world, it is quite impossible the gentlemen can do their duty" (Van Kirk 1972: 10). Two decades later, in the 1840s, he was to return to his stand against the bringing of white wives into the Indian country, on the basis of much longer personal experience and observation. But in the 1820s he had already observed a few cases in which company men had attempted to keep white wives with them during their service and noted problems that could result.

Simpson's Hudson's Bay predecessor, Governor Williams, had left his British family in England for his first four years of service, but from 1822 on his wife and children joined him at Moose Factory. The presence of his family may have been a factor in causing his management of the Southern Department in those years to decline in thrift and efficiency, a complaint that led to his being recalled to England in 1826. Another British wife, Mrs. R.P. Pelly, resided from 1823 to 1825 with her husband at Red River, during his brief governorship of that colony. But after two years her delicate health and failure to adjust to Red River life led Pelly to relinquish his position—a development that certainly influenced Simpson's ideas on the bringing out of white wives (despite his own later experiment in that direction) and probably encouraged him to follow Colvile's advice against marriage at least for a few years thereafter (ibid., 10).

The only other white women in the Indian country in the 1820s were the wives of Protestant clergymen and those among the Red River settlers themselves. By the mid-1820s, four settlers' daughters had become the wives of company men, and Simpson was concerned that these women might prove as burdensome to the fur trade as wives brought directly from Europe. This did not seem the case however. Life in Red River and the Indian country was already familiar to the McBeath girls who married Donald Ross and Robert McVicar (Hudson's Bay clerks of 1821) and to the wives taken by John Clarke after the death of Sapphira Spence and by North Wester Donald McKenzie after he had informally divorced his native wife of several years.

In fact, because these women had adjusted to Red River life and ways, remote from the "civilized world," Simpson was to find that they offered little congenial company for his bride. Early in 1831 he told John George McTavish that Frances had found no friends among the white wives at Red River (Morton 1944: 167–68). Some years later, Simpson's younger colleague and friend, James Hargrave, described one of these Red River women, the wife of Chief Trader Donald Ross at Norway House, north of Lake Winnipeg, as differing but little from the native-born women. Comparing her to his Scottish fiancée, Letitia Mactavish, Hargrave conceded that she was a "tender mother and careful wife" but added:

> In every other respect she is the strongest contrast to what my Letitia is and would be—Deficient in mind and natural taste, uneducated and unpolished,—she has sunk to the same grade as her brown sisters around her; she is fond of gossip and that too often not of the most ladylike description for the collection of which her knowledge of Indian affords her every facility (Hargrave Papers, Hargrave to Letitia Mactavish, 27 May 1838).

Newly arrived European wives, particularly those from a metropolis such as London, were thus likely to be lonely and unhappy in the fur trade country. For Frances Simpson, this sense of isolation was augmented not only by her educated British background but by her high rank as the governor's wife, which set her apart from most potential friends. Additionally, Simpson himself contributed to her isolation by his efforts to keep her apart from the society of the "copper-colored mates" of his officers. In the spring of 1831, Colin Robertson brought Theresa Chalifoux, his fur trade wife of over a decade, to Red River, evidently hoping to pass some time in the company of the Simpsons. The governor's comment to McTavish on this incident was cutting indeed:

> Robertson brought his bit of Brown with him to the Settlement this Spring in hopes that she would pick up a few English manners before visiting the civilised world; but it would not do—I told him distinctly the

thing was impossible, which mortified him exceedingly. . . . He takes his departure I understand tomorrow mortified and chagrined beyond description (HBCA, B. 135/c/2, 15 August 1831).

Simpson's efforts to insulate his wife were probably motivated by at least two considerations. For one thing, he had developed some considerable prejudice, often expressed in racial terms, against natives of the country by the early 1830s. He was not anxious to have Frances associate with "halfbreeds," even of the higher-ranked company families. He also probably hoped to shield her from knowledge of his earlier attachments to native women and from contact with them or their children. Letitia Hargrave wrote in 1840 that Frances evidently had "no idea" of the number of her "encumbrances" in the Indian country, although "she was always terrified to look about her in case of seeing something disagreeable" (MacLeod 1947: 35).

As a consequence, Frances Simpson found little happiness in Red River. A difficult pregnancy, ill health, and the death of her first son at the age of eight months worsened the situation. In May of 1832, Simpson wrote unhappily to McTavish that Frances had "no Society, no Friend, no Relative here but myself, she cannot rove wt. me on my different Journeys and I cannot leave her in the hands of Strangers . . . some of them very unfeeling" (Van Kirk 1972: 21). In 1833, Simpson saw Frances safely home to England, and he thereafter maintained his family life as best he could, by means of trips to England and later to Canada when his family became established at Lachine near Montreal.

Although Simpson's marriage was not the happiest, several of his colleagues were much influenced by his example and attempted to follow a similar course, abandoning fur trade alliances to take white wives whom they introduced with varying success into the Indian country. Significantly, the traders most influenced by Simpson's conduct were former North Westers; the social and company backgrounds of these particular gentlemen predisposed them to follow (or at least morally support) the governor's example more readily than would most Hudson's Bay men.

6

Different Loyalties: Sexual and Marital Relationships of Company Officers after 1821

Although the contrasts between the companies are by no means absolute, the Hudson's Bay traders' country alliances from the late eighteenth century until the coalition period tended to exhibit greater permanence and more signs of mutual affection and loyalty than did those of most North Westers farther inland. Hudson's Bay men often recognized and affirmed the legitimacy of their native families and showed considerable concern for them, even in the face of company rules against such attachments. Certainly practical socio-economic considerations could affect their alliances; the patronage bonds between senior and junior Hudson's Bay men (along with their recognition of the trade-related helpfulness of native mates) have already been mentioned. But these also had affective components, linking colleagues by mutual ties of sentiment. And in the Hudson's Bay Company, alliances solely to expedite trade were not as a rule encouraged.

The greater independence and mobility of the North Westers led them to have less stable and more expedient relationships with native women. And their brief encounters with diverse Indian groups encouraged the formation of unions for short-term trade advantages. Some North Westers' alliances did resemble those of Hudson's Bay men in their strength and durability (for example, those of John Macdonell and Daniel Harmon) or in their patronage bonds. But it appears that many of their relationships with native women were of a casual-exploitative type unstrengthened by bonds with high-ranked fathers-in-law.

When George Simpson came into this environment as an officer of the highest standing, he was able to secure as his partners the lower-status daughters of older company men, exploiting their misunderstandings of his attitudes and intentions toward them. He also influenced the domestic conduct of some of his new colleagues—notably that of certain North Westers. Their behaviour after 1821 showed the effects of his example as well as of their own company backgrounds and reinforced an instrumental view of country alliances and marriage in general, while fostering an emphasis on home (British and Canadian) kinship and friendship ties.

COMMISSIONED GENTLEMEN OF 1821 AND THE SIMPSON SIDE

The former North Westers most conspicuously sympathetic to Simpson's dropping of his country attachments to make a respectable European marriage were his friends Chief Factors John George McTavish and James McMillan. Like Simpson both of these Highland Scots were on leave in Britain in 1829–30, and like him, they were seeking eligible white wives to bring back to the fur trade country.

Of the two, McMillan's conduct stirred less comment, for he had no visible fur trade mate to be directly cast off. He had, however, previously had more than one native mate and had fathered at least six children. Three of these (perhaps of the same mother) were listed in his 1813 will as his "adopted children," a phrase commonly used by traders to refer to offspring of a union without legal sanction. Another, William, was born about 1800 and was later an active member of the métis community in Red River. And a daughter, Victoire, was born in about 1821 to Kil-a-ko-tah, daughter of a minor Clatsop chief on the North West coast. This union probably had short-term fur trade utility and did not persist after McMillan left the area (PAO, McMillan file).

In 1830, McMillan, then in his late forties, married a Scotswoman, Ellen McKinlay, whose brother Archibald entered the company as a clerk at about the same time. Like Simpson, McMillan established his wife at Red River where they lived until his 1834 appointment to a company post in the Montreal region. Ellen apparently remained as much apart from her native-born fur trade peers as did Frances Simpson. In a letter to his Scottish fiancée on 27 May 1838, James Hargrave compared her favourably to Mrs. Donald Ross, the Red River Scotswoman mentioned earlier:

> She on the contrary has preserved during her whole residence here the same delicacy of feeling a good education gave her in Scotland.—Kind to the native women and children she yet maintains her original rank among them and seeks for society only in her own family (Hargrave Papers).

John George McTavish had also had more than one fur trade mate between 1800 and 1830. By one account he had for a time been allied with the daughter of the Hudson's Bay governor at Moose Factory in the early 1800s, during the few years that the North Westers maintained a rival post in the vicinity. And a witness in the Connolly court case mentioned that McTavish had lived for a brief period with a "halfbreed," one Yacko Tinneys (a corruption of the name Jaco Finlay? and perhaps a Finlay daughter) at Spokane House in the Rocky Mountains (*Lower Canada Jurist* 1867: 239).

But his major continuing partnership had been his seventeen-year country marriage to Nancy, native-born niece of his fellow North Wester Donald McKenzie, an alliance that had produced seven children. His colleagues assumed this match was permanent, and Nancy was accepted as "Mrs. McTavish" by James Hargrave and others. In May of 1830, when McTavish was in Britain, Hargrave (who had been serving under him at York Factory) was still sending accounts of "Madame" and the children, who were "well and happy paying all spring a visit to the river side to see when the road shall open for you" (Hargrave Papers). At that point he had not received the letter sent him on 25 February from Edinburgh, where Chief Trader Donald Ross was spending his leave. Ross noted McTavish's marriage three days before and added that Simpson and McMillan also seemed to be "speculating in matrimonial schemes . . . the presence of these ladies will somewhat alarm our poor homespun country squaws, to some of them at least it will be any thing but a gratifying sight" (ibid.).

By early July, Hargrave's information was up-to-date, and he was telling his correspondents of McTavish's marriage to "a white lady from the civilized world" and of his arrival with her at Moose Factory after a voyage from Britain with the Simpsons. For the next four years, McTavish and his Aberdeenshire wife were the highest ranked residents at Moose, and like the Simpsons and McMillans, interposed new social barriers between themselves and the natives of the country. Former Hudson's Bay Chief Factor Joseph Beioley, for example, found that his native-born wife of several years' standing was not considered fit company for the McTavishes (Van Kirk 1972: 17, 19). And like McMillan, McTavish soon found means to remove his wife from the remoter corners of the fur trade world, securing himself an appointment at Lake of Two Mountains within reach of Montreal. Two years after his wife's death there in 1841, McTavish married again, this time choosing the Scottish niece of his North West colleague, Angus Cameron (MacLeod 1947: 156n).

For McTavish, the social and economic costs of his new marital career were considerable. While McTavish was serving at Moose, Simpson at Red River tackled the problem of settling his friend's "old concern" in the same manner as he had managed his own—by arranging Nancy's remarriage to a junior man. Just as Margaret Taylor had been betrothed to Amable Hogue in Red

River, so Nancy McKenzie became the wife of a French Canadian, Pierre
Leblanc, a longtime company servant. But the settlement was not easily made.
Donald McKenzie, in charge at Red River, demanded that she be given a
handsome "dowry" in compensation for her ill treatment, and a compromise
figure of £200 was finally reached (Van Kirk 1972: 17–18). Besides this
expense, McTavish and Simpson both lost their earlier good relations with
McKenzie, and an old friendship between McTavish and Chief Factor John
Stuart was also ended.

Other North Westers accepted McTavish's conduct more readily, however.
James Hargrave remained loyal to his "old Bourgeois," regretted their separation now that McTavish was at Moose, and wrote on 1 December 1831 that he
"rejoiced to hear of the settlement the Gov.r made last spring in your affair in
the north, so proper and suitable to all parties." To Pierre Leblanc, Nancy's
new husband, he had written in June, in cordial if patronizing tones:

> I am happy to hear of your little arrangements and I really consider it the
> most prudent match you could have made.—Madame I am certain will
> make you an excellent wife.—pray give her a kiss from me for old
> acquaintance sake (Hargrave Papers).

The precedents set by Simpson, McMillan and McTavish continued to
have repercussions in the following decade as other officers made or revised
their marital arrangements. In 1830, Mary Taylor, sister of Margaret,
Simpson's erstwhile companion, had been Chief Factor John Stuart's country
wife for some years. Stuart was genuinely fond of Mary and gratified by her
attentions, as his letter of 1 February 1830 to Simpson shows: "she is un-
commonly attentive to me—apparently as caressing and anxious to please as
if I was a young man—indeed I fear that sometimes my soured temper
prevents me from being at all times as kind to her as she deserves" (Strathcona Papers, vol. 3). But although he broke off his relations with McTavish
over his conduct, when Simpson appeared a few months later with his British
bride, Stuart avoided any criticism of Simpson's domestic decisions. While he
maintained his relationship with Mary Taylor, he also took to extravagant
praise of the new Mrs. Simpson (Glazebrook 1938: 57), and made no move to
formalize his alliance—unlike certain other gentlemen of 1821 who had by
1830 begun to have the Red River clergy or other authorities solemnize their
fur trade marriages.

Despite these precautions, Stuart had much annoyed Simpson by supporting Nancy McKenzie and attacking McTavish; and by 1832 he found himself
sent from a comfortable post on the Winnipeg River to the arduous and
remote charge of Fort Simpson in the Mackenzie River district of the far

Northwest. Mary Taylor travelled there with him and was designated his "wife" in the will that he drew up that year. By 1834 he was evidently planning to solemnize their alliance upon their return to Norway House, a post visited by the clergy. But early that year she had an affair with François Annance, a clerk under Stuart's charge, provoking a rupture and incidentally much stir and gossip among fur trade correspondents. Reconciliation soon followed, however, and Stuart was again reported to be with "Mary more loving than ever" (Hargrave Papers, James Hargrave to J.G. McTavish, 1 December 1834). But their alliance was never formalized, despite the fact that Mary even joined Stuart in Scotland for two years during an extended leave that he took before his retirement in 1839. Chief Trader Nicol Finlayson expressed the surprise of many of Stuart's colleagues on learning that even at this point Stuart could not seem to bring himself to give his relationship with Mary the formal recognition that he had evidently decided was necessary for a customary fur trade marriage.

> I was surprised to find on my arrival in London that Old Aesop had determined on sending Mary back to the country. He pretended that his friends wd. not associate with her if he married her, but that is false, they did not wish to do so because he would not marry her (MacLeod 1947: 20n).

Under the circumstances, Mary herself doubtless preferred to return to her own land; she had evidently made it clear that she would not live in Britain without a legal marriage (Van Kirk 1975: 295–96). But Stuart's vacillations left her for a longer period in a more uncomfortable position than had been endured either by her sister Margaret or by Nancy McKenzie when they were set aside. George Simpson himself felt compelled to become Mary Taylor's helper and advocate upon her return by company ship to York Factory. On 20 March 1839, he sent Hargrave the following instructions:

> Should she wish to go to Red River have the goodness to fit her out comfortably with an old Tent, Provisions, &c. and put her under such protection as will guard her against insult. The poor girl has been sadly disappointed and the trifling pecuniary compensation that has been made to her is no cure to her wounded feelings. If in order to save her little means she should desire to pass the winter at York, I think you might manage it, as to place her with Rendall or Gladman or some one of the other Family gentlemen where she could live comfortably free of expense. I feel interested in this poor girl and recommend her strongly to your kind attention (MacLeod 1947: 20n).

Mary accordingly spent the following year with Nicol Finlayson's family at York, then lived with relatives in Red River, and finally married there. When John Stuart died in 1847, however, he had not revised his 1832 will leaving her a legacy and declaring her his wife. As a result of this and other problems (Stuart had also had three children by two other native women before his years with Mary Taylor), the will was subjected to considerable litigation in Britain, as Stuart's sisters challenged the legitimacy of his children and attempted to claim Mary's legacy (Keith Papers, C.4; Van Kirk 1975: 296–97).

A final case among the commissioned gentlemen of 1821 also reflects the manner in which North West Company men's implicit attitudes toward "country" alliances as affairs that could be terminated at will were reinforced or brought into the open under the influence of Simpson's attitudes and conduct. William Connolly's twenty-nine-year Cree marriage, his termination of it to marry his Montreal cousin, and the later legal repercussions have already been outlined. It appears that his decision to marry Julia Woolrich was affected by the news of Simpson's actions in 1830. In 1831–32 Connolly took leave from company service to return to Montreal with his Indian family. By mid-May of 1832, he was married to Julia and had secured reappointment from the far west to a position along the St. Lawrence, where he served until his retirement. Simpson, who was in general favourably disposed toward Connolly, made an interesting private comment on this marriage to his friend McTavish in December, 1832:

You would have heard of Connolly's Marriage—he was one of those who considered it a most unnatural proceeding "to desert the mother of his children" & marry another; that is all very fine; very sentimental & very kind-hearted 3000 miles from the Civilized World but is lost sight of even by Friend Connolly where a proper opportunity offers (Van Kirk 1972: 21).

In a certain sense, however, Connolly's two marriages three decades apart were consistent. The testimony of the Connolly court case indicated that he had taken the Cree, Susanne, as his wife to gain trade advantages with her father. And his later alliance to a Montreal cousin who was a member of a prosperous merchant family suggests that he continued to view marriage as a means of attaining social and economic objectives—an attitude quite in line with the actions of Simpson and several others. This is not to say that affection was absent from the alliances made by Connolly, Simpson, or their colleagues. But it does seem reasonable to conclude that for these gentlemen, more than for some other traders, decisions regarding sexual relationships and marriage were much governed by tactical considerations. Among these men, John Stuart stands out for his endless vacillation about whether to follow a practical course toward a possibly more gainful and prestigious European marriage or to confirm Mary Taylor as his wife. It may be that he had originally taken Mary as his companion with instrumental considerations in mind; his involvement with her began shortly after Simpson's association with her sister Margaret; and Stuart was always eager to curry favour with the governor. But his ensuing personal attachment for her precluded any easy termination of the relationship. Stuart's "unfortunate speculations for happiness in female society," as Hargrave called them in a letter to Stuart on 10 September 1838 (Hargrave Papers), reflected Simpson's influence upon susceptible North Westers and the instabilities of fur trade social life in the 1820s and 1830s.

COMMISSIONED GENTLEMEN OF 1821 AND THEIR WIVES BY CHURCH AND CUSTOM

Many of the 1821 officers maintained more stable domestic relations than Simpson and his friends. There are various means of assessing the degree and duration of these men's attachment to their families and their motives in founding and maintaining these relationships. The wills and personal correspondence which have been preserved indicate their attitudes. Further, the records of early church missions in Red River and the Canadian Northwest indicate whether they had their native wives and children baptized and their customary marriages solemnized.

By the early 1830s, all commissioned officers had probably had opportunities to make use of clergymen's services for marriages and baptisms if they so desired; even those men stationed in remote parts for many years typically returned to Red River or other major centres such as Norway House at regular intervals, either to attend company councils or to go on leave. And the churchmen made constant efforts to be available to the traders, visiting the largest posts accessible to Red River in the busy summer months when they might reach the most people. Despite the private disrespectfulness of some high officers such as Simpson, their efforts received the official backing of the company and bore fruit among traders concerned about the legal standing of their marriages and children. On 12 August 1821, for example, Anglican John West baptized twenty-five children of company men at Norway House. He had already officiated at the marriages of several officers in Red River. Nicholas Garry, the London committee member who visited there in the course of making the merger arrangements, commented favourably on West's success at persuading several officers to marry, "thus introducing more proper Feelings and preventing that Debasement of Mind which must, at last, have rooted out every honourable and right Feeling" (Garry 1900: 137).

Among seventeen Hudson's Bay chief factors and chief traders known to have native-born mates in the years after 1821, at least eight (47 per cent) eventually solemnized their unions. Proportionally fewer North Westers were married in church; only nine (30 per cent) of the twenty-nine men with native mates in these years are known to have formalized their relationships. Because two of the Hudson's Bay Company officers died before 1825, they had no opportunity of participating in Christian marriages, if they had wished. Four of the Hudson's Bay Company officers and three North Westers of 1821 had no known country wife in the period following 1821.

Country Marriages after 1821: the Hudson's Bay Factors and Traders

The failure of seven Hudson's Bay men and twenty North Westers to consecrate their country unions might be interpreted to reflect absence of positive commitment toward the women involved, accompanied by ambivalence about the competing claims of white relatives and the home community (for example, the cases of J.G. McTavish, John Stuart, and John Connolly). Some officers, however, were simply uninterested in or even hostile toward church intervention in their often longstanding alliances. Chief Factor Alexander Kennedy was one senior Hudson's Bay man who evidently did not feel a need for such clerical sanction. At least as early as 1804, he had taken an Indian wife, Aggathas, and had a family of ten children to whom he was devoted and to whose mother he was loyal. On 14 August 1829, Kennedy addressed a letter from Moose Factory to "Mrs. Kennedy," then at Red River, telling her not to "want for anything that I can afford to supply you with, either for yourself, your mother, or the little ones, and be assured that as long as I live I shall never forsake you nor forget you" (PAM, William Kennedy Papers). His will of 15 September 1831 named "my wife Aggathas" and their children as its major legatees (HBCA, A. 36/1B, ff. 11–12). Despite these declarations, there is no record that Kennedy and Aggathas participated in a church marriage before his death in June 1832. Contacts with clergymen were not lacking, however; four Kennedy children were baptized in 1820 and three in 1821 by John West; and Aggathas herself was baptized as "Mary the reputed wife of Alexander Kennedy" on 27 December 1829 (Red River Anglican register).

Two other Hudson's Bay chief factors with native families were also apparently uninterested in consecrating their alliances. Joseph Beioley and Isabella, daughter of trader John McKay, had several children whose lay baptisms were recorded in the Moose Factory register between 1817 and 1822, and it was presumably Isabella with whom J.G. McTavish and his new white wife refused to associate in the early 1830s. Other evidence on Beioley's attachment for his family is lacking; he died intestate leaving no known personal correspondence. In 1859, Her Majesty's Court of Probate did, however, accept the legitimacy of his son Richard, born in Hudson Bay, granting him administration of the estate as "natural, lawful, and only child of the deceased" (HBCA, A. 44/4. f. 7).

The country relationships of Chief Factor Thomas Vincent offer some contrasts. Between approximately 1794 and 1810, six children were born to Vincent and the native-born Jane Renton. Four were registered at Moose Factory in 1809–10. By the 1820s, however, Vincent and Jane had separated. On the eve of his retirement to England in 1826, Vincent made a will listing his "Wife" as "Jane Vincent . . . daughter of the late James Sutherland," although he was still awarding the annual interest on 400 pounds to Jane Renton, "a woman with whom I formerly cohabited & the mother of my children" (HBCA, A. 36/14, f. 54). The relationship with Jane Sutherland apparently received no church sanction despite Vincent's designation of her as his wife. She evidently died before March of 1832. In that month, six days before his death, Vincent made a new will, omitting her name but including bequests to her children by a former husband, to his children, and again to Jane Renton (200 pounds, "for her own sole use and benefit") (ibid., f. 60).

The account that Harriet Gladman, a daughter of Vincent and Jane Renton, later gave Letitia Hargrave of her family supplements this information. Sometime before the merging of the companies, Vincent, like some Hudson's Bay men before him, had attempted to take two women as mates (or perhaps more accurately, a mistress as well as a wife). As Mrs. Hargrave recorded Harriet's story,

> Her mother, his wife as she considered herself got a girl in to help her to work who prevailed on her father to take her too, so the first got malignant and left him. The children were grown up and had left them so she went and lived with Mr. Gladman's mother and widow of one in the same Coy. The father went to England and died, the 2nd squaw having died before him (MacLeod 1947: 82).

Accordingly, in making his first will Vincent denied wifely status to Jane Renton, who had left him, and conferred it on Jane Sutherland, although both his wills showed regard for the welfare of Jane Renton and her children.

It is interesting that, after the deaths of Vincent and Jane Sutherland, Jane Renton, with the help and support of her children and their families, retained status as "Mrs. Vincent" at Moose Factory for many years. In 1837, James Hargrave there visited "Mrs. Vincent and Mrs. Gladman . . . without flattery two of the most respectable Ladies I have met in the land" (ibid., 82n). And on

17 September 1858, the Moose Factory register recorded the death of "Mrs. Jane Vincent from old age." Supported by her former husband's legacy and her family, she had maintained a comfortable standing and independence in the fur trade community. Vincent's loyalty had been imperfect, but he had not completely abandoned or disinherited her. And as usual in Hudson's Bay cases, these familial relationships seem to have been unimpeded and unchallenged by the pressures or demands of white relatives at home.

Information on the four other Hudson's Bay chief traders of 1821 who apparently maintained country wives without benefit of clergy is not complete. John Spencer spent numerous years in Canada with his family, and a record of a church marriage between himself and his country wife may yet be found there. The same may also be true of Jacob Corrigal and his wife (HBCA, A. 36/5, f. 78–79). Chief Trader William Brown, who retired to Edinburgh in 1826 on account of illness, left a will that indicated attachment to his native family but did not attempt to declare their legitimacy. His four "natural" children shared his estate with their mother Josette Bolieu, the latter to receive her share only "until she places herself under another protector." Unlike many Hudson's Bay colleagues, Brown did have several white relatives to claim his attention and compete with his fur trade alliance; his will also benefited his father, a sister, four "maternal half Uncles and Aunts," and three first cousins (HBCA, A. 44/2, ff. 25–28).

Another Hudson's Bay chief trader, John Peter Pruden, maintained a long-term loyalty to a native woman yet appeared to ignore opportunities to consecrate the alliance. In his first will of 10 September 1824, Pruden left legacies to his eight "reputed children" and "their mother my reputed wife" (HBCA, A. 36/11, f. 119). The Anglican church registers of Red River record the baptism of three of these children and of Nancy, again Pruden's "reputed wife," in the 1820s, and the burial of "Ann Pruden," age fifty-two years, in August 1839. Although the alliance lacked church sanction, she was buried under Pruden's name. (His mourning period was, however, fairly brief; four months later he married, in church, a white governess lately arrived in Red River.)

HBC Chief Trader John Lee Lewes and his country wife Jane or Jean Ballenden raised a family of at least eight children during their many years together at various posts. In 1840, nearly two decades after the coalition of companies, the Rev. Robert Rundle married the Lewes at Norway House; and in his will of 1849 Lewes declared Jane to be "my lawful Married Wife" (Dempsey 1977: 23; HBCA, A. 36/8, f. 229). In 1844, a scientist visitor to the Lewes, J.H. Lefroy, gave a vivid account of Jane and her family life at the remote post of Fort Simpson:

She is the daughter of an Indian woman, and much more of the squaw than the civilized woman herself, delights in nothing so much as roaming about with her children making the most cunning snares for Partridges, rabbits, and so on. . . . She is moreover very good natured and has given me two pairs of worked moccassins . . . she also gives me lessons in Cree.

He also noted that Jane ate at table with the men, a practice not typical of larger posts where families lived apart, "the gentlemen . . . being obliged to mess together" (PAC, Lefroy Letters, 29 April: 24 April–June, 1844).

These cases suggest that although there was some variability in the patterns of Hudson's Bay alliances, evidence that the men abandoned native wives or remarried for instrumental purposes is generally lacking. At least four of the five commissioned officers who eventually found white wives among the Red River settlers did so after being widowed rather than by means of casting off native mates. At least one-third of the officers eventually consented to church marriages. Others chose simply to maintain their unions as they had done before the advent of missionaries. Their minor children were in most cases baptized at some point (often in conjunction with being placed in mission schools in Red River); but Christian rites could still be foregone in the fur trade country until the early 1840s, by men who nonetheless showed loyalty and goodwill toward their native spouses. As J.H. Lefroy learned on his visits to various posts and fur trade families, British law courts had begun to accept the legality of unions "according to the custom of the country" on the grounds that clergymen in the Northwest were few and recently arrived and their services not widely accessible. Noting "the want of the means of obtaining lawful marriage," Lefroy observed that "it appears that the absence of the ceremony has been repeatedly held at law as no barrier to the legality of the union, and is therefore none to its moral innocence, inasmuch as the ceremony cannot be obtained" (Lefroy Letters, 15 December 1844). In fact Pruden, Kennedy, and others could have obtained the ceremony sooner or later if they had felt it necessary, as their colleague Lewes finally did, but it evidently seemed superfluous to some of these older traders.

Country Marriages after 1821: The North West Factors and Traders

Among the North Westers commissioned in 1821, country alliance patterns varied more widely. The fates of the country wives of McTavish, Stuart, Connolly, and McMillan have been discussed. And the eventual decision of their colleague Angus Cameron to leave his native family, retire to Scotland, and take a white wife in the early 1840s (Mitchell 1974) may have been governed by similar considerations.

On the other hand, at least nine North Westers did commit themselves to their country alliances. Perhaps the best known case is that of Daniel Harmon, already described. Five of the others brought their wives and children to settle in eastern Canada. Among them were John Dugald Cameron, who wedded his Indian wife of many years in an Anglican ceremony in Red River in 1833, and John Thomson who after having "cohabited together for many years in the Indian Territory" with one Françoise Boucher, native-born daughter of a French Canadian, settled in Lower Canada with six children and there legitimized his union by means of a notarized contract with *douaire prefix* (marriage settlement) (HBCA, A. 36/13, f. 192). One North West chief factor, George Keith, went so far as to take his native wife, Nanette Sutherland, to Scotland upon retiring in 1844. Before leaving Lachine near Montreal, they were formally married, Keith finally observing his brother James's advice of some years before, recommending "his marrying the mother of his Children in order to legitimate them." With some effort and aid, Nanette adapted successfully to life in Scotland (Keith Papers, C. 2, 1836–37; Van Kirk 1975: 320). Chief Factor Roderick McKenzie who, unlike most North West officers, retired to Red River, married his Indian wife of long standing in 1841 (Arthur 1978: 32).

Chief Factor John McLoughlin's eventual church marriage to his longtime wife Marguerite, native-born daughter of former North Wester Jean Etienne Wadin, is of special interest. McLoughlin's alliance with Marguerite dated from before 1812; and a "renewal of their consent of marriage" was solemnized by the Roman Catholic missionary F.N. Blanchet at Fort Vancouver at the mouth of the Columbia River, on 19 November 1842 (Elliott 1935). In 1836, however, McLoughlin had refused to allow the Anglican Herbert Beaver to perform the ceremony. A man of no tact or country experience, Beaver strongly condemned the domestic arrangements of his hosts at Vancouver from McLoughlin (chief at the post) on down, as concubinage and urged the officers to set good examples by solemnizing their unions. His approach won little sympathy, and during his two years, he succeeded in performing only nine marriages.

Indeed McLoughlin (who in any case had Roman Catholic leanings) conspicuously boycotted Beaver by having Chief Trader James Douglas act as justice of the peace and perform a secular marriage between himself and Marguerite (Jessett 1959: 58, 77, 86). Beginning some years before, the company had approved a secular contract form to be employed for recording marriages (see HBCA, B. 239/z/1, f. 33; B. 89/z/1, ff. 1–3). McLoughlin was therefore following an acceptable company procedure, albeit one intended for use in the absence of clergy and in general practice applied only to newly initiated alliances.

McLoughlin's temporary rejection of clerical intervention in his marriage was outdone by that of another former North Wester, Peter Skene Ogden.

Ogden would have been counted among the chief traders of 1821 had his rivalry to the Hudson's Bay men not been so violent in the years immediately preceding the merger. However, in 1823 he was allowed to join the new company. Shortly before the merger, while in the Columbia district, Ogden had taken a native wife, Julia Rivet, Nez Percé stepdaughter of an old Canadian voyageur (Cline 1974: 29). Despite the opportunities for church marriage, Ogden died in 1854 without having formalized the long-lasting union. There was no question of his loyalty to his wife and family; much to the ire of his white relatives, he left his estate mainly to Julia and their children and specified that "should any relation of mine or any other individual attempt to dispute this my Last Will and Testament I . . . declare that I disinherit them as fully as the law authorises me" (ibid., 214–15). His failure to solemnize his marriage, then, reflected not a lack of seriousness but a lack of interest in or sense of need for the ceremony. By one account, Ogden objected to the aspersions cast by clergy such as Beaver upon traders' country alliances and firmly rejected their judgment of such unions as "sinful" until blessed by their hands (Binns 1967: 355). His friend Samuel Black, who like Ogden also belatedly became a chief trader after the merger, evidently was similarly disinclined to church marriage with his native wife, Angélique Cameron, and after his death, his will too was subjected to the challenges of white relatives asserting the illegitimacy of their part-Indian kin (HBCA, A. 36/3, ff. 78–112; Cline 1974: 139–40).

The other North Westers who did not pursue church marriage exhibited a considerable range of attitudes. At one end was Chief Factor John Haldane who, upon retiring in 1827, abandoned his country wife and even reneged on the annuity he had promised her (Van Kirk 1975: 229). Chief Factor Alexander Stewart followed a different course with his native wife, Susan Spence. Although no church marriage is on record, five Stewart children were baptized by the Red River Anglican clergy on occasions in 1823, 1825, and 1828. And in 1829, Stewart made a visit to Canada, the "principal object" of which, as he reported to Robert McVicar on 11 July, "was to procure a situation for my Family" (McCord Museum, McVicar Papers). His attempt to settle Susan in Montreal, however, bore sad results; she died there in January of 1830.

Several North West officers of 1821 died before their native wives, without having entered Christian marriages. Nevertheless, they provided for their families in their wills as Ogden and Black had done. The varied provisions reflect loyalty and attachment to the women involved but indicate differences in the ways in which these alliances were conceptualized. Chief Trader John Warren Dease died in 1829 leaving a will that provided for his "Dearly beloved Friend Jenny Beignoitt" and his "adopted children by her," five in number, born between 1818 and 1827. In return he expected her to continue to reciprocate his loyalty: "Let it be clearly understood that if the said Jenny

Beignoit Mother of my adopted children . . . marry or cohabit with any man during my lifetime, she then forfeits the provision made for her in the foregoing will." Both Dease and Jenny had had previous country alliances; the will also provided legacies for his two "reputed" daughters by Mary Cadotte and for Jenny's son, Peter Goulet (HBCA, A. 36/1B, ff. 4–8).

Other North Westers either applied no label to their native mates, or explicitly affirmed their wifely status, especially in later years. Chief Trader Joseph McGillivray (d. 1832) took the former course, leaving a legacy to "Mme Frances Bouche," relationship unspecified, in his will of 1830 (HBCA, A. 36/9, f. 75). Despite the attitudes and actions of Governor Simpson and certain of his colleagues, in these years Hudson's Bay Company country unions had won some legal standing in Britain. The question of their legality could not be left open, since the law imposed a 10 per cent duty on the legacies of all heirs who were natural children or "strangers in blood" to a deceased party. The company was therefore obliged to indicate whether its late employees had been legally married in those cases in which it became involved in estate settlement. In the McGillivray case, as in others, company secretary William Smith defended the legality of the country wife's status as widow and her right to exemption from the duty along with her children. Helping to settle McGillivray's affairs in 1832, Smith wrote from London to McGillivray's Montreal executor, advising the latter to have Mme Bouché, mother of two sons by the deceased,

> subscribe to her name Widow in which case I hope to be able to close the matter without subjecting the estate to the Claims of Legacy Duty, under the circumstances of the deceased and Made having lived together as Man and Wife in the Indian Territories, according to the customs of that country and acknowledged as such and further that there were not any resident clergy within some hundred miles of the places at which they resided; if she terms herself Spinster she as a Stranger in Blood will be liable to a duty of 10 pct which by the before arrangement I hope to avoid.

The reply soon came from Montreal that "In accordance with your very proper suggestions, Madm Boucher has signed herself widow." And on 13 April 1833, Smith was able to reply in turn, "I have prevailed upon the office to pass Mde Bouche as the Indian Widow of the Deceased which saves the duty" (ibid., ff. 127, 132, 137). Despite Smith's arguments, McGillivray and Frances had not been without opportunity to marry in Christian form. In August 1822, while McGillivray was stationed at Norway House, John West had baptized his son Murdock but did not accomplish a marriage between the parents.

It is probable, although not on record, that the country widow of Joseph's brother, Chief Trader Simon McGillivray, also gained a widow's exemption after Simon's death in 1840. In his will of 1833, Simon had left a substantial legacy "To Mme Therese Roy, who has lived with me 18 years on the most affectionate terms" (ibid., f. 146). Like two of her children before her, Therese was baptized in Red River in 1836 and designated at that time as the "Reputed [wife] of Simon McGillivray"; no marriage is on record.

The two wills of Chief Trader Alexander Roderick McLeod show an important terminological shift within a short period. In February 1823 McLeod was about to depart on a hazardous journey in the Mackenzie River district and accordingly made a will to provide "for my family Concerns which consist of a Woman and 4 Children." In June 1828, while serving at Fort Vancouver, McLeod made a will listing his "Wife" and six children, one yet unborn, as legatees. He further instructed that the mother was "to be considered my legitimate wife which I hereby declare to be my serious determination that no plea be adduced in any shape to alter my view." Following McLeod's death in 1840, a legal opinion on the validity of his marriage "in a remote part of the Colony, where there were no Established Clergymen" was sought and delivered from Doctors Commons on 28 December 1841, as follows:

I cannot undertake to say that no question may by possibility arise respecting the Legitimacy of the Testators Children, but assuming that the marriage took place as stated in a remote part of the Colony, and that it was solemnized in conformity to the custom of the country, and previous to the birth of the children, I am of the opinion that it must be deemed a valid marriage, and consequently that the children are legitimate (HBCA, A. 36/10, ff. 9–18).

McLeod's native family, more fortunate than those of some North Westers, received their full legacies without challenge or litigation.

The case of Chief Factor John Rowand, another chief trader of 1821, provides a final example of these North Westers' varying actions and attitudes regarding their families and the clergy. Rowand was said to have acquired his native wife, Lisette Humphraville, when she saved his life after he was thrown from his horse. They had at least seven children in the years 1808–32 and remained together until Lisette's death in 1849. Like John Warren Dease, Rowand did not characterize Lisette as his wife, although they remained mutually loyal. In writing of her death, he deplored the loss of "my old friend the Mother of all my children" (Van Kirk 1975: 256). And in making his will in 1853, he described his children as "reputed" (HBCA, A. 36/11, f.

286), a term used often by traders (and clergy) to acknowledge that church marriage had not occurred.

Four of these children were baptized at Fort Edmonton when Rowand played host to Roman Catholic priests Blanchet and Demers on their trip to the Columbia in 1838. But unlike his colleague John McLoughlin, Rowand did not marry Lisette in a rite of his own church when the chance came. And one piece of evidence, an 1840 letter to James Hargrave shortly after the latter's Scottish marriage, suggests that despite his ultimate loyalty to Lisette, Rowand had considered other options:

> If I am too old to find a wife when I go down it is likely I may settle in Columbia but if I get a wife below or in England or elsewhere, the Columbia shall not see me, it shall be as she may think proper . . . let others do as they please but this will be my way if ever I get such a wife as your or as our friend D. Finlayson &c. (Glazebrook 1938: 316-17).

Some general patterns emerge from these Hudson's Bay and North West Company examples. Among the Hudson's Bay commissioned officers of 1821, William Brown was the only one whose will consigned his native family to illegitimate status (description of children as "natural" rather than "natural and lawful" or simply undesignated, classed them as "strangers in blood" and subjected their legacies to duty; see also the case of James Tate in 1833 [HBCA, A. 36/13, ff. 18, 40]). Chief Factor Thomas Vincent had had more than one fur trade mate during the years before 1821, like a few of his senior colleagues. But there is little evidence of desertion or of either casual or instrumentally motivated mate-changing among the Hudson's Bay officers, either before 1821 or in the better documented years after the merger. Most of their familial relationships, even if not church-sanctioned, were characterized by stability, loyalty, and monogamy, traits generally consistent with the character of pre-1821 Hudson Bay and its large factory-household communities, isolated yet British in their antecedents and dominant values.

The North Westers of 1821, of course, did not lack examples of stability and devotion in familial matters, as the examples of J.D. Cameron, George Keith, Stewart, Thomson, Harmon, McLeod, and others have demonstrated. But their ranks also included such men as J.G. McTavish, William Connolly, and John Haldane, for whom Hudson's Bay counterparts are difficult to find. The greater variability of attitudes and behaviour among North Westers than among their old rivals regarding native families is a matter of record, and is consistent with earlier patterns.

After the merger, however, the two social worlds were no longer separate. Contrasts along old company lines persisted for some years but were bound to become attenuated as older men retired and as new officers, lacking their distinctive backgrounds and old loyalties, rose through the ranks. Some of these new arrivals such as James Hargrave, who had joined the North West Company in 1820, strongly supported the new fur trade social order that Simpson, his friends, and the clergy were bringing about, as the voluminous Hargrave correspondence well demonstrates (Brown 1976*a*).

THE GENTLEMEN OF 1821 IN PERSPECTIVE: OVERVIEW AND CONCLUSIONS

Changes with broad and important consequences were occurring in the fur trade world between 1821 and 1850. Even those men whose actions followed older patterns could not ignore or be unaware of the new pressures, particularly insofar as they came from their own governor or senior colleagues. Officers who maintained old loyalties, consecrated their country unions, or found new brides among the women of the fur trade did so with a consciousness that they were choosing among alternatives rather than following (as formerly) the main or only course open to traders in the Indian country. Increasingly they realized that their choices might have important effects upon their careers.

The forces for change were of course not solely a few individual agents. Their personal influences and examples must be placed in a broader perspective. Before the establishment of Red River with its white settlers, the advent of clergy, and the merger of companies, the fur traders had been relatively insulated from the "civilized worlds" of Britain and Canada. By the 1820s, however, the barriers between these worlds were much broken down, and the fur trade country, no longer divided by conflicts, was laid open to the influences of a uniformly British culture emanating both from Britain and from eastern Canada. The merger itself helped to multiply the total number of contacts between the Indian country and the outside world; now Hudson's Bay men and North Westers shared channels of communication via both Hudson Bay and the Great Lakes. Choices of travel routes and of locations to spend furloughs and retirements were broadened. Private correspondence to and from the country became easier and more frequent, as did the transport of books and newspapers.

At the same time, the British and Canadian social worlds that came to impinge more directly on fur trade life were much changed. The acceleration of the Industrial Revolution led to increased mobility and to the diversification of jobs. Aspirants for the new careers in business and industry were in turn likely to be better educated, reflecting rising literacy rates in Britain. And, most importantly, those young men who found their way into fur trade careers now represented a nineteenth-century Britain in which social patterns, values, and ideas later to be known as distinctively Victorian were already becoming visible. With improved communications, these new recruits did not become as isolated from British society as their predecessors, which facilitated the continued infusion of late pre-Victorian and Victorian ideas into the fur trade.

Of all the nineteenth-century British values that penetrated the fur trade country from the 1820s on, perhaps the most significant was the growing importance attached to the quest for upward mobility (Houghton 1957: 4–7). This emphasis on personal advancement encouraged a corollary adherence to certain broader ideals. As Beatrice Webb later recalled,

> It was the bounden duty of every citizen to better his social status; to ignore those beneath him, and to aim steadily at the top rung of the social ladder. Only by this persistent pursuit by each individual of his own and his family's interest would the highest general level of civilisation be attained (ibid., 188).

Respectability and progress toward a civilized life became important personal goals and aims for society in general.

In the fur trade, Governor Simpson, James Hargrave, and several other nineteenth-century traders left ample evidence of their support of this complex of values. With the help of friends or relatives as patrons, they surpassed less well-advised and less well-organized rivals. As they rose, they placed increasing value on the accoutrements and amenities of civilization for themselves and for others. This led them to support, among other things, organized religion and its missions and schools, although they were sometimes privately sceptical of the prospects of the latter endeavours for success. On 12 November 1830, Hargrave told his father that he much regretted the "absence of a Church Establishment" at York Factory. He went on to note that even where clergymen were present in the fur trade country, their efforts were hampered by the limited understanding, prejudices, and superstition of the Indians, and especially by the fact that "attempts at conversion must commence from Childhood, Civilization in all the departments of a settled life must lend its aid, and . . . several generations must pass away before the native savage can be transformed into the enlightened and pious Christian" (Hargrave Papers). This company clerk may not have fully shared the optimism about civilization and progress characteristic of many British Victorians, but on numerous occasions he gave expression to a piety similar to theirs.

In nineteenth-century Britain, one of the concomitants of the emphasis on upward mobility was the view that rising young men should delay marriage and chose mates prudently (Cominos 1963: 28)—a belief that also influenced the behaviour of Hargrave and the Simpsons and McKenzies. It is true that late in life Hargrave recognized problems and costs incurred by delaying the founding of a family so long; as he told Edward Ermatinger on 3 February 1853, "Like most of the *overwise,* I remained single, through the prime of my days, in order to secure the means of providing for a family before I had one:— my children are therefore still young . . . while their number is as yet *unlimited;* and the education of the whole . . . will require for some years the *lions* share of my independent income—" (Ermatinger Papers, ser. 2, vol. 1). But he had seen good reasons for his delay. By 1835, the case of his friend, clerk George Barnston, was illustrating the pitfalls of early marriage; "His family is sprouting up poor fellow like many others before his fortunes are secured" (Hargrave Papers, Hargrave to Richard Grant, 10 December 1835).

The growing numbers of late marriages by men in Britain and in the fur trade had broader consequences than the delayed effects noted by Hargrave— consequences that caused growing concern to the Victorians. The celibacy of the upwardly mobile was not particularly associated with sexual continence. In Europe, the search for non-marital sexual partners probably contributed greatly to the increased rates of prostitution and illegitimacy observed by various scholars. Edward Shorter (1971) has traced conspicuous jumps in illegitimacy rates in various parts of continental Europe from the eighteenth to late nineteenth centuries; and Houghton has noted high levels of illegitimacy and prostitution, accompanied with much anxiety about these problems, in mid-nineteenth-century Britain.

The arrival in the Indian country of gentlemen carrying this complex of social values had particular potential for harm as customary fur trade marriage was challenged, as many native-born women were placed in new, uncertain, and ambiguous social positions, and as these women faced unfavourable comparisons with their "fairer sisterhood" and developed new anxieties about the legitimacy of their marriages and children. Infanticide was occasionally a response to these stresses. On 20 April 1837, James Hargrave recorded that in Red River, "The Courts of Justice have of late had full employment in cases of infanticide—a crime which of late has made its appearance to an alarming extent" (Hargrave Papers, James Hargrave to John Charles). A letter of 20 June to Thomas Simpson added further details:

the crime of infanticide seems to have taken possession of the poor frail ones of the place, 16 different cases we are informed having been discovered in course of the season—The unnatural mothers have I believe in few instances been found out.—This is a dreadful state of things (ibid.).

Infanticide was not new in the Indian country; Indian groups had practised it upon unwanted children and in multiple births, particularly in defence against privation and hunger. But its growth and apparent peak in Red River at this time was doubtless related less to privation than to the social pressures and problems facing native women. When Jane Heckenberger, daughter of former Hudson's Bay factor William Hemmings Cook, was convicted on 19 February 1853 of contriving and concealing the death of her daughter's natural child, she related the act mainly to social factors: "She . . . said she was not well used and that people did not think well of them" (Public Interest v. Jane Heckenberger, Red River court records).

Illegitimacy, in sum, was increasingly defined as a worrisome problem in both Britain and the fur trade in these decades. Its stigma adhered most strongly to the women involved—and most particularly, of course, to those "unnatural mothers" who resorted to infanticide. There is little sign that men who fathered illegitimate children were subjected to any particular censure or disability as a consequence; and their children, if they survived and were given a home, might join the ranks of the upwardly mobile without any noticeable prejudice. Governor Simpson himself, Nicholas Garry (deputy governor of the Hudson's Bay Company in Britain from 1822 to 1835), and former North Westers Alexander Fraser, James Douglas, and the native-born chief traders Simon and Joseph McGillivray all rose to respectable positions without being legitimate. Their mothers, however, were generally confined to lower-class obscurity or anonymity (as was Simpson's mother), with few marriage prospects. In the fur trade, women of mixed descent who lacked Indian connections to fall back on and had hopes of rising in white society suffered particular disappointment and isolation if set aside by officers intent on advancing their careers. If they did eventually marry, it was often downward, below the social levels of their fathers and of their previous partners.

These values may be linked to another broad phenomenon of the period—the generally low and subordinate position of women. In the fur trade context, the introduction of nineteenth-century codes of conduct diminished the standing of native women. In earlier days, their importance had frequently been considerable. In some cases such as that of Thanadelthur (Van Kirk 1974*b*), their autonomy and leadership qualities were striking, and in many others, their assistance was critical to traders' subsistence, survival, and fur production. Some women continued in similar roles well into the nineteenth century; witness the wife of Chief Factor John Lee Lewes who pursued her accustomed Indian style of life in the 1840s in the far Northwest. But at the other extreme, some completely lost their former roles and social positions.

In 1843, for example, Letitia, the Scottish wife of James Hargrave, sympathetically recorded the plight of the former mate of a North West clerk, Kenneth McKenzie, who had gone from Red River to St. Louis in the 1820s, where he rose high in the American Fur Company. The two McKenzie daughters had been taken from their mother and placed in a Red River school with strict moral standards:

> if the mothers are not legally married they are not allowed to see their children. This may be all very right but it is fearfully cruel for the poor unfortunate mothers did not know that there was any distinction and it is only within the last few years that anyone was so married. . . . [The father of the McKenzie sisters] left the service and their mother . . . some years ago. The two girls were sent to school and of course prohibited from having any intercourse with their mother who is in a miserable state of destitution. The poor creature sits in some concealment at MacCallums with deers head or some such Indian delicacy ready cooked for her daughters and they slip out and see her, and as she is almost naked they steal some of their own clothes and . . . give them to her. . . . At 13 years old taking them from her and placing them where they heard her called anything but genteel cannot be a very good plan (MacLeod 1947: 177–78).

Between Mrs. Lewes and this extreme were numerous native women who lost the familiar country roles of small-scale hunters, gatherers, and fur producers yet escaped debasement. Some acquired European domestic skills and a modest education, found loyal fur trade husbands, and could begin to claim the respectability so esteemed by Hargrave and others, even if still consigned to a lower rank than "our British Ladies."

Eventually Red River itself, earlier looked down upon by Hargrave and others, began to be viewed as a place where company officers might find suitable and respectable marriage mates (PAC, Anderson Papers, vol. 1, file 1, p. 57). Women drawn directly from Indian groups were now unacceptable as wives. But the native-born women of Red River, whatever their degree of Indian blood, had now in many cases been exposed to sufficient civilizing influences to be regarded as suitable wives for mid-nineteenth-century company officers. In the 1840s Simpson himself, after seeing the numerous adjustment problems of European wives, had begun to admit the suitability and even the superiority of the locally born women as wives for men obliged to adapt to the conditions of life in the fur trade country (HBCA, D. 4/115, ff. 116–17).

Whether white or part-Indian, however, wives chosen by aspiring fur trade officers from the 1820s on into the Victorian period were increasingly consigned to the subordinate protected positions of their counterparts in Britain, subjected to rigorous moral standards and expected to be "frail" (an oft-used word) and properly domestic. Elements of love and affection often entered into these relationships, but an instrumental component might be quite frankly articulated, particularly by men with links to the circle of Simpson and his friends and relatives and with North West Company backgrounds. One final example of these men's views, a description by Chief Factor Donald McKenzie, governor of Red River, of his new wife, the Swiss-born Adelgonde Droz, expresses some of the views of the place of women current among these leading officers of the new Hudson's Bay Company:

> People here [Red River] are very rigid in such particulars [about chastity] and it became me to hold a good example. I therefore possess a piece of very valuable live furniture upon my premises. The lady is a person out for this country by a series of reverses . . . the daughter of a Swiss gentleman on the commissary department. . . . She is well informed and possesses strong intellects, but you are not to think she is a muse for wit. Much thought of as to looks but is anything except a paragon for beauty, of mild and easy simplicity of manners . . . expert with her hands in all that females are accustomed to perform on the continental parts of Europe from the bonnet to the slippers. She is strict and exemplary in her conduct, the acknowledged model of the sex in this quarter, industrious, studious, devout, never missing a sacrament by any chance . . . sings psalms, gets whole strings of hymns by heart and prays and meditates by herself in lonely places by moonlight. She is going on twenty years of age. She has gained upon the estimation of everyone and for my own part I esteem her also in consideration of her habit taciturnity for you may rely upon it that nothing can give greater comfort to a husband than the satisfaction of having a wife who is nearly mute (St. Louis, Missouri Historical Society, Hunt Papers, Donald McKenzie to Wilson Price Hunt, 25 June 1827).

Company women, then, native or white, were to be judged by conservative European standards of the time, standards that could now reach Red River and beyond with increased rapidity and force. But fur trade women were not the only ones affected by these social changes. Their children were equally subject to changing values, as the situations of fur trade offspring in the years before and after 1821 demonstrate.

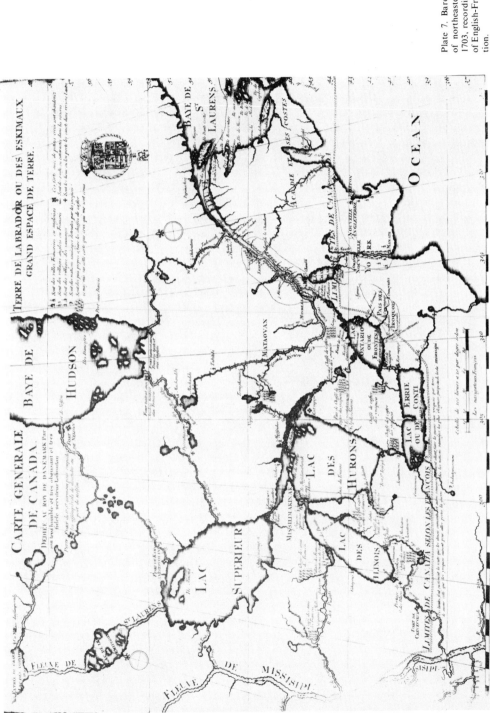

Plate 7. Baron de Lahontan's map of northeastern North America in 1703, recording early posts and foci of English-French fur trade competition.

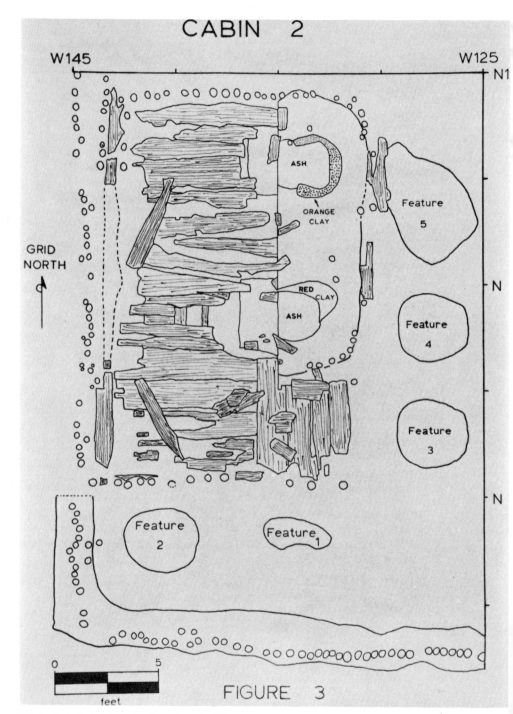

Plate 8. Archeological floor plan of a cabin used as living quarters by NW Co. traders while trading with the Chippewa Indians on the Yellow River in northwestern Wisconsin from 1802 to 1804, perhaps the one that apprentice clerk George Nelson and other XY Co. traders dismantled and relocated inside the NW Co. compound because of a threatened Sioux Indian attack in the spring of 1803 (Oerichbauer 1979).

Plate 9. HBC brass tokens, representing one prime "made beaver" pelt and fractions, which formed the basis of the accounting system used to equate the value of furs received with goods traded. Photograph from Christy Collection, State Historical Society of Wisconsin.

Plate 10. Meeting place of the Beaver Club, Montreal, where the NW Co. winterers met for social gatherings and to entertain distinguished guests. Redrawn from a picture formerly in the possession of Adele Clarke, daughter of Chief Factor John Clarke.

Plate 11. Portaging a brigade of York boats. Introduced in the late eighteenth century by Lowland Scottish and Orkney HBC servants, the boat form can be traced back to Norse antecedents. Lantern slide painting by J. E. Laughlin.

Plate 12. The Rev. and Mrs. James Evans and their daughter in a north canoe, about 7.5 metres long, between Lakes Superior and Winnipeg en route to Norway House in 1840 to establish the Methodist mission there.

ate 13. *Canôts de maître*, about 11 metres long, on Lake Superior. Passengers in the rear canoe are the artist Frances Ann
opkins and her husband, Edward Martin Hopkins, longtime personal secretary of Gov. General Simpson.

ate 14. Voyageurs in canoe in front of Fort William, Lake Superior. Note distinctive headgear. Photograph dated 1860 (State
istorical Society of Wisconsin).

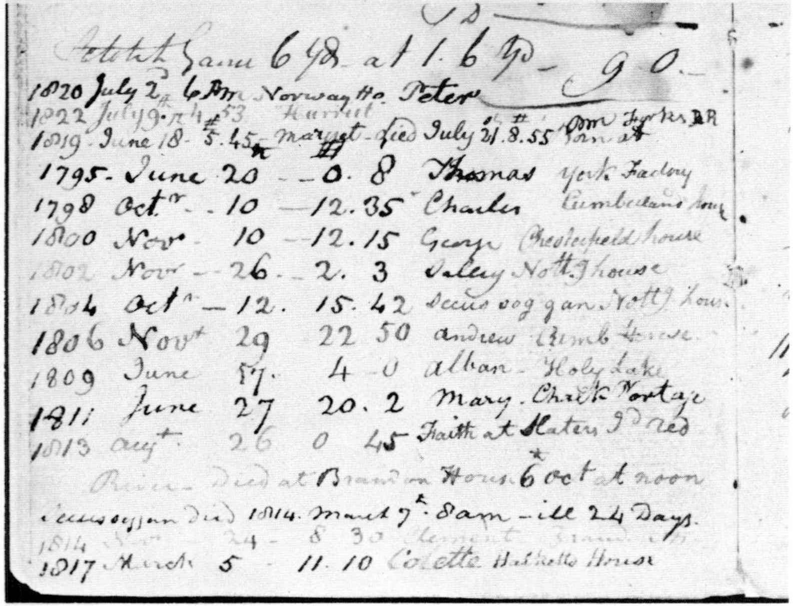

Plate 15. On a small notebook page, HBC surveyor Peter Fidler (1769–1822) recorded the times and places of birth of the children born to him and his Indian wife, Mary, whom he married by Anglican rite at Norway House on 14 August 1821.

Plate 16. This drawing, entitled, "Winter dress of Red River half-breeds," was sketched in 1851 by

counter-clockwise from left

Plate 17. James Bird, Jr. (Jemmy Jock), became an interpreter and leader among the Blackfoot and Peigan (*see pages 175-78*).

Plate 18. Augustin Grignon (1780-1860), a noted member of one of many French-Indian families that settled in Wisconsin (State Historical Society of Wisconsin).

Plate 19. Chief Jacob Berens and his wife, c.1909. The surname comes from that of HBC governors Joseph Berens, Jr., and Henry Hulse Berens.

Plate 20. Isabella Sophia (1825-1914), daughter of HBC officer Richard Hardisty and his native wife, Margaret Sutherland, married HBC clerk Donald A. Smith, later Lord Strathcona and Mount Royal.

Plate 21. Alexander Kennedy Isbister (*see pages 184-85*).

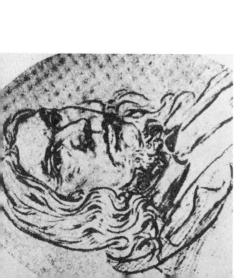

Plate 22. Winter travellers used two main types of sled, the passenger-carrying cariole and the baggage sled. Drawing by J. E. Laughlin of a journey made under northern lights in the Edmonton area in February 1865.

Plate 23. This late nineteenth century Indian dwelling, possibly in the vicinity of Norway House, illustrates the mixing of Indian and white material culture in that period.

7

Fur Trade Parents and Children
before 1821

Parent-child relations and the social positions of fur trade children have already been mentioned at scattered points: by the end of the 1700s, for example, the study of fur trade wives also becomes in good part a study of fur traders' daughters—women of mixed parentage born at the posts. The lives of the children, however, merit more focused attention.

FUR TRADE FAMILY SIZES

One problem in examining these offspring is to determine their approximate numbers and rate of increase during the century (c. 1750–1850) in which they emerge as a significant demographic subgroup. The task is not easy, given the limited data. The paucity of census materials, parish registers, and other such compendia means that intensive study of fur trade demography is extremely difficult. Nonetheless, the sources, if patiently pieced together, do yield a considerable amount of information and indicate some interesting divergences in pattern along company lines.

In the years from 1791 to 1800, Hudson's Bay families, as far as known, surpassed in size their North West Company counterparts (Brown 1976*b*). By 1800, particularly in the residential post communities along Hudson Bay, it was normal for officers to take native mates and establish families. Lasting cohabitation led to greater numbers of offspring and to more open recognition of them.

The lower average family size for North Westers in the same decade may reflect somewhat more transient sexual alliances. It may also reflect sampling deficiencies, less complete record-keeping and preservation, and perhaps the North Westers' lesser interest in recording and recognizing their native-born offspring.

The data for the decades from 1801 to 1820, in contrast, suggest a North West Company rate of increase closely paralleling the Hudson's Bay rise that began in the 1790s and imply that the North Westers were becoming equally involved in more lasting alliances. Some North Westers were also bringing native children (and sometimes whole families) home for baptism and education, as did John Macdonell and Daniel Harmon.

The following decades indicate substantial and fairly consistent growth rates for Hudson's Bay officers' families and a lesser but continuous growth of North Westers' families (ibid., figure 1). Analysis by company cannot proceed beyond 1850 since after that year few childbearing families can be distinguished by their separate company origins (that is, by having belonged to one or the other firm before the 1821 merger).

Although the data and samples are necessarily limited, fur trade family size increases and mixed-blood population growth were major demographic phenomena in the sparsely populated Canadian Northwest between the late 1700s and 1850 (table 3). As such, they had broad social, cultural, and political implications for the fur trade social field. Many of the children born to these families stayed in the Northwest to influence the course of later Western Canadian history. Others went to live with Indian groups or passed into Canadian or British society. Their biographies are complex and varied. Yet they exhibit some common themes and patterns. Numerous offspring found themselves in similar situations and roles, facing similar problems, with which they and their parents coped in recurringly similar ways.

TABLE 3: COMPANY OFFICERS' COMPLETED FAMILIES WITH TOTAL NUMBERS OF THEIR KNOWN CHILDREN

	1750s–1820	1821–50	Total
HBC	53 families (200 children) Av. size: 3.8	50 families (397 children) Av. size: 7.9	103 families (597 children) Av. size: 5.8
NWC	27 families (77 children) Av. size: 2.9	46 families (302 children) Av. size: 6.6	73 families (379 children) Av. size: 5.2
Total	80 families (277 children) Av. size: 3.5	96 families (699 children) Av. size: 7.3	176 families (976 children) Av. size: 5.5

HUDSON'S BAY AND NORTH WEST COMPANY OFFSPRING TO 1790

The earliest company families are the fewest, smallest, and least known. A few Hudson's Bay cases have already been mentioned, and there is little to add regarding these children born before 1750. After being briefly noted in wills or as sources of trouble or expense (for example, the child of Robert Pilgrim), they seemed to disappear into Indian society (with the apparent exception of Joseph Adams's daughter who travelled to England), presumably to live as Indians with relatives near the company posts. Several writers have cited Moses Norton, governor of Churchill and presumed native-born son of officer Richard Norton, as an exception to this pattern; but Moses' Indian ancestry is not proved (Van Kirk, personal communication); he may have been as British as all the other early Hudson's Bay employees.

In the middle to late 1700s, options for some native-born Hudson's Bay children began to diversify, as their numbers grew and as their fathers' interests in their prospects increased. Company fathers' growing attachment and concern in the face of rules against forming country alliances and, after the Pilgrim case, against bringing native families to Europe may have had two origins. Because the long-term isolation of many Hudson's Bay men created problems in founding and maintaining families in Britain, it was understandable that some should find familial companionship, as well as sexual relationships, at the posts. But their evolving attitudes toward their families, and especially toward children, may also reflect cultural and social changes in Britain itself. J.H. Plumb has observed that in England, "by the 1740s, a new attitude to children was spreading steadily among the middle and upper classes." There appeared to be "a greater emotional investment in children by parents" and less of the older stern emphasis on discipline and on breaking the child's will. As economic opportunity and social mobility grew, children also became "vehicles of social emulation" of whom new accomplishments and achievements were desired and expected (1975: 70, 67–68). Children accordingly received more education and personal attention than before.

A marked paternal concern for native-born offspring was demonstrated in the case of Charles Price Isham, son of York governor James Isham. Charles was born in 1753 or 1754 (HBCA, B. 239/f/3, f. 11, and B. 239/f/6, ff. 23, 40, 64). When James died in 1761 at York Factory, he left his estate in trust for Charles and in charge of his brother Thomas (HBCA, A. 36/1A, f. 13). In the summer of 1763, Charles travelled to England to receive three years of education under Thomas's guardianship; he then returned to Hudson Bay and a long career as trader and master at inland posts (HBCA, A. 1/42, f. 92; Brown in press *b*). Thanks to the concern of James and Thomas Isham and company friends, Charles became a literate officer classed among "Englishmen" and could list his home address as Bloomsbury (HBCA, A. 30/4, f. 20) and retire to England. Like several British-born colleagues, he left a will granting annuities to his four children in Hudson Bay.

Isham is the first certain case of a native-born company son achieving a fur trade career of any note. Most children of his time took up Indian lives, any specific record of their partly white ancestry being preserved only fortuitously. A possible contemporary of Charles Isham at York Fort, for example, was the grandfather of the Cree Anglican clergyman, James Settee. Settee was baptized as an "Indian" at Red River on 24 June 1827 (Red River Anglican register no. 644). Had he not left a personal account identifying his grandfather as the son of one "Captain Smith," officer at York, and an Indian girl, this aspect of his background would have remained unknown (Brown 1977). Similarly, Settee preserved the information that one of his grandmothers was the daughter of John Newton, who had preceded James Isham in the charge of York (Southesk 1969: 323).

Such materials suggest that two options were open to early Hudson's Bay officers concerned with the placement of native-born children. The first, easier, and by some accounts kinder choice was to encourage them to keep their Indian attachments and identity—an alternative that Samuel Hearne thought advisable. The other was to seek to equip native-born offspring with sufficient British education and culture to enable them to become "English," at least within the fur trade context.

This polarity of choices tended to follow sex lines in the later 1700s; fathers were more likely to find means of providing transatlantic passage and a British education to males than to females. The two children of officer Ferdinand Jacobs illustrate this contrast: Samuel went to England and eventually entered the British East India Company, while the daughter Thu'cotch remained in the York Factory vicinity and married a Cree "Home" Indian (Smith in press; HBCA, A. 11/117, f. 60). Other cases of the period show similar divergences. Isaac Batt's "Indian" daughter Nostishio and Matthew Cocking's daughters remained in the Indian country with Indian names and with one exception married company men there, while Malchom Ross's son George was, after his father's death, granted permission to come to England if his father's executors so desired (Brown in press *a*; Spry in press; HBCA, A. 6/16, f. 129). George Atkinson provided for his two sons Sneppy (George) and Shesheep (Jacob) to go to England but did not seek to have his daughter Jenny leave Hudson Bay (Public Record Office, PROB 11/1238 18857). Paternal concern for their sons' futures led officers to make efforts to provide for their travel, education, and advancement; for daughters they were more likely to try to arrange a secure fur trade marriage, with support from annuities after the father's death. Once in a while, a native-born daughter was brought to England, as was Andrew Graham's daughter at age six in 1772 (Williams 1969: 347–51). Once in England, however, such daughters, unlike their brothers, were not to have the privilege of returning to Hudson Bay. A London committee dictum of 25 May 1803 reaffirmed the policy that not only forbade "Woman natives" (that is, country wives) to come to England, but added, "nor have any Female Children born in that Country [Hudson Bay] been permitted to return to it after receiving their Education in Great Britain" (HBCA, A. 6/16, f. 160). These rules seem to have been followed at least until after Red River was established and women became more frequent transatlantic travellers. For native-born females, then, perhaps even more than for males, the polarity between "English" and "Indian" or "native" was strong indeed, even though all were often the recipients of paternal attention.

Few North Westers' native children born before 1790 seem to have received as much parental support. Nor were they the objects of as much concern to the company. Nicholas, son of Nicholas Montour, and Jaco, son of James Finlay, both received enough training to hold company clerkships for a few years. Neither appears, however, to have maintained strong ties with his father. The elder Montour had a white wife and three children in Lower Canada; the elder Finlay had a wife and four children in Montreal (Wallace 1934: 487–88, 440). The younger Montour and Finlay founded native families in the fur trade country and apparently died there.

A third early North Wester, Jean Etienne Wadin, a Swiss Protestant who had apparently come to Canada with the British army, also had both a wife and children in Montreal and a daughter, Marguerite, born in the Indian country. In 1782 he was killed in a dispute with another trader. Marguerite Wadin became for some years the country wife of Alexander McKay. After they separated, presumably upon McKay's retirement from the North West Company in 1808, Marguerite married John McLoughlin, first according to "the custom of the country" and later by Christian rite.

Marguerite's eldest son, Thomas McKay, married a daughter of Nicholas Montour, Jr., at Fort Vancouver in 1838. The bride's mother, according to the marriage record, was "Susanne Ompherville," doubtless the descendant of Edward Umfreville, who, after a decade of service with the Hudson's Bay Company, had joined the North Westers in 1782 and then retired to England. His other descendants included Canote Umphreville, a guide at Fort Vancouver in the 1830s and Louise (Lisette) "Humpherville," country wife to Chief Factor John Rowand in the Saskatchewan country (Barker 1948: 326; Warner and Munnick 1972: 44, A–37–38, 8–9, A–72). Umfreville's oldest son may have been Thomas "Umferphille," who was hunting and trapping for York Fort in the 1790s (HBCA, B. 239/a/102, f. 21). Umfreville's children, like most others of early North Westers in the fur trade country, appear to have separated from their father and made their own livelihood without benefit of European education other than what sympathetic traders may have taught them at the posts (for example, Harmon's teaching in 1801 of the son of partner A.N. McLeod [Lamb 1957: 50]), and without support of legacies or annuities.

The children of Patrick Small provide some further details on North West Company offspring born before 1790. When Small retired from the fur trade in 1791, he left behind his Cree country wife, a son, Patrick, who although "deficient in education" later served as a clerk and died in the Northwest, and two daughters. The daughters, despite their father's absence, made lasting fur trade marriages. At age fourteen, Charlotte married David Thompson, a North Wester who was originally a Hudson's Bay Company apprentice, and eventually settled with him and their large family in Lower Canada. Nancy married John McDonald of Garth and retired with him to Upper Canada.

These cases suggest that offspring born before 1790 were placed in somewhat differing social circumstances according to their company context. Hudson's Bay sons and daughters were likely to be given more guidance and direction, whether by the company's regulations or by interested fathers combatting company rules to secure their advancement. Their fathers and other company agents had active roles in determining their identity as "English" or "Indian" and maintaining them in it, once established (witness the rule that daughters, if educated in England, must remain there permanently). Furthermore, the "Indian" status was of a specific type. "Indian" sons and daughters of traders became "Home" Indians, members of the mainly Cree bands whose lives increasingly centred upon particular posts. Hudson's Bay fur trade children then, whether "English" or "Indian," were subject to a generally benevolent and well-intentioned paternalism emanating either from their own fathers or from the company, which was concerned with the order of its posts.

Early North West Company children faced rather different prospects. The geographic mobility and the home ties of their fathers might mean that they would be left with equally mobile Indian relatives or as dependents of company posts whose personnel might or might not be interested in their prospects. This looser structure perhaps provided more personal freedom; a fur trade son might win favour either with the traders or with some of the numerous independent Indian groups contacted by the North Westers. His surname might help him obtain a clerkship, he might be a more casually employed guide or interpreter or "freeman," or he might remain with Indian relatives. Similarly, a North Wester's daughter might be assimilated to Indian life, or she might enter a marriage with another trader's native-born son, a voyageur, or perhaps a wintering partner on a more or less lasting basis. Neither sons nor daughters, however, were likely to be educated in Canada or Britain or to receive annuities, legacies, or other forms of recognition and support from their fathers or from their fathers' estates; nor could they join or move upward in white society.

In the decades between 1790 and 1821, the social positions and adult career patterns of many fur trade offspring changed markedly. In both companies their numbers rose conspicuously; and much evidence indicates that parental and company attitudes toward them showed a new recognition of this distinctive demographic group, its problems, and its potentialities.

Varied source materials regarding Hudson's Bay offspring of the 1700s to early 1800s have provided information on two hundred native-born individuals known to have survived birth (table 3); ninety-six males, ninety-nine females, and five of unknown sex (a ratio that suggests relatively unbiased recording of births of both sexes). This section surveys children born no later than about 1805, that is, offspring who matured and were educated, if at all, under the "old regime" in Hudson Bay. It also focuses more upon sons than daughters since sons were particularly affected by changes in personnel practices.

To a certain extent these cases are self-selected; quirks of data preservation and of infant and child mortality mean that often important biographical information has either been lost or was never generated in the first place. It is not possible to measure mortality rates among these children with precision, but clearly accident and disease claimed many of their lives before they reached maturity, sometimes striking heavily at particular families. The Moose Factory register records, for example, the deaths of five of the seven children of William Bolland (d. 1804) and Penachequay between July 1808 and April 1810 and the burials of three of the six children of Andrew Moar and Imockquay between January and May 1815. George and Mary (Moore) Gladman lost two of their eight children in infancy at Eastmain Factory in 1806–7 (HBCA, B. 59/z/1, p. 185).

The histories of surviving Hudson's Bay offspring suggest that an important shift away from the simple dichotomy of choice between English and Indian identity began to occur as early as the 1780s and 1790s. A class of company sons of mixed descent emerged who were described neither as English nor as Home Indians, but instead as "natives of Hudson's Bay." Anglicized to some degree and having some fur trade skills, numbers of these youths began to be employed intermittently and sometimes permanently by the company. They kept their British surnames and were included on the same servants' lists as British-born personnel. Clearly they were not classed as Home Guard Cree; indeed, in this period the company is not known to have carried Home Indians on its regular payroll, and persons in that category, whatever their racial descent, would not have been hired except as temporary servants. But they also did not attain the more privileged status of "Englishman" that Charles Isham had gained thanks to his father's high standing and support.

Among the best documented cases of this new class are those of John and Thomas Richards, born in the 1760s to William Richards, a company surgeon from Wales. William Richards served the company from the 1750s to 1769, but then, being suspected of smuggling furs, he was not rehired until 1794, despite his repeated applications. Meanwhile his sons remained in the Albany area and requested on several occasions to enter the company as Englishmen. By 1784, John, who was at least minimally literate, had received a five-year contract as labourer at £6 per annum. Fifteen years later, when his father returned to the Bay, John was a "trader" at £18 per year and "beloved by the Indians" although at times "irregular." After his year's service in 1794 to 95, William Richards returned permanently to Britain, and John sailed with him to spend a year in England and Wales. He returned to the Bay the following summer, and company work occupied him till June 1797, when he left his inland post duties to go off with some Indians. His departure did not surprise his immediate superior, who had found that John was "Impossible to keep from Indians and at present he is more turbulent than any other Indn. belonging the place" (Johnson 1967: 6–7; HBCA, B. 155/a/12). He later served with both Canadian and Hudson's Bay traders at intervals but disappeared from view after 1799. John's brother, Thomas, was a more steady employee but always of low rank, serving in such capacities as canoeman from 1794 until his death in 1812 (Johnson 1967: 6; Moose Factory register).

The Richards brothers were among the first fur trade sons to appear in servants' records as natives of Hudson Bay and to have a separate standing and a commonly low rank that went with this identity. John, in particular, was close to Indians yet not one of them, and at the same time he was not British enough in education or culture to gain easy entry into or advancement in the company. His "irregular" habits and eventual lack of company loyalty may have been related to incompatibilities with his British peers, a sense of frustration at his prospects, which was perhaps heightened by his visit to Britain and renewed association with his father, and to competing offers from rival Canadian traders impressed by his influence with Indians. John's and Thomas's descendants continued in similarly low ranks as post servants and dependents. Of their twenty or so children and grandchildren on record in the Moose Factory register from the early 1800s to 1840s, only one might have proved an exception to that pattern if he had survived past his mid-twenties. William, son of John Richards, not only became a good cooper through a term of apprenticeship to a company tradesman but was also, for the last four years of his life, husband of the eldest daughter of John Thomas, chief officer at Moose Factory. By some unknown means he also became a skilled watercolour painter and, probably with Thomas's encouragement, made some detailed pictures of the James Bay posts that provide a unique visual record of these establishments and were perhaps painted for the information of the London committee (Brown in press *b*). Upon his death in July 1811, after a long illness, Thomas described him as a "useful servant and remarkable for his genius in drawing" (Moose Factory register).

The careers of George and Jacob Atkinson, born in 1777 and 1779 to George Atkinson, officer at Eastmain Factory, and Necushin, an Indian, are comparable in some respects. The older son appears to have spent two winters in England before his father's death at Eastmain in late 1792. In 1790, his father sent George to England to "shake off a little of the Indian" and equip him to be a useful assistant to inland officers. The boy returned to the Bay in 1791, but by then his father was preparing to sail home on sick leave. Both George II and Jacob accompanied their father to England that summer and back to Eastmain in 1792 (Davies 1963: 329).

After his father's death, George was employed in hunting, fishing, and trading for Eastmain and inland. He then received an appointment as trader at £20 per year in 1794, although an inland colleague doubted that he would ever "be of any service ... for he delights always in the company of the Indians, and not in the Englishmens" (ibid., 330–31). After a year in England (required by the terms of his father's will), George continued as an inland trader, assisted at times by his brother Jacob, who, helped by the London committee's approval of hiring sons of "old servants," had entered the company as a labourer in 1794 (ibid.; HBCA, A. 30/9, f. 21). His success in trade and against encroaching rival North Westers secured him an annual salary reaching £50 by 1805–6; and in December 1806 he was in London to report to the committee on Canadian trade rivalry. His good relations with the Indians and knowledge of the country made him a valued trader and even at times "District Master" until 1821 (HBCA, A. 30/12, f. 17; Davies 1963: 340–41).

There were, however, recurring signs that George, like John Richards, experienced personal difficulties with his British-born associates and felt the strain of sometimes divided loyalties. Disputes between him and others over who should conduct a whale fishery at Eastmain led the London committee in 1813 to remark on the need for his co-operation ("the influence of Atkinson over the Indians is such that unless they can be brought to cooperate there would be but little prospect of success"), while expressing fear of "some difficulty in establishing a cordiality between Atkinson and any European officers for long continuance." One of Atkinson's superiors felt that since he was not accustomed to "business managed with a view to profit," he could not "be expected to manage the fishery in a manner conformable to our present views." In subsequent years, Atkinson conducted inland surveys, although he spent much time with Indians and was thought to be "too much possessed of Indian ideas" (Davies 1963: 335–36, 338n). He drew a salary, however, until he was retired with an annuity in 1821.

Shortly thereafter, James Clouston, a former colleague, again criticized his conduct. Atkinson was reportedly fostering discontent among local Indians, telling them that they were cheated in trade and urging that they not "hunt furs till they are better paid." Clouston later added that the Indians "esteem his knowledge to be equal to that of the Spirit which enters the Conjuring House and his words equally true." The company officers must understandably have been ambivalent about Atkinson. In the mid-1820s they encouraged him to remove from the Eastmain coast and take land for himself and his large family (an Indian wife and fourteen children) in Red River. Still, he continued to render valuable service to the company as late as 1828 (ibid., 340, 341).

Atkinson finally moved to Red River in 1829 and died there in 1830. The Moose Factory register and later nineteenth-century servants' records (HBCA, A. 32/20, passim) list several Atkinsons, evidently his descendants, as residents of the James Bay and Red River areas and as low-level employees at the ranks of labourer, canoeman, guide, and interpreter. George's illiterate younger brother Jacob, however, remained on the James Bay coast; and he and his family, like numerous traders' descendants in earlier days, seem to have tended back toward Indian life. A list of Indians belonging to Eastmain in 1827–28 included Nooquattamagan, son of Jacob Atkinson (Davies 1963: 75n). And a list of Indians at Great Whale River in 1846 included the names of Jacob Atkinson, two Indian wives, and a son (Moose Factory register).

These cases outline some of the career patterns followed by native-born sons growing up in the 1780s and 1790s. John and Thomas Richards and George and Jacob Atkinson all matured, however, in times when training, apprenticeship, education, and hiring of traders' sons were uncertain matters not yet supported by company policy. Although led away from Indian life and given various chances at employment, the Richardses and Atkinsons were not consistently encouraged within the company. John Richards and George Atkinson in particular showed signs that they were frustrated in their aspirations and that they developed conflicts of allegiance.

During these years, however, senior officers and the London directors were beginning to become more aware of the collective presence of native-born children and to recognize that offspring such as the Richardses and Atkinsons presented both problems and possibilities. From about 1800 to 1810, the company developed a cluster of new policies and practices concerning them, with the intention of making them more consistently loyal and useful (and even more British and Christian) than men such as the Richardses and Atkinsons were proving to be.

The changing positions of native-born offspring in the Hudson's Bay Company may be traced in some detail in post records. Some of the most complete and most interesting of the relevant post journals originated at Moose Factory where, from the late 1700s on, traders and their descendants had begun to form an expanding web of marital and kinship links (figure 3). From the 1780s until his retirement in 1813, the keeper of these journals was almost continuously one man, John Thomas. Over the years his records reflect some significant social changes in the fur trade community of Moose Factory.

From 1785 to 1789 (HBCA, B. 135/a/70–74), for example, Thomas generally made no direct reference either to native-born children of traders as such or to native women as traders' partners, although both were by then amply represented at Moose, and although he himself had a native wife and a growing family (eventually totalling nine children born between 1780 and 1807—Moose Factory register). But by 1797, he was regularly and openly referring to these persons and describing their activities. On 28 July "with the assistance of some of the Women and Children, we got some more of the Hay dried." Later, "three of the Factory Boys [a new category] and four Indian Lads" left on a local boat trip. In the same period, the shipwright and cooper were plying their trades with the help of their respective native-born sons—a sign that tradesmen too now had Hudson Bay families to an increasing extent (HBCA, B. 135/a/84, ff. 34, 35, 39).

The following winter's journal noted other diverse tasks given to the Moose Factory children. Sometimes they were getting firewood, setting rabbit snares, or pheasant hunting with Thomas himself. On 22 January 1798, "three of the Boys yoked one Team of Cattle and sledged home firewood and Timber," and on 12 March, some of the boys were helping the women with ice-fishing (HBCA, B. 135/a/85, ff. 6, 10, 14). From this period on, children were much mentioned and often named as they acquired locally needed skills and trades and contributed in various ways to subsistence and other work at Moose Factory.

Of equal interest are certain other activities, first mentioned in this period. While three boys were bringing home firewood on 22 January 1798, "the other Boys & Children" were "at their Books." References to schoolwork thereafter recur intermittently during the relatively slack winter seasons. In December 1799 John Thomas summarized the children's studies and other work as follows:

in order to avoid daily repetitions concerning the Boys & other Children, I shall here remark, that except when their Services are required out of Doors they are kept at their Books—the larger Boys at times . . . are sent round the Fox Guns, rabbit snaring &c, Gill's [the shipwright's] Son is now Framing a Boat, they likewise attend on Chief's Table—lead the hauling Cattle, & in short are employ'd in any little offices they are Capable of (HBCA, B. 135/a/86, f. 11).

The 1790s, then, were years in which Factory children were both making

small-scale economic contributions and receiving some training and schooling. The London committee had previously supplied the posts with religious
books, and chief officers had been encouraged to hold Sunday services and
promote "Virtue, Diligence, and Sobriety" (HBCA, A. 6/16, f. 29). Now it was
to consider attempting, more specifically, to educate the children to play
useful roles at the posts and in the trade, a move encouraged by interested
fathers who were already beginning to train their sons in practical skills. These
native-born youths, as they found their own niches within the posts,
supplanted an older category of company servant. In its first decades, the
Hudson's Bay Company had commonly brought out young apprentices from
England who matured and learned trades while serving the company. By
around 1800, such apprentice roles were increasingly being filled locally.
George Ross and John Sutherland, sons of officers in the York district, were
granted apprenticeships at York by 1800 (Brown in press *a, b*). And on 17
November 1800, John Hodgson, chief at Albany Factory, recorded that he
had apprenticed three boys "now past 14 Years of Age" (one being his own
son) to the Albany shipwright, house carpenter, and cooper respectively:

> as their Inclinations tend toward the several Trades they are put to, I
> have hopes in a few Years, they will be Capable of being useful, in these
> several Branches, and trust your Honors will approve of my Actions in
> this respect towards these Youths Educated and Brought up in the
> Factory (HBCA, B. 3/a/104).

These apprenticing actions and other changes regarding native youths
corresponded closely in time to a new hiring policy that the company directors
were establishing. On 21 February 1798, the London committee ended its long
practice of recruiting British servants in their early or mid-teens by resolving
that "after this day no person shall be engaged as a Servant to the Company
who is under the Age of Eighteen" (HBCA, A. 1/47, f. 107). Whatever their
other reasons, the directors must have begun to realize that the Bay posts now
held their own growing populations of potential apprentices and junior
servants and that personnel policies could be revised accordingly. It is certain
that on various occasions they were hearing of the usefulness of these fur trade
sons. In 1803, John Thomas wrote to London, doubtless with the Atkinson
brothers as well as others in mind, "The services of . . . Native Youths are
becoming every year more & more conspicuous . . . they are almost our sole
dependance both for supplying & supporting the Inland Stations, as well as
otherwise opposing the Canadians" (HBCA, B. 135/f/1, Moose Servants
requests and resolves).

With these developments, the company moved to support a more formal programme of schooling at its major posts. Its motives were mainly practical. In May of 1806, Bay officers were asked to respond to a proposal to instruct servants' children in the rudiments of religion and in reading, writing, and "arithmetic accounts." The directors hoped this would "attach them to our Service & in a short time become a Colony of very useful Hands." They added that while "the nature of the country & Service" precluded sending out ministers, they saw "less difficulty in sending out persons merely to serve as Schoolmasters" (HBCA, A. 6/17, f. 69).

Bay officers responded favourably, and in May 1807, London letters outward noted that parcels of schoolbooks were being sent to all the factories. Regular schoolmasters had not yet been hired, but the surgeons of the different posts were to use their leisure time for teaching, with "proper Remuneration to be added" (ibid., f. 94). By the fall of 1807, some post journals were making more frequent reference to the instruction of traders' children. At Albany, for example, William Spence on several days acted as "Schoolmaster" along with "Mr. McCormick Surgeon, who . . . has paid particular attention to the Children whenever his professional duties would allow it" (HBCA, B. 3/a/110, f. 8).

During the same period, the London directors were formulating more specific policies and procedures regarding their new schools in the Bay and determining the resources they would commit to these enterprises. It was now unquestioned that "Factory boys" should receive basic practical instruction; furthermore, no one seems to have suggested denying basic schooling to the girls. There was, however, some discussion over how much special attention should be allocated to them—discussion suggestive of traders' growing aspirations for their children and of the kind of life and community for which they now hoped to see them prepared. The York officers raised these issues most explicitly in their London letters of 1807, communicating their "Sentiments on this most interesting subject," deploring "The present helpless Condition of our Children," and offering to contribute toward the extra costs of the following proposal:

this is the anxious desire of every Parent that the Happiness resulting from Education and Religion should be imparted without distinction to the Children of both Sexes and that the female Youth in particular should experience that delicacy and attention to their persons their peculiar Situation requires—Native Women as Attendants on these young persons seem improper—their Society would keep alive the Indian Language and with it, its native superstition which ought to be obliterated from the mind with all possible care.—It is therefore suggested that a female from England of suitable abilities and good moral character accompany the Schoolmaster would obviate the necessity of employing such attendants and the cleanliness of the Children and domestic Economy of the Seminary under the superintendance of a respectable Matron would we have no doubt . . . promise to the undertaking that Success which could not be expected from a more limited regulation.—The expenses necessarily incurred in forwarding this benevolent design would as far as your Honors thought proper be cheerfully sustained by those whose Children received the benefits of the Institution. The Residence of the Children and their Instructors would be most convenient at a short distance from the Factory . . . such retired Situations would not only estrange the Children from their Indian Acquaintance but present other advantages friendly to the progress of Education, Morality, and Good order.—(HBCA, A. 11/118, f. 3).

The request for an entirely separate "Seminary" with a British matron did not win approval; aside from the costs involved, white women were still excluded from Hudson Bay. When London sent forth its "School Instructions" in 1808, however, it instructed that all children of currently employed servants were to be admitted to school "without distinction at the age of 5 Years complete" to remain for seven years or until done with their course of studies and, in the case of boys, "useful to be employed in the Service." A schoolmaster was sent out to each major post, with orders to instruct not only servants' children but also those of the "Chiefs of Trading Tribes friendly to the Company" if the chiefs so desired, to cultivate their "Friendship & Gratitude" (HBCA, A. 6/17, f. 119).

The results of these well-intended efforts can best be described as mixed. For a brief period marked success and progress were reported. On 15 September 1809, the York officers sent home some schoolwork as "Samples of Progress" and wrote that "the School Establishment is proceeding under the happiest presages of Success—The amelioration already taken place is sufficient to justify the Hopes of the Well Wishers of the Institution and to fix in us a firm Belief that the Results tho distant will be eventually beneficial to your honours Concerns" (HBCA, A. 11/118, f. 8). But later York school records are lacking. At Eastmain Factory an Orkney schoolmaster, James Clouston, taught a class of about fifteen children from October 1808 to early 1811, using books that ranged from scriptural subjects and Mrs. Trimmer's *Sacred History,* to *Moral Sketches for Young Minds,* to grammar and spelling. But by mid-1811, Clouston's activities had become entirely centred upon the fur trade itself and remained so until he retired at the rank of clerk in 1827 (Davies 1963: 342–43; 352).

The Albany school seems to have been the best recorded, thanks to the efforts of its master, William Harper. His "School Journal," kept from August 1808 to September 1809, records the varying attendance and progress of twenty-three pupils (fifteen boys and eight girls), among them two Indians. He began with eleven children who already knew the alphabet. But some later entrants presented a greater challenge; Mary Prince, aged about fourteen, scarcely knew the letters and Margaret Goodwin, aged about thirteen, entered in April 1809 "not knowing one Single Letter" (HBCA, B. 3/a/112, ff. 1,3). Four students eventually began arithmetic, but Harper found that subject "the hardest to make them understand of anything." By August 1809, however, five boys (three being sons of factory chief Hodgson) and one girl (Harriet Vincent, later Gladman) were capable of writing "Copy Books to go to England." Harper's effectiveness must have been restricted by his students' irregular attendance; in December, one officer withdrew both his children because he was leaving the factory "to go a hunting." Another temporarily withdrew his daughter in April to go goose hunting; and soon after, John Hodgson, Jr., left to be "employ'd working with the Cooper." In few cases was attendance continuous (ibid., ff. 3–5). No subsequent school journals survive to record later developments, but it is doubtful that these problems were overcome.

No comparable school journal survives from Moose Factory, but John Thomas's journal in 1808–9 documents the extent to which regular post and trade-related activities competed with schoolwork for the attentions of the pupils and even, in this case, of the schoolmaster himself. On frequent occasions the master and boys were out after winter provisions, fishing, and partridge hunting (HBCA, B. 135/a/97, ff. 9, 10, 16). In May and June 1809, the schoolmaster was at times "teaching his little School" (then four boys and a girl) and at times acting as steward, since the steward had been set to other activities such as making buoys. In July, always a busy time, the schoolmaster was helping both as steward and in the packing of furs, while the boys were gardening and fishing (ibid., ff. 19, 21–23). In October he was again a steward while the steward helped to build the new schoolhouse (a project begun a year previously and probably much interrupted—it was not completed until late in 1810 [ibid., ff. 5, 2, 34]). He also helped the boys to reap barley and stow potatoes, then assisted in the warehouse and writing room while the boys ground oatmeal, hunted geese, and fished. Not until 2 November did he again begin "teaching his little school"—now four boys and four girls. Schoolwork was again subject to major interruptions in the springtime, when the master was called upon to replace the steward who was away with the inland boats. The children received instruction on 12 May, but "at these busy times the School cannot be regularly attended." On 14 May, Thomas recorded, "the School Master besides acting as Steward assists me in the Warehouse & when at leisure Instructs the Children." Finally, an entry for 6 August summarized the problems besetting these infant educational enterprises in Hudson Bay. On that day, "The School Master began teaching the Children again which many unavoidable interruptions & circumstances have almost totally prevented for above three Months past" (HBCA, B. 135/a/98, ff. 3, 5, 25, 34).

Despite good intentions, then, it was most difficult to organize and maintain an effective educational system. The company directors and fur trade fathers, like growing numbers of Britishers in general, increasingly saw education as useful; yet providing it in Hudson Bay would have consumed much more time, energy, and money than the company could or would readily spare. As a result, the minimal literacy acquired by Hudson Bay pupils was not comparable to the education that Britain could have provided. At a time when the general literacy of company servants was increasing, few native-born youths could compete with their British-born peers for advancement. In earlier years apprentices from Britain had been able to rise through the ranks perhaps acquiring some literacy at the same time; the native-born apprentices of the early 1800s found themselves in a much less favourable situation, even if supported and encouraged by interested fathers, fathers-in-law, or friends at the posts. Possibly a Hudson Bay "education" may have proved proportionally more useful for women than for men. Harriet Vincent, one of William Harper's best pupils at Albany, later ranked relatively high as an officer's wife and was the closest companion of any mixed-blood woman to the well-educated, Scottish-born Letitia Hargrave at York Factory in the 1840s; and it may be that some slight education also improved other fur trade daughters' chances for higher positions and better marriages.

It may be questioned why the company did not follow up more consistently on its educational efforts after about 1811; once the initial plans and invest-ments were made, costs of maintaining the programme presumably would have stabilized. However, it was in these years that Lord Selkirk first proposed to bring colonists from Scotland and elsewhere into the Red River area and to provide a place, equipped with schools and churches, for company servants to settle with their native families. The first colonists arrived at York Factory in 1811 and wintered there under the leadership of Miles Macdonell. Macdonell found the York officers, like the company itself, supportive of the project, and wrote to Lord Selkirk on 1 October 1811:

> They, as well as a great number of the Company's officers and other servants in the country, feel interested in its success and look towards it as a future asylum for themselves and their numerous offspring.—I am informed that many of the Company's Servants . . . who have served their time, and have families with Indian women will be induced to join as soon as they see a Settlement begun on a permanent basis (Miles Macdonell Papers, ff. 263–64).

These hopes for Red River may accordingly have diverted attention from the further development of local schools.

It was another full decade, however, before Red River became firmly established in the face of the North Westers' opposition to both its land claims and its Hudson's Bay Company sponsorship. In the meantime, Hudson's Bay offspring in increasing numbers were maturing, and their livelihoods came mainly from what company employment they could get. Fortunately, the company was still hiring employees fairly liberally to meet North West Company rivalry. But it was also evident that even those sons of high officers who had managed to get some British schooling might not gain or retain company positions.

One problem was that the fortunes of these youths tended very much to be linked to the vicissitudes of their fathers' careers, as the Richards' case shows. The family of John Hodgson, chief at Albany, provides other examples. Two Hodgson sons had early received company and paternal encouragement to qualify for responsible positions. The elder spent some time at school in England, returning to Albany in mid-1800. The London committee noted on that occasion that he was still "too Young to be engaged as a Writer," but that Hodgson might place him on the books at £8 a year as an "Assistant Writer." They added, "In due time he shall meet with the proper Encouragement" (HBCA, A. 6/16, f. 111). In May 1807, the committee allowed Hodgson to bring his son Thomas home with him on leave, "being ready to facilitate your views in educating & qualifying your Son for the Company's Service (HBCA, A. 6/17, f. 115). And in 1808-9 four younger Hodgson boys were listed as attending the Albany school (HBCA, B. 3/a/112, f. 5).

In 1810, however, the prospects of the Hodgson offspring were much changed by the removal of their father from his Albany command on a charge of mismanagement. Rather than return to England, which he had left thirty-four years before as a Grey Coat School pupil and apprentice, Hodgson and some of his family took up land at Lac des Chats on the Ottawa River. Later travellers on that important water route wrote vivid accounts of this ex-governor and his inelegant establishment. Colin Robertson, travelling inland from Montreal on company business, found his mode of life little different from that of the Indians: "One room served him for dining room, bedchamber and kitchen." Hodgson conversed "upon a grand scale— . . . but in the middle of his harangue a large Pig entered the room, which cut the thread of his discourse . . . he informed me that he was many years Governor at Albany, but really I think the upper works of his excellency is a little deranged." On a later visit, Robertson met three Hodgson sons. One of them, Thomas, "leaning on a paddle," eyed "the company or bottles with no small degree of interest." Tom had a wife, "a lady with a ring in her nose," who was an excellent trapper of muskrats (Rich 1939: 220, 52). Given the circumstances of their forced retirement and isolated life at Lac des Chats, it is not surprising that the Hodgson sons, whenever they served the company in later years, served in low capacities.

Some sons fared somewhat better, especially if they were able to maintain their positions after the merger and the advent of George Simpson as governor and through the difficult 1820s and 1830s. Several individuals had attained clerkships by 1821, and a few managed to retain officer rank thereafter. Others were victims of post-merger retrenchments. George Bird, son of James Bird, a chief factor of 1821, entered service as an apprentice in 1805, rose to be an assistant trader in 1812, and then served as a clerk from 1815 to 1825, when he retired to Red River. He was not highly regarded by Simpson, who found him in 1823 a "tolerable clerk and trader not steady fond of liquor" (HBCA, A. 34/1, f. 29). John Bunn, son of Londoner Thomas Bunn and apparently a grandson of John McNab, surgeon at Albany, was one of the best educated fur trade sons of this period. He was sent to Britain in 1809 and returned to the Bay in 1819 as a licenciate of the Royal College of Surgeons, Edinburgh, and a clerk and ship's surgeon. Although his character as a gentleman and officer was praised in 1821, the company found "no farther occasion for his Services" in 1823. He joined his retired father in Red River, where his medical skills proved useful for many years (HBC Library, file on John Bunn, M.D.).

Joseph, son of William Hemmings Cook, served the company for twenty years before the merger. Evidence on his educational background is mixed. In 1822 he was on record as "Steady and active deficient in Education but a tolerable trader will be retained." In 1823, he was judged "Active and Steady but neither good Clerk nor Trader," and he retired to Red River as had his father (HBCA, A. 34/1, f. 57). His occupation there was later listed as "Schoolmaster" although, curiously, he signed his will of 1847 with an X (HBCA, A. 36/5, f. 1).

Clerk John Vincent, son of Chief Factor Thomas Vincent, fared poorly, particularly after his father's retirement in the 1820s. In 1827, after over a decade of service, he was described as "A Halfbreed, weak, timid and useless—not sufficiently educated for a Clerk . . . Retained for the present out of feeling and respect to his father, who has been many years at the head of the Department." As soon as his father left the country, John was reduced to the lower rank of postmaster (HBCA, A. 34/1, ff. 76d, 131). As happened with some other sons of officers, his prospects declined once he lost the benefit of the immediate presence and patronage of his father.

NORTH WEST COMPANY OFFSPRING: THE 1790s TO 1821

The North West Company did not concern itself with moral and practical education of company offspring. North West posts did not receive schools or schoolmasters; individual traders took what responsibility they could or would for educating their offspring. Those who undertook to do so, however, did not face company rules against transporting native-born children home; it was easier for them to place offspring in the summer canoes bound for Montreal than for Hudson's Bay men to secure their children's passage in company ships across the Atlantic. Additionally, North Westers might be able to enlist the assistance of their often numerous relatives in caring for these children. Daniel Harmon, for example, could readily send his young son George home to relatives for schooling in 1811 (Lamb 1957: 138).

Montreal church records indicate that, beginning at least in the 1790s, several North Westers' children (notably sons) had begun to arrive there for baptism and presumably some education. James, son of partner Cuthbert Grant, was baptized in 1798 in the St. Gabriel Street Presbyterian Church of Montreal and was later sent to Scottish relatives for education. His younger brother, Cuthbert, Jr., was baptized in 1801 after their father's death and placed under the guardianship of William McGillivray in accord with the father's will, which also instructed that the sons be brought up as Christians and educated (MacLeod and Morton 1974: 4–5). By 1810, close to thirty other children born to Montreal traders and women of the Indian country had been baptized in the St. Gabriel Street Church (PAO, church registers), and some in other churches. Simon and Joseph, sons of William McGillivray and later chief traders in the 1821 coalition, were baptized at Christ Church, Montreal (O'Meara 1968: 259). Four mixed-blood children of Charles Chaboillez were baptized in Terrebonne in 1811, the same year in which their father took a wife of Scottish-French descent (Wallace 1934: 432). And the baptisms of the native-born children of Alexander Fraser were noted earlier.

Several North Westers' mixed-blood children spent varying lengths of time with relatives in the Scottish loyalist area of Williamstown, Glengarry, in eastern Ontario. Thomas, son of Alexander McKay and Marguerite Wadin, was baptized in the local Presbyterian church in 1804 at the age of six (ibid., 473–74). Glengarry offered opportunities for schooling, for example with the Scottish schoolmaster Alexander Ross who taught there from 1805 to 1810 before joining the fur trade as a clerk (PAM, Alexander Ross Papers, B1). In the years before 1821, several children of John McDonald le Borgne, later a chief trader in the new company, were being boarded and educated with relatives there. A letter from McDonald to his brother James dated 6 August 1819 provided evidence of his concern for his children's prospects. He and their mother were, he noted, sending down three buffalo robes for the boys and shoes for them and their sisters. And his brother was to "tell the little boys" that

> I hope they will be good boys, obedient and attentive to their Superiors. They must break themselves of their propensity for playing—and solely bind their minds on their education. If so they will find me to discharge

my duty towards them by giving them every support according to their merit (John McDonald le Borgne Papers, box 6, item 2).

Several North Westers' sons of this period later returned to the fur trade country as clerks and sometimes to become "freemen" or intermittent employees like the mixed-blood descendants of the earlier French and Scottish Montrealers, who had more commonly left their offspring at the posts among Indian relatives. These growing numbers of offspring, whether or not they had visited Canada, cannot always be easily traced as individuals; they left few written records and might be more mobile geographically than native-born families at, for example, Moose or Albany Factory. By the early 1800s, however, Canadians in the Northwest recognized them as members of a distinct social and racial category. It was in North West Company contexts rather than in Hudson Bay that the term "halfbreed" was first used. This word, used in the southern United States by 1780, first appeared in North West Company records in the first decade of the 1800s (Brown 1979), becoming more commonplace in the following decade. In 1812 North Wester John Macdonell used the term in reference to mixed descent people of the Red River area, in a letter to his brother Miles, who was at that point leading into the country the colonists sponsored by Lord Selkirk and the Hudson's Bay Company. Like other North Westers, Macdonell was intent on discouraging the founding of the colony and sent his brother an unflattering description of the various native groups:

> I much fear your followers will curse the day they entered the HB ships— ... The Country you intend settling is what I alude to. It is thinly inhabited or rather overrun by some rascally Savages . . . and some Canadian free men & half breeds. The savages in general great villains & most of the free men not to be trusted & in general outcasts from our employ (Miles Macdonell Papers, 27 June 1812).

The increasing use of "halfbreed," along with the older French Canadian terms, *métis* and *brulé,* to refer to North West Company offspring as a group, corresponds temporally with some early efforts by members of this group to assert themselves socially and politically, particularly in the Red River area where, as John Macdonell noted, they were beginning to settle as semi-independent buffalo-hunters and suppliers of the fur trade, as well as intermittent North West Company employees. In the rivalries that intensified over Red River colony from 1814 on, the North Westers found it useful to seek their aid, pointing out that the colony and the Hudson's Bay Company threatened their lands and livelihoods as well as the trade of their fathers' company. Hudson's Bay man Peter Fidler's Red River journal of 1815 documents that the North Westers encouraged this group in efforts to intimidate him and his colleagues and to assert métis rights to the area. On June 19, "Grant, Shaw, Bonhemme, Bostona [sons of Cuthbert Grant, Angus Shaw, Nicholas Montour, and Peter Pangman], and Hoole ½ breeds, but all clerks and interpreters to the North West Company told us by the directions they had previously received, that they had come to the resolution of not allowing a single colonist or servant of the HB Co to remain. . . . These half breeds are held up by the North West Company." In July, Fidler was asked to assent to some "articles of agreement" between "the half breed Indians of the Indian Territory" and the Hudson's Bay Company, which specified that the colony was to be removed. The signers of this document described themselves as "The four chiefs of the half Indians by the mutual consent of their Fellows." Fidler, however, recognized the document's handwriting as being that of North West partner Alexander McDonald and its signers not as chiefs but as "Shaw, Grant, Bostona Pangman, and Bonhemme Monteur, the 2 former are the sons of Partners and now serving their apprenticeship, and the other two . . . are acting as interpreters" (PAM, Peter Fidler's Red River journal).

But while the North Westers were making political use of these native-born men for their own ends, the latter were also using the occasion to formulate and express their own demands. These demands make clear that the Red River métis already identified themselves with a distinctive lifestyle and with values emphasizing the freedom to claim the benefits and privileges of both their maternal and paternal heritage, whichever they should choose. The document received by Fidler demanded not only removal of the colony but also that the writers and their supporters keep "the full liberty of running Buffalo and living according to the custom in which they have been brought up"; that they "not be subject to any local Laws that may hereafter be established, unless they finding the good effects of living a civilized life shall come forwards and asked to be admitted into our society, then they shall be considered as one of us and shall enjoy all the privileges we may possess"; and that it be "promised that whatever presents may be given annually to the Indians, that the Half Breeds shall have an equal share with them" (Fidler's journal, Selkirk Transcripts, pp. 18,430–18,536). This early assertion of identity, seeking guarantees of distinctive rights, highlights some of the wide social and cultural differences between the North West and Hudson's Bay Company offspring of the time; the latter still lacked this kind of political consciousness and sentiment of social distinctiveness. The themes of the 1815 declarations were to assume prominence at several later dates in Red River, when "halfbreed" descendants of both companies combined to define and defend common interests and finally to take military action in the Rebellions of 1869 and 1885.

Several North West Company offspring, whether or not they engaged in political activities, joined their company's ranks as junior officers, as did some of their Hudson's Bay counterparts. Besides Chief Traders Simon and Joseph McGillivray, there were several clerks. Cuthbert Grant, Jr., had first joined the North West Company in 1812. Because he was involved in violence at Red River in 1816–17 and was later subjected to criminal charges, he was not a desirable employee in 1821. In 1822, however, Governor Simpson met Grant, discovered that he might be politically useful in Red River, and secured his admission as a clerk at £120 annually, noting that he would make not only "A tolerable Clerk good trader" but would be "extremely usefull in Red R on account of his influence with the Half Breeds" (Williams 1975: 210n; HBCA, A. 34/1, f. 133). In 1824 Grant left his clerkship to become a Red River settler. But in 1828 he was given a new position for reasons Simpson described in 1832:

we allow him a saly of £200 p Annum as 'Warden of the Plains' which is a Sinecure offered him intirely from political motives and not from any feeling of liberality or partiality. This appointment prevents him from interfering with the Trade on his own account which he would otherwise do in all probability; it moreover affords us the benefit of his great influence over the half breeds and Indians of the neighborhood which is convenient inasmuch as it exempts us from many difficulties with them.

Grant retained this position until 1849. In 1832 he was still listed as a clerk, although at twice the usual clerk's salary, and was, according to Simpson, "perfectly satisfied with what has been done for him which is quite sufficient and has no prospect of advancement" (Williams 1975: 210–11).

Several other native-born North West clerks were retained after the merger for political and tactical reasons. Chief Trader Donald McIntosh's son John became a clerk in about 1818 and was said in 1827 to be "deficient in education" but useful. In 1832 Simpson specified his value: although a "low blackguard lying fellow," he was retained "to prevent his being troublesome to us in Opposition on the shores of Lake Superior where he was born and brought up, and related to many of the Indians in that quarter" (HBCA, A. 34/1, f. 153; Williams 1975: 217). As with some Hudson's Bay sons, John's career was also dependent on his father's support. In January of 1822, one of McIntosh's associates noted that this paternal bias could cause problems, even if beneficial in the short run. Alexander McTavish told Duncan Clarke that McIntosh had removed a certain man from his post to give "the entire Charge to his worthy Son, the foolish man conceives this to be an act of applause, however, I fear it will turn out as every man of sense might previously judge—whatever his Errors may be this Year—the father will naturally cover them, his Successor may not have the same sympathy, when his downfall will be as sudden as his Elevation" (PAC, Duncan Clarke Papers). In 1831, Simpson complained strongly about McIntosh's partiality for John and for another son then seeking to enter the company as a clerk (Williams 1975: 188n).

Three other native-born North West Company clerks were also retained after the merger on account of their local trade connections and knowledge, although found wanting in other respects. Donald McKay had entered the company in 1807, having had some education in Canada. In 1827, he was said to be "Addicted to liquor, not to be trusted with the charge of a post," but he was "retained, because he might be troublesome in the hands of petty traders." Simpson elaborated in 1832: "An active useful Man at Kenigumissie, to the Indians of which place he is related and with whom he has much influence . . . altho not steady fond of Liquor and given to falsehood" (HBCA, A. 34/1, f. 116; Williams 1975: 217). Patrick Small, Jr., and John McKay also had liquor problems, besides lacking education. Small was valued for his knowledge of several Indian languages and his good relations with the Plains tribes of the Saskatchewan, but he had "no prospect of advancement" (Williams 1975: 227). McKay, demoted from clerk to postmaster by 1832, was nonetheless retained "as he would be troublesome in opposition from his knowledge the country and influence over the Principal Indians in the District to whom he is related" (ibid., 236).

In sum, several North West Company native-born clerks who entered the fur trade before the coalition of 1821 resembled their Hudson's Bay counterparts in being said to lack sufficient education for their jobs, but they differed in having political and tactical uses in the trade. Their connections with a variety of native groups, Indian and mixed-blood, led Simpson to cultivate their usefulness much as earlier North Westers at Red River had done. Native-born Hudson's Bay employees, in contrast, seem to have offered fewer useful ties with autonomous and semi-autonomous native groups, perhaps because they had often matured as members of more closed post communities. A few sons of Hudson's Bay officers who served inland in the late 1700s to early 1800s did become close associates of Indian groups—for example, "Jemmy Jock" Bird, one of the eldest sons of Chief Factor James Bird, whose shifting loyalties and links with American traders were deplored by Hudson's Bay men of the 1830s and 1840s (Hargrave Papers, John Rowand to James Hargrave, 11 January 1834; HBCA, D. 4/113, ff. 324–25, George Simpson to James Evans, 27 July 1841; Kane 1968: 288). But such instances were more rare among the sons of Hudson's Bay men, reflecting, again, the differing fur trade social contexts, organization, and domestic patterns of the two companies. North West sons were likely to be better Indian traders and more important means of liaison with native groups; their Hudson's Bay contemporaries such as the Gladman brothers more often aspired to follow conventional paths of advancement within the company.

Conditions were changing, however, for children growing up after 1821: old company contrasts weakened and new patterns and influences appeared. Increasing numbers of company offspring were placed in Britain and Canada for education and employment in this period, and they faced new and varied problems in making transitions from the "Indian country" to the "civilized world."

8

Patterns and Problems of "Placing": Company Offspring in Britain and Canada after 1821

In their private correspondence, fur trade officers of the early to mid-nineteenth century frequently discussed their concerns for "placing" their children in an environment where they could gain schooling or technical training. These concerns became more pronounced as the newly merged company, no longer seeking personnel increases, provided few openings for fur trade sons and also as fathers interested themselves in maintaining or raising the social standing of their families both within the company and in the world at large.

Growing numbers of traders' children began to be placed for schooling in Red River itself. But Red River proved to have several deficiencies from the viewpoint of traders concerned with their children's advancement. Aside from the questionable quality of its schools, it did not yet hold the kinds of well-established business and professional figures whose teaching and patronage would be of assistance; nor was there much secure and "respectable" employment available. As a consequence, officers preferred to place their offspring in Canada or Britain if they could manage to do so.

Placing children for schooling or apprenticeship confronted company families with difficult choices and uncertainties, particularly if the father was absent in active service and unable to supervise the process directly. Many fathers were obliged to rely on the advice and aid of relatives, home clergy or teachers, or friends in Canada or Britain. These parties varied greatly in their helpfulness and solicitude, and the children in turn faced sometimes difficult adjustment problems in strange new environments. Families that successfully weathered these difficulties to see their offspring at last "well placed" were grateful for their good fortune.

In these years of large families, it was also a financial trial for most traders to board and educate their children in some distant place. As a result, some families contained both educated and uneducated siblings, as Letitia Hargrave noted at York Factory in 1840 regarding the sons of Hudson's Bay Chief Factor James Bird and of former North Wester John McLoughlin:

> The state of society seems shocking. Some people educate and make gentlemen of part of their family and leave the others savages. I had heard of Mr. Bird at Red River and his dandified sons. One day while the boats were here a common halfbreed came in to get orders for provisions. . . . Mr Hargrave called him Mr Bird to my amazement. This was one who had not been educated and while his father and brothers are Nobility at the Colony, he is a voyageur and sat at the table with the house servants here. . . . Dr. McLoughlin one of our grandees at a great expense gave two of his sons a regular education in England and keeps a third a common Indian. . . . I daresay the heathen is the happiest of them as the father is constantly upbraiding the others with the ransom they have cost him (MacLeod 1947: 84).

Such bifurcation of siblings' careers was often to some degree related to the fact that they might differ in age by as much as two decades or more and might have matured in very different circumstances with different alternatives open to them. Bird's older children such as Joseph, mentioned by Letitia Hargrave, and Jemmy Jock grew up several years before Red River was founded while their father was serving far inland; Bird's younger seven or eight children, however, were born after 1821 in the settlement itself (Red River baptismal register).

Using Letitia Hargrave's observations as a point of departure, fur trade offspring of the period may be divided into two groups: those who remained in Red River or elsewhere in the Northwest and are the subject of the following chapter, and those who left the fur trade country to be trained for and take up other occupations and perhaps never returned. Those who left went on to pursue, with mixed success, a greater variety of careers than those who remained. The fact of their dispersal makes them more difficult to follow, but several may be traced in some detail, at least in their younger years.

RELATIONS AND STRANGERS

By the 1830s, several fur trade sons and daughters had left their native land more or less permanently. The 1832 will of Chief Factor Thomas Vincent, made in Hartlepool, Durham, alluded to seven Hudson's Bay natives who by then were resident in England. One was his son James, "of Hackney near London Gentleman," who ran a school that probably emphasized practical clerkly and related skills like many others that had begun to spring up in the eighteenth century. Another was his daughter Jane, the wife of a former company employee in the Orkneys. Another son, Thomas, was a clerk to one of Vincent's executors in Sedgefield, Durham. Faith Prince of Hartlepool, who had been listed in 1808 as a pupil in the Albany school along with two of Vincent's own daughters (HBCA, B. 3/a/112, f. 5), was a legatee; so was Sophia (Sutherland?) McCormick of the same town, perhaps a stepdaughter and "Widow and relict of Charles McCormick late of HB aforesaid Surgeon deceased" (McCormick's Hudson Bay family is also mentioned in HBCA, A. 6/16, f. 160).

The most unfortunate legatee named by Vincent as resident in Britain was his stepson, John Sutherland. After his death, the implementation of Vincent's will was delayed by creditors' charges and by disputes between his sons James and Thomas. Meanwhile Sutherland, who had been boarding in Gravesend, fell desperately ill. His landlady's husband became jealous of the attentions she was paying the young man "and which his unfortunate situation so indispensibly required" and, as the lady wrote to the Hudson's Bay Company secretary in London, "turned us both pennyless from his door." In the fall of 1833, while charitably lodged by the landlady's daughter, John died, leaving his accounts much in arrears and his benefactresses in dire straits, unable to get money from the estate even for decent burial: "having kept the corpse until so offensive as to endanger the health of the family, we have been compelled to apply to the parochial authorities for the means of burial . . . a most heart-rending thing to see a young man whose manners were those of the perfect gentleman, and whose connexions were apparently respectable consigned to a scanty grave like the poorest pauper on earth" (HBCA, A. 36/14, ff. 60, 94, 143, 146).

Correspondence over the Vincent estate records the situations of two other Hudson Bay relatives in Britain in less vivid detail. Thomas Vincent, Jr., evidently did not keep his Sedgefield clerkship long after his father's death, was reprimanded by the company secretary, William Smith, in 1834 for his dilatory habits and his neglect of his affairs, and was much in debt by 1835 (ibid., ff. 145, 149, 202). In May 1837, his brother James inquired of the company whether Thomas could be found employment in the fur trade "as he is in great distress and wishes to return to Hudson's Bay." Secretary William Smith, perhaps recalling Governor Simpson's earlier complaints about another brother, clerk John Vincent (HBCA, A. 34/1, f. 131), responded, however, that there was "no chance of his obtaining the situation you allude to" (HBCA, A. 36/14, ff. 213–14).

The Vincent records also note the presence in England of still another Hudson's Bay native—David Vincent Stewart, grandson of Thomas Vincent and son of Harriet Vincent Gladman by her first unhappy country marriage. Vincent had placed the boy in the school run by his son James near London in 1831, asking that James give him "as good an education as if he was your own." David was still there after Vincent's death but his account had gone unpaid, and in early 1833 James sued Company Secretary William Smith, one of Vincent's executors, for payment (ibid., ff. 225–29). David's career thereafter is unknown; he may have returned to his own father, then living in Canada.

Because Thomas Vincent died leaving several debts as well as legacies and because of subsequent disputes and requests for payments of accounts due, his estate records serve as a rich source on several company offspring who reached England in the years immediately preceding and following the merger. It is evident that fur trade children, sons in particular, often faced problems in finding and maintaining positions in white society. Schoolmaster James Vincent evidently succeeded in his profession; his brother did not, and eventually hoped to withdraw to Hudson Bay. Their stepbrother, John Sutherland, was one of numerous casualties among fur trade children placed abroad.

For the last few years of his life, Vincent at least had the advantage of residing in England. Many other officers were obliged to supervise their children's affairs at a distance. Anxious to provide for their security and wellbeing, North Westers in particular drew where possible on their networks of relatives. But relatives sometimes seemed to fail in their duties (being either over-indulgent or neglectful), and fathers whose offspring disappointed them might, correctly or incorrectly, view the relatives involved as responsible. After leaving his children for several years in the care of his brother James, Chief Factor John McDonald reacted bitterly against the fur traders' practice of entrusting their children to relatives in a letter to his brother dated 27 August 1827:

Respecting my ordering my children from under your protection; it was a necessary step, and I am only sorry that it was not done 5 years sooner. If so, I should not have the mortification to hear them branded as vagabonds, They were as promising children as ever left this country when they went down and had I then placed them with strangers as others did they would not have turned out otherwise. . . . But they are not the only ones when placed with their relations who turned out in the same manner. Witness Donald McIntosh's Son . . . Mr. McLellan's boys, your cousin John and many others in Lower Canada who were sent to their relations who never did any good.

McDonald went on to assert that fur trade children "sent under the care of strangers [non-kin] . . . invariably turned out well," among them a son of John McGillivray schooled for four years near Montreal and "now one of our first-rate clerks," a son of Roderick McKenzie who was three years at Terrebonne (Quebec), Patrick Small, Jr., a son of James Hughes, and two of Donald McKenzie, a son of Sir Alexander Mackenzie, a son of John Dugald Cameron, and finally, "two sons of Mr. William McGillivray, who are now partners in this Company besides a great number of half breeds from Hudsons Bay who were sent to England to be educated and all have turned out well with the exception of one Joseph Cook and he was sent to his relations . . . the deceased Ranald Cameron's Sons were brought up at their grandfather's at Sorel—and they have turned out to be the greatest vagabonds that ever were in this country. After all these examples and many others . . . how can you presume to tell me but that those children have been spoiled and badly brought up?" (John McDonald le Borgne Letters, box 6).

It is not possible to test the validity of all McDonald's assertions about relatives and "strangers," but his long Glengarry and North West Company experience probably gave him a broad view of his colleagues' placing practices and their results. In his own case, disputes over his children's upbringing seem to have caused a lasting rift with his kin. Upon McDonald's retirement, a friend, Donald McIntosh, correctly predicted to Duncan Clarke on 16 August 1827, "It is a doubt with me if he settles amongst his relations, I am disposed to think that he will settle upon his lands at Lake Simcoe" (Clarke Papers, file 1).

Donald McIntosh himself later found that relying upon "strangers" was not the panacea McDonald had thought. Possibly influenced by McDonald's experience, McIntosh had placed his younger boys under the guardianship of a minister, Fraser, in eastern Canada. After Fraser died in April 1836, however, McIntosh learned that his trust had seemingly been misplaced:

By accounts from my relations he did not as the protector of my children acquit himself with that view to the ultimate respectability, which had been my object when I had selected him to superintend their morals & education. He treated them more like menials than like Gentlemen's children & allowed them to go through the country worse clad than the poorest farmers son in the Parish, notwithstanding that I afforded means to Keep them as decently Cloathed as any Country Gentlemen sons in the Neighbourhood.

Further, one son had been obliged to leave school because Fraser had "neglected to make the necessary remittance for his maintenance and education which is rather strange as he had drawn last summer upon my

Agent at Lachine the sum of £70 on my Account." McIntosh told Clarke on 20 July 1836 that he was reluctant to suppose that Fraser had "any sinister motive for treating my boys as he did," but that he was most unhappy with the results (ibid.).

One major difficulty facing McIntosh, McDonald, and others was that traders long absent in the Northwest did not have many options in placing their children. Even after ordering his children from his brother's care, in August 1825, John McDonald was still obliged to ask James for other aid in his plans to place his sons Donald and Angus in some respectable employment:

> If Donald can be reclaimed I wish he would attend schooling at Williams-town with his brother all winter there to study writing and accounts. . . . [Governor Simpson] promised to me . . . that he would give him a passage up in his canoe . . . for God's sake let him exert himself this winter . . . that he may be able to hold some situation above the laboring class. . . . Tell Donald that I expect he will behave himself so as to meet the Governor's approbation. . . . Mr. Simpson has also promised to try his endeavors to find some situation for [Angus]. . . . His whole study must be to please his employers and to learn whatever is useful with Commercial Concerns (John McDonald le Borgne Letters, box 6, item 2).

Thus, John McDonald still depended upon James to see the boys properly prepared to impress a potentially more valuable advocate and protector, George Simpson, "a true Highlander from Ross-shire and one to whom I am under many obligations." The help of Simpson or some similarly well-situated person was invaluable in solving problems of placing and could play a critical role in any young man's advancement, as John McDonald well knew. The prospects of Donald and Angus would have been much affected by Simpson's advocacy or indifference toward them.

For company fathers of the period, the suitable placing of children was not only a matter of duty and of laying a basis on which family social standing could be maintained, but also a form of insurance in case of a trader's death. Several traders' wills specified guardians and schooling arrangements for minor children. When Chief Trader Alexander McTavish, a former North West clerk, died in December 1832, he left as heirs two native-born sons. One of these, Donald, was "Yet in the country," but in the case of his father's death, was "to be sent to the Highlands of Scotland, and educated along with his Brother Duncan who is now there, both to live with their Grandmother till they arrive at an age capable of providing for themselves." After McTavish's death, the grandmother and a cousin took charge of the boys' affairs and their schooling. Unlike some North Westers' relatives, McTavish's cousin took his duties seriously; nor did he challenge payment of part of the estate to "the Widow in the Bay." In 1837 he even opened some communication with her, regarding "how her children have been attended to" (HBCA, A. 36/10, ff. 124–46, 155–59).

He also took on the task of finding the boys proper employment. A letter of 8 December 1837 asked the advice of William Smith regarding the older boy, now done with education: "I am at a very great loss what employment he should follow, and have often thought of consulting you . . . whether there might be any probability of getting him to Hudson Bay . . . I believe he has a great inclination to return to his native country—but . . . I am a stranger to any of the partners or Directors of the Company." Smith replied that the youth might apply, but added that he must "candidly state that it may be some years before he attains an appointment, as there are already many applicants . . . if I may be permitted to give an opinion I would recommend both the Lads to be made Tradesmen in preference to Clerks, the market being completely overstocked with the latter." In June 1838, the boys' guardian informed Smith that he had accepted this advice and had entered Duncan "to be a Cabinetmaker in Inverness, thinking it the most profitable trade to which I could bind him." By June 1839, however, both young men had taken up a more clerkly "line of profession." Donald was "in a writers office in Inverness." Duncan "shewed a great inclination to go to New South Wales, which I encouraged and have taken him with myself for a year to be instructed in the management of different kinds of stock" (ibid., ff. 160–61, 163, 167). Under the continuing care of their cousin and grandmother, both boys eventually seemed to enter secure livelihoods.

It is usually more difficult to trace the careers of daughters; their upbringing did not require discussions of trades or livelihoods. And it is probable that fewer daughters than sons travelled outside the fur trade country in the first place; many married young and remained in Red River or at the posts. Some fathers, however, favoured educating both sons and daughters. The two daughters of Hudson's Bay Chief Factor Alexander Christie both travelled to Britain for schooling, where "kind friends" watched over "their health and education" (Glazebrook 1938: 409). One daughter later married a cabinetmaker in Edinburgh; the other married John Black, Red River recorder and judge, during her father's governorship of that colony in 1844–48 (HBCA, A. 36/4, f. 137).

After the death of former North West Chief Trader Alexander Roderick McLeod in 1840, his three youngest daughters resided in Canada, as had an older sister before them, and there was some dispute over their future education. Governor Simpson evidently inquired of a Roman Catholic convent in Montreal whether they, although protestant, might be accepted there and was informed by the Lady Superior that there would not be "the least objection to the admission of the Young Ladies in question if recommended by a Gentleman of your Standing. Their Creed . . . is by no means an obstacle." Others argued, however, that they would be better off and better educated in the hands of a Mrs. Kendall in Quebec, with whom they had already lodged. The eldest sister, Eliza, aged sixteen, herself wrote to Simpson, "I feel much hurt at the thought of a removal as we are very happy here and I cannot bear the thought of a nunnery as we [would be] shut out from any of the duties of our religion and obliged to conform to the catholic worship" (HBCA, A. 36/10, ff. 11, 17, 38–50). The girls thus remained in Quebec, but Eliza soon died of "an inveterate cough she had brought from the Indian country." Former North Wester James McKenzie wrote Simpson that she was buried "along side of my deceased children." Her younger sisters remained with Mrs. Kendall for some years and apparently did not return to the Northwest, although they could have joined an older sister, Sarah Ballenden, in Red River, where she resided with her company officer husband (ibid., ff. 52–55).

The numbers of North West and Hudson's Bay children in Britain were small enough and they were sufficiently dispersed that they did not suffer social or racial distinction as a category. After 1821 or so, many of them were of less than half-Indian ancestry and not necessarily highly distinctive physically. But it also seems that after several years' schooling, they could gain acceptance as members of the British middle classes. Clearly some had problems of adjustment and hoped to return to Hudson Bay. But others disappeared without particular difficulty into diverse trades and professions (or homes in the case of daughters) in various parts of Britain, as did Mary, daughter of former Hudson's Bay man Nicol Finlayson, who accompanied her father when he retired from the company to Nairn, Scotland. In 1858, she married "a young gentleman who is a Banker and Lawyer" and was reported to be "very happy" (PAO, Nicol Finlayson Letters, box 1, item 2, Finlayson to John Finlayson, 17 May 1859).

From the 1830s on, children were more likely to be sent to Canada than Britain. Before turning, however, to an examination of them, one final Hudson's Bay son who ultimately settled in Britain but made himself a distinctive reputation in both Britain and the Canadian Northwest, deserves some attention.

Alexander Kennedy Isbister, born in 1822, was the grandson of Chief Factor Alexander Kennedy and his Indian wife and son of their daughter Mary and an Orkneyman, Thomas Isbister, who had entered the company as a labourer and later reached the rank of postmaster (Williams 1975: 234). Before his death in 1832, Alexander Kennedy took an interest in his namesake and arranged for the boy to be educated in the Orkneys with his own younger sons (HBCA, A. 36/8, ff. 104–5, 119–20, 145). Alexander Isbister left the Orkney school in 1834, joined relatives in Red River, and then entered the

Hudson's Bay Company in 1838. His rank, however, was, like his father's, only postmaster, a servant's rather than a gentleman's rank that, as Simpson had described it in 1832, generally held "no prospect of further advancement" (Williams 1975: 232). In 1841 Isbister left the service because "he does not find the station he holds therein agreeable to him." His far northwest travels and observations in those years still gave him material for papers later on—in the *Journal of the Royal Geographical Society* and before the British Association for the Advancement of Science. In 1842–44, Isbister was a student at Kings' College, Aberdeen. He received his M.A. from the University of Edinburgh in 1858 and his LL.B from the University of London in 1864, meanwhile also becoming a teacher and headmaster and author of twenty-one textbooks covering practically all school subjects of the time (Knox 1956: 19–21).

From the late 1840s until his death in 1883, although he was resident in Britain, Isbister kept up a lively interest in the affairs and problems of Red River and its mixed-blood population and assumed the role of its advocate in London at several points, as the dominantly native-born people of the colony sought free trade and less company control. He sponsored petitions, met with Earl Grey and other government ministers, and gathered and presented evidence for parliamentary investigations of company administration in the 1850s. As one company man wrote as early as mid 1849, "What do you think of . . . Isbister's doing in England he has contrived to kick up a row. I think the Co's monopoly runs a hard chance in these free trade days" (ibid., 22). Isbister also managed to interest such groups as the Aborigines' Protection Society in the conditions of the natives and in the issue of the Hudson's Bay Company's sometimes hostile attitudes toward missionaries and their work (*The Colonial Intelligencer or Aborigines' Friend,* vol. 2, 1848: 29–31, 35, 41, 325–26, 389). While most company sons in Britain disappeared into the populace, Isbister became an effective advocate of his countrymen. His early education was financed by his grandfather; but Isbister appears to have forged his later career largely on his own. His numerous Kennedy relatives remained for the most part in their native land, in Red River or in company employ, except for one unmarried sister who was living with him in London at the end of his life (Knox 1956: 18).

"ATTEMPTS TO MAKE GENTLEMEN OF THEM"

By the mid-1830s, the number of Hudson's Bay and North West officers' children being schooled in Canada was rising noticeably, as educational opportunities expanded in southern Ontario and Quebec (then Upper and Lower Canada) and as marriages "according to the custom of the country" were increasingly formalized and seen to entail parental responsibilities for the education and Christianizing of the children. Offspring sent to eastern Canada tended to cluster in communities to which older fur traders had already retired—Montreal, Terrebonne, Williamstown in Glengarry county, Ontario, in the case of North Westers, and later, St. Thomas, Port Hope, Cobourg, and Brockville, Ontario, in the case of Hudson's Bay families (although from the mid-1800s onward, families of the two old companies were less separate geographically and socially). In communities long dominated by the fur trade, these offspring were accepted and seem not to have suffered any particular discrimination. Other non-fur-trade communities may have been less tolerant. In the 1830s, for example, the small Ontario town of St. Thomas contained several company offspring who were probably conspicuous and strange to the local populace, and certain ones faced problems.

The first fur trade children sent to St. Thomas were those of some of the associates of Edward Ermatinger, who had joined the Hudson's Bay Company in 1818 and retired from the service in 1830 to become a prosperous banker with a white wife and family. Because he was the brother of another company clerk and the friend and correspondent of several other officers, Ermatinger was for many years consultant and confidant on his former colleagues' familial and financial problems and took under his care several of their children. For example, his brother Francis, who did not retire until 1858, had a native-born son, Lawrence, born about 1828. This son, said to be sickly and a little deaf, was placed in the Ermatinger home in St. Thomas for care and education (Munnick 1971: 163–64).

In the 1830s, Ermatinger became involved in aiding the English clerk Thomas Dears and his native-born family. Dears first wrote to Ermatinger on 5 March 1831, inquiring whether the latter might act as his agent in locating farmland that would allow him to "by my own Industry keep my head above water and secure myself and Children a wholesome meal of food" after his retirement (Ermatinger Papers, series 2, vol. 1). Upon completing these arrangements, Dears retired to the St. Thomas area in 1836, but he was ailing. His colleague John Tod, observing him at Norway House near Lake Winnipeg, wrote to Ermatinger on 25 July 1836, "it is really melancholy to see poor Dears—here with a flat head [his Indian wife from the New Caledonia district], a family of fine children and himself quite helpless with the gout." Later Tod expressed his relief "that poor Dears had reached you in safety with his family, and is likely to take root and thrive under your wing, he talks feelingly of your kindness to him" (ibid., 25 July 1837). By March 1840 Dears had died, however, and Ermatinger doubtless assumed an important role in the care of his dependent family (ibid., to Ermatinger, 1 March 1841; George Gladman to Ermatinger, 27 July 1840). The 1860–61 census of St. Thomas listed a Mary Deers, aged twenty-five, as a servant and the cemetery of the St. Thomas Anglican Church attended by the Ermatingers contains the grave of

Joseph Thomas Dears, aged twenty-three, who died in 1858; both were doubtless children of this unfortunate clerk.

Ermatinger also provided advice and aid to John Tod and members of his family. In 1831, Tod was considering plans to retire to Canada, "where my savage habits and mode of life will be less under . . . observance and where my liberty is not likely to be hemmed in by Game laws, and where also a few hundreds would put me upon a par with some of my neighbors" (ibid., Tod to Ermatinger, 10 April 1831). Tod eventually settled in British Columbia in the 1850s; but in the 1840s he acquired land near St. Thomas, to be cleared by a brother newly emigrated from England. It was also Tod's plan that his son James, by a country wife from whom he had separated, should help to work the farm. When James left the Northwest in 1841, Tod described him as "an able and willing lad—and tolerably efficient either as a ploughman or ploughmaker. . . . I have his welfare very much at heart, and on his success depends a good deal of my own happiness" (ibid., Tod to Ermatinger, 1 March 1841). A later letter, although it expressed reservations about the potentialities of mixed-bloods in general, characterized James as "a well disposed hard working lad . . . should you be of opinion he can do better by working at his trade (a carpenter) than on the farm, with his Uncle, perhaps you can find him employment" (ibid., Tod to Ermatinger, 10 March 1842). This Ermatinger was apparently obliged to do, for James and his English uncle "could not agree." Tod's letter of 20 March 1843 indicated that James had his own ties to the Northwest and did not adjust happily to life in St. Thomas, and that Ermatinger must have had continuing and difficult responsibilities in the matter:

> I should be very glad if he would stick to his trade, and get reconciled to the place but I doubt if anything short of matrimony will do the last—he thinks, am told, he has been treated with cruelty because he has not been made a gentleman! I am sorry he should entertain such an erroneous impression, for God knows, all my plans hitherto with him, have been with a view to his ultimate good—if he carries on a correspondence with his relations in Red River, as I suspect, he well never be satisfied till he gets back once more amongst them, in this case it would be an act of humanity to suppress the correspondence.

James finally left St. Thomas for the Northwest and later settled near his father in the Columbia district.

The most celebrated company son to come under the Ermatingers' care was Ranald, son of Hudson's Bay officer Archibald McDonald and Koale'xoa, a daughter of Concomly, an important chief in the area of Fort Vancouver on the Columbia. McDonald had married Koale'xoa ("Princess Sunday") in 1823; she died in 1824, shortly after Ranald's birth (Knox 1944: 42). Ranald was brought up by McDonald and his second wife, the native-born daughter of a Canadian company employee, with their own large family, and educated first in a small school founded at Fort Vancouver and then at Red River (Ferris 1957: 14).

McDonald first broached the idea of sending Ranald to St. Thomas in a letter to Ermatinger on 1 April 1836. McDonald was by then well aware of the problems fur trade children could face in the "civilized world" and had begun like some other officers to make an association between their difficulties and their racial background: "All the wealth of Rupert's land will not make a *half-breed* either a good parson, a shining lawyer or an able physician, if left to his own discretion while young." Asking Ermatinger to "take him in hand," however, he expressed confidence that Ranald could not "be under a better guardian" (Lewis and Murakami 1923: 27).

In March 1839, having completed arrangements with Ermatinger, McDonald (still stationed in the far Northwest) drafted a letter for Ranald to convey with him to St. Thomas. Although Ranald had so far done well, McDonald wrote, "I cannot divest myself of *certain indescribable fears,* which you can conceive as well as I can." His plan was to apprentice Ranald directly to Ermatinger until "the fall of '41, which will either confirm all our plans of making a gentleman *tout de bon* of him or have him enter on a new apprenticeship at any trade he may select for himself." In 1840 McDonald again expressed anxiety over his son and added "I do not like this [fur trade] country for them, yet how many of them have done well out of it" (ibid., 31, 33). In 1841, news of Ranald's inattention and notions toward other occupations seemed to confirm McDonald's fears, causing the father to ask Governor Simpson whether the youth could be taken into the company. While Ranald's application was pending, McDonald begged his friend, "For God's sake don't lose sight of my son, until he is fairly embarked in that concern [the company] which I believe is the most suitable for every mother's son of them, bad as it has proved to so many" (ibid., 34–36). It was Ranald's case that prompted John Tod to send Ermatinger his own developed views on "halfbreeds" and the problems they presented on 20 March 1843:

> I was sorry to learn that Mr. McDonalds Son had conducted himself so badly, truly Mrs. Ermatinger and yourself have had your hands full with the bois brulés. . . . Well have you observed that all attempts to make gentlemen of them, have hitherto proved a failure. The fact is there is something radically wrong about them all as is evidently shown from mental science alone I mean Phrenology, the truths of which I have

lately convinced myself from extensive personal observation (Ermatinger Papers, ser. 2, vol. 2).

Tod generalized and McDonald despaired: "If he can only keep out of egregious acts of impropriety till we can once more have him back in the Indian country, I shall consider it a great point gained.... Here... he may just crawl through life as the Black Bear does—lick his paws. We are all most unfortunate parents" (Lewis and Murakami 1923: 37). But Ranald, now nearing twenty, had his own plans and motives. His remarkable autobiography, which he never succeeded in having published in his lifetime, and other records of his early life relate that he gave up his "Bank stool" out of distaste for money and a desire to travel, particularly to Japan. His curiosity about Japan and its people, who must, he believed, be related to the North American Indians and to himself, had been stirred in his boyhood by the arrival of three shipwrecked Japanese sailors at Fort Vancouver in 1834. Ranald evidently became still more acutely aware of his Indian descent once placed in St. Thomas (in part because a white girl there reportedly rejected his attentions) and resolved to visit "the land of his ancestors" (ibid., 118–21, 39).

In March 1844, Ranald's father received word that his son had begun a sailing career. Unknown to McDonald, this was Ranald's first step in a design devised "while sitting, like a Simon Stylites, on my high stool in the Bank of Elgin, with little money or means . . . no friends or influence . . . a stranger amongst strangers. . . . In the monomania of the project I had sagacity enough to keep it to myself." Believing the Japanese "similar to the Indians and probably ignorant, so that an educated man might make himself something of a personage among them" (ibid., 39–40), he hoped to become a teacher among them.

Japan was of course closed to all foreigners at the time. After a few years of sea service, Ranald secured a place on a ship passing near the Japanese coast and arranged with the captain to be set adrift with a few books and supplies in a small boat in June 1848. Presenting himself as shipwrecked to the Japanese who discovered him, he found that his books saved him from harm, "for seeing me ever reading, a man of books, they drew to me: the books magnetized them: *and they made me their teacher!*" (ibid., 150, 133). He spent the next year in Nagasaki under guard, teaching English to a number of Japanese, some of whom later used their training to serve as interpreters in negotiations with Commodore Perry and others. In mid-1849, Ranald was allowed to leave Japan on an American ship, through the mediation of a Dutch factor at Nagasaki (ibid., 226, 248–49). After continuing a sailing career for some years, Ranald returned to British Columbia and the Washington area where he engaged in various small business enterprises until his death, unmarried, in 1894.

Even more than his Hudson Bay contemporary, Alexander Isbister, Ranald McDonald was a lone independent figure. Both discouraged company superiors by discarding conventional careers after considerable amounts had been invested in their education. And both found individual ways to express a continuing consciousness of their part-Indian identity and their affiliations to the Northwest without becoming assimilated to or classed with "halfbreeds" or métis as a social and political group.

NORTH WEST SONS AND THE INDIAN LIBERATING ARMY

In the same years in which Isbister and McDonald entered upon their careers, certain North Westers' sons in Canada became involved in a venture expressive of a sense of collective identity that seemed more characteristically North West than Hudson's Bay Company in its antecedents. Several sons of former North Westers joined an enterprise called the "Indian Liberating Army" led by a man known as General Dickson (or sometimes Montezuma II) in 1836. Dickson, perhaps a mixed-blood son of Col. Robert Dickson, British trader and War of 1812 leader in Minnesota, had first appeared in Washington, D.C., in the winter of 1835–36 and later turned up in other eastern cities, including Montreal, seeking support for his causes, variously described as aiding Texas and seizing California to found an Indian kingdom. He planned to lead an expedition westward from Buffalo, starting in July 1836 and travelling across the Great Lakes to Red River and beyond, gathering supporters as he went, particularly from the Indian and mixed-blood populations (Nute 1923: 127–28; Arthur 1970: 151–52).

In Montreal, Dickson won several recruits whom Governor Simpson described as "wild thoughtless young men of good education and daring character, half-breed sons of gentlemen lately and now engaged in the fur trade" (Arthur 1970: 151–52). These included Dickson's "Brigadier-General," John George McKenzie, native-born son of a North West partner who had retired before the merger, and two "captains": Charles McBean, stepbrother to McKenzie, and Alexander Roderick McLeod, Jr., older brother of the McLeod girls whose Canadian education was discussed earlier.

There were also two "majors." One was Chief Factor John McLoughlin's son John. He had studied medicine in Paris and at McGill University, but in 1835 his extravagant living caused quarrels with his uncle, Simon Fraser, who was overseeing his affairs while his father served in the Columbia district (Chapin 1936: 49–57; Elliott 1922: 369). Discontented in Canada, John applied to Governor Simpson to enter the company and was refused. His father was ready to give up on him at this point: "Is he such a fool as to suppose that people will Engage a person in this Service who has shown so Untractable a Desposition as to Disagree with his Relations and Guardians . . . to shew you the little spirit he has . . . on seeing he could not get a passage to come up to this Country nor be taken in the service he offered to come up as a Common Engagée" (Chapin 1936: 62–63). In joining the Dickson expedition, then, John showed both his interest in the cause and his eagerness to return to the Indian country and leave behind his difficulties in Canada. The second "major" was Martin, son of John McLeod of Lower Canada, and the only white among Dickson's Canadian officers (backgrounds of the Americans in the group are not known). Martin McLeod was a friend of Charles McBean and John McLoughlin, Jr., although he joined the expedition separately from them (Nute 1922: 353, 355).

Dickson and his Canadian and American recruits, numbering about sixty, left Buffalo on 1 August 1836. Numerous vicissitudes delayed their progress as Martin McLeod's diary records, and by the time the party left Sault Ste. Marie in September, desertion and sickness had lowered its numbers to no more than twenty. A major loss was that of McKenzie who was obliged by an illness that proved fatal several months later to return to relatives in Lower Canada (Arthur 1970: 152; Nute 1923: 129–30; 1922: 372).

By this time the expedition had attracted the attention and concern of various authorities. Newspaper reports of "pirates on the lakes" had come to Governor Simpson's eye, and he and others feared that Dickson's people would incite trouble, particularly at Red River. At Sault Ste. Marie, Chief Trader William Nourse also realized that they had no sanction to pass through company territories and recorded for his superiors as much detail as he could on their aims. His letter of 15 September 1836 provides the clearest statement of Dickson's previous activities and of his plans and goals at that time. After obtaining "from one or two hundred Recruits, mounted & armed" in the Red River and Pembina regions,

> he would then proceed to the junction of the Yellow Stone River with the Missouri . . . then continue till they reached the Southern pass of the Rocky Mountain. . . . He says that while at Washington he saw many of the Chiefs of various Indian Tribes . . . and made arrangements with them (particularly the Cherokees) to join him at a designated point . . . his object is to obtain possession of California, for the Indians now about to be removed from the United States and make it an independent kingdom.

If joined by the "halfbreeds of Red River," Dickson hoped to capture and plunder Santa Fe, then claim California for his followers and the Cherokees and other Indians. There he would set up "a Military Government, preventing all except those of Indian blood, from possessing an acre of land. All Whites only to be received as Officers of the Govt" (PAC, RG7, G1, vol. 78: 520–23).

Nourse correctly predicted the already shrinking expedition was "likely to end . . . in smoke" (ibid., 524); in December, its last eleven members reached Red River in considerable distress. Dickson disappeared southward; Martin McLeod went into fur trading in Minnesota and later served on the council of that territory; Charles McBean returned eastward to join his father, then a chief factor in the Lake Huron district (Arthur 1970: 153).

The last two of these company sons, now appearing capable of being troublesome if in opposition (like some other North Westers' sons), were brought into the company. John McLoughlin, Jr., was hired as a clerk and surgeon for five years (PAC, HBC Minutes of Council, Northern Dept., 1837: 194), and joined his father and brother in the far west. In 1841, he was murdered by his men while in charge at a small post. Governor Simpson let much of the blame rest on John's own head for presumed misconduct of his charge; and Chief Factor McLoughlin, who had so far found his son's record satisfactory, never forgave Simpson for omitting to make a full investigation and lay charges against those involved (Chapin 1936: 70–73).

Alexander Roderick McLeod, Jr., was made an apprentice clerk for five years (Minutes of Council, Northern Dept., 1837: 194), but his company career was soon ended because of sexual conduct more accepted in older North West Company days than in 1840. Chief Trader Alexander Fisher reported in a letter of 29 December 1840 that McLeod "has got himself into some trouble by marrying a woman with a large family, who was already the wife of . . . Houle Interpreter at Fort Halkett . . . there appears to be some little fault on both sides. I forward Mr. McLeod to Red River that he may explain matters and defend himself" (PAC, Charles Napier Bell Collection, file 3, Fisher to Donald Ross). In about 1842, McLeod appeared in Minnesota, and thereafter apparently remained in the United States. In 1862 he entered the Union Army, and died of disease in 1864 while serving in Missouri (Nute 1923: 136).

While numbers of company sons faced individual problems in settling in Canada for education and employment, the Dickson expedition seems to be the only occasion upon which any of them combined to assert a common identity. And even in this instance, John McLoughlin, Jr., and the others apparently had differing motives. John George McKenzie in particular was known to have strong grudges against the company, and some influence over his stepbrother, McBean. It was a matter of concern that he might use the Dickson enterprise to stir up Red River, already a centre of some disaffection, and to assert a claim to "the whole of the Company's territory as their inheritance by birthright" (Arthur 1970: 155, Nute 1923: 133–34); he was probably quite uninterested in Santa Fe and the Cherokees.

"CANADA-WARD, THEIR FAVORITE ROOSTING PLACE"

Toward the 1850s, it appeared increasingly unlikely that company offspring placed in Canada would join or form such enterprises as Dickson's. Canada was growing in population and wealth, and company sons began to find a diversity of careers there like their counterparts in Britain. And unlike the situation in the fur trade country, references to racial distinctions and handicaps were decidedly rare in the context of eastern Canada. Nor did Canadian whites seem to make subtle distinctions based on gradations of colour; individuals with dark complexions and Indian mothers were not assigned a lower status than, for example, light-skinned persons with mothers of mixed ancestry. The apparent success of the family of North West Chief Factor John Dugald Cameron and his Indian wife in southern Ontario is of interest in this regard. Shortly before the Camerons themselves retired to Ontario, their daughters and sons were becoming well established there, as Cameron reported in a letter of 5 May 1843 to James Hargrave:

> Clouston [Orkney husband of Cameron's daughter Elizabeth] is going down to settle on his farm at Cobourg. . . . My daughter Margaret lives with her Aunt at Toronto . . . my two youngest boys are now at College—and coming on well, the eldest of the two is now nearly qualified for any of the learned Professions. . . . My son Ronald is on a good Farm—is quite up to the practicable part and is a hard working man—he had the good fortune to marry a lovely Lassie . . . a native of England—the daughter of a very respectable farmer—Clouston will be within a short distance of Ronalds (Glazebrook 1938: 435–37).

Shortly thereafter, Cameron himself and his wife settled in the nearby village of Grafton.

A broad tendency of senior officers with native families to follow their children to Canada to look for favourable retirement prospects was remarked by John Tod in a letter of 21 March 1844. Canada was growing; the fur trade was not, and by some estimates it was even waning. "Old Factors" were retiring, "guided, no doubt, by the same instinct that teaches rats to leave a falling house—Canada-ward, seems to be their favorite roosting place" (Ermatinger Papers, vol. 2, ser. 2, Tod to Edward Ermatinger). The Cobourg area of southern Ontario became the home of several families—the Camerons, Cloustons, and others of both old companies. In 1840, Hudson's Bay Chief Factor Jacob Corrigal retired to Cobourg. His will of 1844 named as one executor a former North West Company trader, Robert Henry, and a Hudson's Bay son-in-law, William Nourse, who was to retire to Cobourg in 1851 (HBCA, A. 36/5, ff. 78-79; Williams 1975: 224). Nourse's will in turn mentioned the names of George Gladman, Jr., and Thomas Gladman, of the neighbouring towns of Port Hope and Lindsay respectively. After some consultation with Edward Ermatinger and others, the Gladman families, all descendants of Hudson's Bay Company officer George Gladman (d. 1820), had taken up residence in that area.

Another cluster of families settled in Brockville, an eastern Ontario town with easy access to other former traders who gravitated toward Montreal. Former North Westers James Hargrave and George Barnston retired to Brockville and Montreal in 1859 and 1863 respectively, and Hudson's Bay factors Robert Miles and the native-born William Sinclair II retired to Brockville in 1861 and 1862, all bringing their families from the Northwest (Hargrave's, however, being white). Various letters, particularly those of George Barnston to James Hargrave and Edward Ermatinger, suggest the kinds of lives that these officers were building. Before Barnston's retirement, some of his family had preceded him to Canada. In 1846, two sons were at Lachine, "now placed with a Mr Simpson the presbyterian minister." In 1848, another son was at school in Montreal while a daughter was receiving "a plain education" in Lachine (Hargrave Papers, Barnston to James Hargrave, 12 April 1846 and 7 April 1848). In 1858, Barnston expressed hope to Ermatinger in St. Thomas that the latter might help to find "a situation . . . for my son Aleck . . . whom I wish to place in some Banking concern. He has distinguished himself sufficiently in the McGill College to shew his abilities. but the delay will probably be too great before he can get into Business as an Engineer or Surveyor, and my circumstances do not admit of my maintaining him longer. I am therefore desirous of having him placed somewhere where he may support himself" (Ermatinger Papers, Barnston to Ermatinger, 6 October 1858).

A later letter to Ermatinger, dated 11 September 1872, gives an impression of the diversifying lives and careers of the large Barnston family (originally eleven children) and of certain other company offspring in Canada and elsewhere, and of the continuing responsibilities of a company father:

> I find that the cares and anxieties of life have not decreased with my exit from the Country, and my retirement from the Business of the Fur Trade My numerous family (the Youngest now Sixteen) has occasioned me much thought and exertion to bring up to Years of Maturity, when each should be able to play his own or her own part on the Stage of Life. . . . [Dunlop and our eldest daughter] have a family of four daughters and a son, some of whom will come home for education next Year.

Dunlop was Clerk ten Years in the fur Trade. . . . He is now . . . thriving in Colombo, Ceylon, as a Commission Merchant. . . . Helen has been ten months married to a . . . manager of the London and Lancashire Life Assurance Co. in Canada. . . . Maggie the eldest unmarried will . . . be Bridesmaid to Hannah Miles the Youngest Girl of our old and lamented Deceased Friend [Chief Factor Robert Miles]. . . . She will be back . . . to act the same agreeable part for [retired Chief Factor John] Swanstons eldest Daughter (ibid.).

Barnston added that John, his eldest living son, was practising law in British Columbia; Peter (Ermatinger's "old acquaintance") was bookkeeper in the Bank of Montreal in Belleville, Ontario; Duncan was "Custom House Clerk and collector &c" for a firm of dry goods merchants and importers in Montreal; and Willie "will soon be at some such work also, as soon as I can find a place for him." An older son, James, had earned his M.D. in Edinburgh and a professorship of botany at McGill University in Montreal, before his death, aged twenty-six, in 1858 (Brown and Van Kirk in press).

The Barnston letters and other materials provide some detail on the variety of non-company careers into which fur trade offspring were finding their way in Canada and elsewhere and some view of the British-Canadian social life into which company families were eventually absorbed. The retiring officers' attitudes and concerns generally mirrored those of the society to which they and their families were now joined. One central feature of this society was its strong distinction between "gentlemen" and non-gentlemen, corresponding to the distinction between company officers (or gentlemen) and servants that became increasingly important within the fur trade after 1821. Much of traders' private correspondence in these decades showed active worry over whether their sons would maintain or attain gentlemanly status or sink to the level of labourer or (in fur trade terms) "a common engagé." Gentlemen were of course educated and literate. They might have a variety of occupations—teacher, banker, clerk, government official, businessman, landowning farmer—but in any case they were expected to be able to support themselves and their families comfortably and respectably. Within the fur trade or in other firms, only those of clerkly status and above were gentlemen, as Alexander Isbister well realized when consigned to the company rank of postmaster in 1838. Interestingly, references to the racial origin of company children did not usually occur in discussions of their social standing in Canada or Britain; such references seemed more common in the fur trade country itself—in the writings of George Simpson, in the phrenological determinism of John Tod, and in the anxious letters of Archibald McDonald—than elsewhere. Nor were questions of legitimacy raised in assessing gentlemanly standing, although they might have been expected, given the backgrounds of many fur trade marriages. While it came most easily to those of good family and connections and to those who had been well placed, gentlemen's status depended much on individual achievement and conduct; failure in these realms could remove the best connected of youths from gentlemanly standing.

At the same time, access to such standing depended much upon opportunities for advancement, which might be restricted or expanded by others' perceptions and knowledge (or ignorance) of one's fur trade familial background. A potential patron, especially if he was not directly connected with the company, might be relatively free of tendencies to prejudge a youth on the basis of criteria other than his abilities, being unacquainted with details of his family history. The remoteness of many fur trade families from the children being placed left open more occupational and status options than these children might have had within the orbit of the company.

A converse example illustrates this point. Thomas Taylor, native-born son of a Hudson's Bay Company sloopmaster, served for ten years as Governor Simpson's body servant, beginning in the early 1820s. In 1832, Simpson noted that he had also become "one of the most effective Postmasters in the Country." Although postmasters typically had no prospects of advancement, Taylor's abilities and his personal connection with Simpson enabled him to attain a clerkship and become "Mr. Taylor" in 1843 (Williams 1975: 233). Simpson continued to take an interest in him and his family while Taylor was stationed at Buckingham on the lower Ottawa River, not far from the governor's offices at Lachine. There were signs, however, that Simpson's view of Taylor as his former body servant caused him to remain insensitive to Taylor's own rising aspirations for his children. Taylor's letter of 17 September 1850 to his father-in-law, Chief Factor James Keith, then retired to Scotland, vividly described his unhappiness about having placed a son under Simpson's care:

> George [aged twelve] is with Sir George at Lachine—it was my earnest wish to put him to some place for benefit of Education but my means were not sufficient. . . . I reluctantly complied with Sir George's request to let him have him as his servant Boy. . . . I didn't let the poor Boy go without Sir George promising he would give him some education, I was not at all pleased with the Boys usage last summer—while Sir George was off to the Interior . . . not having Sir George or Lady Simpson to attend to, instead of being put to attend school he made a slave of . . . to every body in the House at Lachine, and loosing his best time for schooling (Keith Papers, C.4).

Simpson's well-intentioned offer of a servant's post to George was no doubt influenced by his long familiarity with George's father in a master-servant relationship, but it also indicated his narrow perceptions of the children's potentialities. (James Keith had expressed some awareness of this danger in a letter of 17 April 1831 to Taylor [ibid., B.4]). In this instance, it is also possible that Simpson's earlier identification of Taylor as a "halfbreed" may have affected his view of the family's standing, as would have evidently been true in the fur trade country itself. In any case, Taylor lacked the advantages that sometimes accrued to company officers placing their children at a distance among people who knew little of their familial background or occupational history.

CONCLUSIONS

The placing of children outside the family was by no means confined to fur traders in northwestern Canada, but was apparently a customary practice all across the British Empire in the nineteenth century and probably before. Sending children, both white and of mixed descent, homeward for schooling, and the resulting long separations between parents and children are themes that emerge sharply elsewhere, for example, in Rudyard Kipling's poignant autobiographical story, "Baa Baa, Black Sheep," concerning children sent home from India.

There are also striking parallels with older British and British-American patterns of parents sending children into other homes as boarders, servants, and apprentices. The fur traders may have taken up the custom of placing the more readily because of familiarity with similar practices that served to provide children with a suitable "calling" in other British and American contexts (Morgan 1966: 76–78). Besides finding a child a place in the work world, these separations in general may have served, and were perhaps even to some extent intended, to remove children from the dangers of parental over-indulgence and sexual and other rivalries within crowded large families (Illick 1975: 330, 344), thus aiding their independent psychological and personality development. Perhaps some such motives also underlay some traders' placings of their children, although the sources make clear that educational, economic, and status considerations were certainly dominant.

In comparative perspective, similar socio-economic considerations have evidently motivated and perpetuated somewhat similar child-placing practices elsewhere. The common West African practice of the "purposive fostering" of children serves, among other things, to broaden their education and to strengthen ties with kin who are better off (Goody 1973: 3). (Both these considerations influenced some nineteenth-century fur traders, particularly the kin-oriented North Westers.) In the past, West African fostering was reflective of mutual kin links and obligations, but the more recent trend has been to place children with "strangers who can provide either training in modern skills, or a chance to gain familiarity with urban, western ways," particularly in southern Ghana. Many West Africans residing in London maintain this practice there, placing children with English families for care, language training, and education (ibid., 14, 21, 24–25). These patterns do not involve the creation or substitution of new sets of primary ties for those of parent to child, and Goody's statement on West Africans would apply as well to the families of the fur trade: "The delay of fostering . . . until the child 'has sense' at six or seven is consistent with this pattern of augmenting existing ties rather than creating a new set of primary bonds" (ibid., 49). Fur trade fathers did not surrender parenthood in the placing process, but instead reinforced their secondary ties to carry out their parental duties more effectively. In so doing, they followed patterns that have interesting parallels in other historical and comparative contexts.

Those company children who were not placed for long periods outside the fur trade country faced rather different prospects and conditions of life. Children placed abroad created individual problems for parents and other parties involved, but those who remained in the fur trade country from the 1820s to the 1860s confronted local social and economic conditions that could not readily be escaped.

9

Fur Trade Sons and Daughters
in a New Company Context

Certain socio-economic and political changes beginning in the 1820s had important effects upon and implications for company families in the fur trade country from the time of the merger until the end of the company rule and the annexation of the Northwest by Canada. One was the reorganization of the new company both as a monopoly and as a *de facto* colonial government engaging in more administrative activities with more authority than either of the old companies had had. Further, Red River itself became at least an outpost of "civilization" with its schools, churches, and other appurtenances. Communications with Canada and Britain improved, and British and American culture also began to penetrate the fur trade country from the west as settlers and missionaries entered the Oregon Territory and British Columbia (Fisher 1977).

Other developments, particularly the continuing steep growth of the mixed-descent population and company retrenchments, also had important effects. The pruning of surplus personnel in the 1820s was predictable; "The number of servants employed by the contending parties was triple the number required in quiet . . . times, and, more especially, when the business came to be managed by one firm" (Donald Gunn, quoted in Innis 1970: 288). But even after the pace of post-merger cuts and early retirements slowed, other problems confronted those dependent on the fur trade—shortages of fur-bearing animals in once rich areas, increased incursions of American and other independent trappers and traders as transport routes improved, and, finally, changes in fashion and market demand, notably the rising preference for silk hats after 1839.

COMPANY CONTEXTS, OLD AND NEW

Before the merger, neither company tried to govern the Northwest in more than a very limited way. Each firm had begun with the deliberate plans of a few men interested in commercial gain. Although the Hudson's Bay Company was a royally sanctioned colonialist enterprise, it had soon divorced itself from colonial goals to concentrate on narrower economic objectives, and it was repeatedly censured by parliamentary and other parties for pursuing its private aims under the cloak of its charter, without fostering broader British colonial and commercial advancement. The North West Company, being a coalition of private business partnerships, was even less interested in governmental administration. The specialized aims of both companies set them apart from their social surroundings in their homelands and in the Canadian Northwest. Unlike their home communities or the Indian groups whose furs they sought, they were formal organizations, narrow in scope rather than all-encompassing. They were of course built upon and their personnel carried with them broader implicit cultural models and values drawn from their home societies, but their intent was only to pursue certain restricted company interests.

This specialization meant that for many decades other social domains in which these companies were willy-nilly to become involved were dealt with either not at all or in a distant and not very comprehending manner. The social, sexual, and familial desires of their men and the interests and expectations of Indian groups in these domains were scarcely given formal attention by the North West Company proprietors but rather were left to direct themselves in whatever way they might. The Hudson's Bay Company attempted to impose regulations to resolve these matters wherever they seemed to threaten company aims, but the London directors were too remote and too busy with other concerns to take up the detailed study of social conditions in Hudson Bay. Its men therefore devised their own informal responses, based on immediate situations, on Indian pressures, and on British cultural notions of household, hierarchy, and domesticity. The relative lack of direct rule in these domains permitted the institutionalization of marriage "according to the custom of the country" and of related customs and practices adapted to local circumstances.

The net result was that in the last two decades of their separate existence, the two organizations were presented with *faits accomplis* with which neither could effectively cope. The progeny of the employees of both companies were increasingly numerous and could no longer be assimilated into the scattered Indian population, absorbed within company employ, or simply shipped *en masse* to Britain or Canada. By the early 1800s, the Hudson's Bay Company was acknowledging the situation and turning toward means of educating, employing, and settling its fur trade families—hence its efforts toward schools and its support of Red River Colony. The North West Company had begun to react more slowly, first trying to curb its traders' alliances with Indians, then defending, along with its own rights, the rights of their offspring to congregate, settle, and hunt buffalo in the Red River area. But neither company dealt with these matters in a more than reactive way.

This situation changed with the merger and the growth of Red River; the whole context in which company families lived was much modified. Conscious organization now extended into many areas of domestic life as well as commercial activity. The new monopoly was not just a trading concern; it also took over the colonial administration of Red River. By extension, and in the absence of any other British or Canadian governing agent, its administrative power and duties spread to encompass the whole of the Northwest. As a colonial agent, the company in turn became responsible to the British government and was also caught up, sometimes unhappily and unwillingly, in contemporary British movements to spread the blessings of civilization and Christianity. As Andrew Colvile reminded George Simpson in 1824, after the governor had complained about missionary interference in the fur trade country, "it wd be extremely impolitic in the present temper & disposition of the public in this country to show any unwillingness to assist in such an object" (Merk 1968: 205).

This uniting of British-based economic, political, and colonial interests in one powerful organization placed the people of the Northwest in an increasingly dependent position. And it meant that brokers and middlemen assumed roles of increased importance as they generally do in interactions between strongly dominant political structures and those that they surround or encapsulate (Bailey 1969: 168–75). The emerging and diverse political roles of mixed-bloods such as Cuthbert Grant, Jr., in Red River and Alexander Isbister in London exemplify some of the complex and often adversary relations that developed after 1821 between the new company and the local population.

Changes in the internal social order of the fur trade and in the roles of the Hudson's Bay Company were also visible. Red River and the development of its religious and educational facilities became central matters of concern. The company's involvement in Red River had already been deepened by two developments just before the merger. When Lord Selkirk died in 1820 he left as executors two of his brothers-in-law, Andrew Colvile and John Halkett, who were both important members of the London committee. In the same year two other committee members, men of strong evangelical sympathies, encouraged a decision by the Church Missionary Society to provide "large sums" to make the "North West America Mission" one of their new fields of mission work. With this support, the company hired Anglican John West to go to Red River "to afford religious instruction and consolation" to the natives and settlers of Red River and to company servants, active and retired. Northwestern Canada, like the territories of the British East India Company in the same period, was to be newly opened to Christian endeavours, and company directors and officers faced new decisions on how to support, direct, and sometimes control them (Thompson 1970).

Minutes of a council held at York Factory on 20 August 1822 also noted that new administrative structures were to be set up in Red River. Besides having the guidance of clergy and of a governor of Assiniboia, commissioned as chief administrator, the inhabitants were now to be "under a regular Police and Government, by the Establishment of Magistrates under the act passed the last Session of Parliament" (PAC, Andrew Bulger Papers, vol. 2: 251). The company was also involved in allotting lands to new settlers, in promoting the establishment of a "School of Industry" and of a boarding school to educate "Female children natives of the Indian country," and in other tasks (Fleming 1940: 95). By this time John West was already occupied with religious instruction and conducting church rites. Between the summers of 1820 and 1823, when another clergyman replaced him, West baptized 297 persons, most being the country wives and children of active and retired traders, and performed (or reconfirmed by Christian rite) 65 marriages (Red River registers).

Along with all this new activity, the company, oriented toward economy, efficiency, and good order under the rule of George Simpson, now involved itself more directly in the personal conduct of its employees, both active and retiring. Simpson and the London committee expressed concern about the high costs of the large numbers of employees and the sizes of their families and worried about possible disorder. Trimming personnel rolls by removing surplus or ill-qualified men from service involved making sure that they and their dependents (along with any earlier traders' unemployed descendants around the posts) either left the country or were placed where they could provide their own means of subsistence under organized leadership without interfering with trade or challenging company authority. Between 1822 and 1824 the company dismissed numerous men and laid down several new policies. At York Factory on 20 August 1822, George Simpson and his officers agreed with the London committee that it was now a "Matter of serious importance" to decide upon,

the most proper Measures to be adopted with regard to the men who have large families and who must be discharged, and with the numerous half breed children whose parents have died or deserted them. These people form a burden which cannot be got rid of without expence, and if allowed to remain in their present condition, they will become dangerous to the Peace of the Country and Safety of the Trading Posts.

It will therefore be both prudent and oeconomical to incur some expense in placing these people where they may maintain themselves and be civilized and instructed in Religion [i.e., Red River] . . . it would be impolitic and inexpedient to encourage or allow them to Collect together in different parts of the Country where they could not be under any proper superintendance (Bulger Papers, vol. 2: 249–51).

In 1824 the Council of the Northern Department laid down particular rules governing retiring servants and families: all men leaving children in the country were to "make such provision for the same as circumstances call for and their means permit," and all those "desirous of withdrawing their children from the country" were to be granted "every facility for that purpose." Simpson and the council also formulated rules to keep track of and control expenditures on families residing at the posts. All traders in charge of posts were instructed to "keep accurate and distinct accounts of the issue and expenses of Provisions attending the Families of Officers, and . . . those of the Engagees." And contractual terms to govern all new marital alliances in the country were put in effect; no officer or servant was to "take a woman without binding himself down to such reasonable provision for the maintenance of the woman and children as on a fair and equitable principle may be considered necessary not only during their residence in the country but after their departure hence" (Fleming 1940: 95).

While promulgating personnel measures favouring economy and efficiency, the council also brought the company with new vigour into the realm of domestic relations by instructing that education and religion be integrated into post family life. There were good intentions in this move, but it was also based on a consciousness that the fur trade country was now less isolated and more observed and that its posts were increasingly in reach of visiting clergy and other Britishers. Divine service was to be read on Sundays at all posts whenever possible, "for the more effectual civilization and moral improvement of the families attached to the different establishments." In addition, "in course of the week all irregularity, vicious or indolent habits, particularly among the women & children" were to be "checked and discountenanced." Officers were to "endeavour to provide such regular employment for the children as is best suited to their age & Capacities," encouraging those who excelled "so as to excite and keep alive a spirit of activity emulation and juvenile rivalry." Mothers and children were always to be addressed in and to use "the vernacular dialect (whether English or French) of the Father" to pave the way for their education; and traders were in their leisure time to teach their children at least the alphabet and catechism (ibid., 60).

These requirements remained in effect among the "Standing Rules and Regulations" with little change for at least the next two decades. One addition, a rule appearing in 1841, reflected both the continuing concern that families not accumulate at the posts and also the desire that native-born sons still living with their parents be early separated from them for company work, perhaps to promote their attachment to the company so that they would not be drawn into opposition trading or otherwise become troublesome:

> Much inconvenience having arisen to the service from Lads remaining with their parents until arrived at an advanced period of Life . . . no Lad be permitted to remain with his family when exceeding the age of 15, but that he be then received into the Service as an Apprentice Labourer or Tradesman; And if the parent does not consent to this arrangement, that he be removed from the service (PAC, Minutes of a Temporary Council, 25 May 1841, Michipicoten, Southern Department, p. 12).

Such rules no doubt stimulated traders' efforts to place their children outside the fur trade country if possible, where options and opportunities would be more numerous. They were also manifestations of the general socio-economic order in which fur trade families were now enmeshed and the pressures and influences to which they were subject, an order that many company parents and offspring found uncomfortably confining.

PARENTAGE, RACE AND RANK: "HALFBREEDS" IN RED RIVER AND THE COMPANY

The decades from the 1820s to mid-century were perhaps the most difficult of any period for company offspring. Before the merger, many traders' sons and daughters had found fairly secure positions. In the Hudson's Bay Company in particular, the relatively strong vertical social integration of the large residential posts frequently included native-born offspring who remained individually identified by their parentage rather than by race. The tendency to increase manpower and the move to extend the apprenticeship system at the main posts rather than to continue importing young British hands opened training and employment opportunities to many company sons. Even if their educational deficiencies meant that many of them did not have a great chance of advancement, several native-born sons from both companies had attained clerkships by the time of the merger, and there was no evidence at that point of any discrimination against them as a racial group. Although some North Westers' sons had begun to see political potentialities in asserting a distinctive racial identity at Red River in 1815, this weapon had not yet been turned against them.

Company daughters had similarly been individually assimilated into the fur trade social order as the country wives of traders or their sons. Unthreatened by the presence of white women or of clergy to challenge the legitimacy of "the custom of the country," many had become wives by all the criteria that Canadian and British courts could later apply in evaluating their status—*nomen, tractatus, et fama*—name, enduring cohabitation, and repute. They also assumed productive subsistence and economic roles for their families and for the posts. In sum, although subject in some cases to abuse and exploitation, both daughters and sons commonly benefited from the individual attentions of fathers, fathers-in-law, and fathers' colleagues, from supportive familial bonds centred within the fur trade country, and from the resulting nepotism that Simpson later deplored.

The 1820s and 1830s, in contrast, were conspicuous for the rise of racial categorization and discrimination and for the economic and sexual marginality of native-born sons and daughters to the new order. They were also years in which the social stratification characteristic of the North West Company (figure 2) and incipient in Hudson Bay before the merger appears to have been generalized to the new company as a whole.

FUR TRADE SONS IN THE NEW COMPANY

The sharpest employee distinction in the new company was between gentlemen and servants. Whereas eighteenth-century Hudson's Bay apprentices and labourers could aspire to high positions, it now became almost unheard of for any "servant," white or native-born, to become a "gentleman." Various regulations enforced social separateness; in 1824, "In order to draw a line of distinction," it was ordered that all commissioned officers and clerks mess separately from lower-ranked servants (Merk 1968: 238). It was knowing the strength of these distinctions that made Chief Factor John McLoughlin angry when his son offered to enter the company as a "common engagé" in 1835–36 and caused Archibald McDonald's great efforts to have his son Ranald appointed to the company by "their Honors" in London, thus "being placed on the footing of *apprentice clerk,* instead of apprentice, as is the case with all those received into the service from the country" (Lewis and Murakami 1923: 36). The same knowledge led James Hargrave to advise a British acquaintance, Mrs. Lane, strongly against having her son enter the firm as "a common labourer" when he might, if patient enough to let his name stand awhile on a waiting list, attain a clerkship. As a labourer, he would be "descending to the same rank as the most uneducated of our people . . . in short lose caste and descend from the respectable rank in which he has been brought up to a level with the lowest of the peasantry" (Hargrave Papers, 22 May 1840).

More rigid stratification was soon matched by equally rigid racial distinctions applied to "halfbreeds" in company service. These differentiations appear strongly related to changing economic pressures. In a suddenly expanded company striving for recovery after costly rivalries, economy demanded, for example, that wage outlays be reduced. Besides forced retirements, one means of cutting wage costs was to draw on the lowest ranked (and lowest paid) employees who could possibly qualify to perform middle-level fur trade tasks. The solution in this case was to create the new category and rank of postmaster. The words of Governor Simpson himself in 1832 best define the content of this "Class . . . between Interpreters and Clerks":

> we have removed to this Class several persons from the List of Clerks who were not qualified to perform the duties of the Situations they nominally filled. and other vacancies have been filled up by Young Men the half breed Sons or Relations of Gentlemen in the Country who could not obtain admission to the Service as apprentice Clerks. Those who enter the Service in this Class . . . have no prospect of further advancement, nor is it intended that they shall be removed from this Class except in vary particular cases of good conduct coupled with Valuable Services (Williams 1975: 232).

Most postmasters received an annual wage of forty to sixty pounds, about half to two-thirds of a clerk's salary.

The company also began to devise general criteria by which to assess and predict the utility and future performance of employees already on company books as well as of future applicants. Simpson had early begun to form private opinions regarding men of mixed descent; in a letter of 1822 he had observed that "even the half Breeds of the Country who have been educated in Canada are blackguards of the very worst description, they not only pick up the vices of the Whites upon which they improve but retain those of the Indian" (Merk 1968: 181). And by 1827 it was clear that one major criterion used in judging employees was race. Company lists of clerks and postmasters from 1823 to 1832 (HBCA, A. 34/1) included numerous mixed-bloods of good, bad, and indifferent qualifications. By 1827 to 1830, their qualities and deficiencies were typically described in the context of their racial origins; and Simpson's characterizations of 1832 show clearly that he was now viewing the performance of these clerks and postmasters in terms of a set of prejudices that had taken form in his first decade of government. "Halfbreed" failures were now judged as predictable, while successes occasioned surprise. And certain unflattering character traits began regularly to be attributed to these people or were expected to emerge if not already visible—conceit, unsteadiness, lying, laziness, and lack of propriety. The rise of these stereotypes certainly contributed to the economic and social marginality of native-born company sons. As a sorting device, the stereotypes eased problems of screening new applicants for clerkships, of whom there were usually far too many from the 1820s to the 1840s, and native-born sons were rejected out of hand, unless they were extremely well educated and Briticized, with powerful advocates within the company.

To complement these negative stereotypes, there emerged positive ones by which to identify successful applicants. Like older North Westers, the successful candidate was one whose relatives, patrons, or friends (themselves of good repute with Simpson or his associates) were willing to recommend him. By such means did Simpson himself secure the entries of his cousins, Thomas, Aemilius, and Alexander, into the company. Similarly James Hargrave advocated the candidacy of the orphan son of an old friend and "Benefactor of my early days," informing Simpson of his "good conduct and carefully superintended education" in Scotland (Hargrave Papers, 1 March 1838). And another young apprentice clerk, R.M. Ballantyne (who proved more successful as a novelist), arrived in company service in 1841 with a letter from Lady Simpson describing him as her cousin, "a very clever boy . . . straight from the Stockbridge Academy" (MacLeod 1947: 99).

These two sets of stereotypes had considerable social implications. Racial or colour bars never became as codified as in, for example, the Caribbean slave or former slave societies. But racism certainly became to some extent a pretext for economic exploitation. As in nineteenth-century Cuba, a connection could "be detected between changing economic needs and intensity of discrimination" (Martinez-Alier 1974: 6). In the fur trade, the halfbreed label became a means of classifying the population hierarchically and occupationally. A few "halfbreeds," generally of North West origin, could sue successfully for higher pay by threatening to join rival traders in certain areas where they had influence among the Indians. But most had limited markets for their services and could be dealt with accordingly. Alexander W. McKay threatened desertion in 1832 but without effect; he "will probably be allowed to make the discovery that he cannot mend his fortunes by a change of Masters." Likewise, George Gladman had "brought his Services to an excellent Market and . . . is fully paid for them" (Williams 1975: 219, 209).

These kinds of judgments soon stirred opposition, both from the "halfbreeds" whose prospects they darkened and from others who saw them as unjust. The growth of Red River and the development of its educational institutions (even if slow and beset by many problems) offered many fathers the hope of educating their children at lower cost and with less permanent separations than occurred if the children were sent to Britain or Canada—an opportunity particularly appreciated by those traders (notably Hudson's Bay officers) who lacked strong home ties and were themselves retiring or contemplating retirement to Red River. And by the 1840s, it could provide the basic liberal and practical education that clerks would require to enter the company. It was thus a sore point with company fathers (and sons) that native-born offspring so trained could enter the company only with difficulty and at low rank. Sons trained in Red River had few contacts in the outside world and were usually obliged to find livelihoods and employment within the company domains. It was a serious enough problem that sons educated in Britain or Canada should have difficulty rising in the company, but numbers of these youths could at least consider other options. Those schooled in Red River alone, however, moved in a much more confined social field. In the early 1840s, old North Wester Charles McKenzie complained bitterly about the company's treatment of his son and schoolmates who had completed courses of study at the Red River seminary:

> It appears the present Concern has stamped the *Cain mark* upon all born in this country; neither education nor abilities serve them. . . . The Honorable Company are unwilling to take Natives, even as apprentice clerks, and the favored few they do take can never aspire to a higher status. . . . There are now 60 or 70 boys in the Red River seminary, a dozen of whom are ready yearly to enter the service in the same capacity—if they can. . . . I do not see the use of so much Greek and Latin for these postmasters, since neither artificial nor natural requirements are of any avail (Masson 1960, I: 318–19).

A later officer, Chief Trader James Anderson, complained directly to Simpson about the matter in a letter of the early 1850s:

> It has occurred to me that there is something very unfair—and certainly impolitic—in the way the young gentlemen educated at the RR School have been treated, and they must be something more than human, if this treatment do not rankle in their minds—In general their education is fully equal to that of the ap: Cl: from Europe, and they perform precisely similar duties, but have only the rank, pay, and allowances of ap: Post Masters . . . half that of an ap: Clerk. . . . The whole of Mr McCallums [Red River] eleves in this quarter are able and excellent officers (PAC, Anderson Papers, vol. 1, file 1: 58–59).

Persistent in criticizing the injustice, he returned again to the matter in subsequent letters. Finally, in 1858, he urged that the rank of apprentice postmaster be abolished and that "banishing all Consideration of origin that education, ability, and *character* should be the qualifications required for granting apprenticed clerkships" (ibid., file 5: 276–77). It may be recalled that it was Anderson who had criticized the over-rapid advancement of those officers fortunate enough to be in Simpson's circle, observing in 1846 that "Interest" seemed to be "the Main Channel of Promotion." Anderson had perceptively deduced the sets of stereotypes, negative and positive, by which personnel were being judged.

Although Simpson and his associates possessed much power and influence and conducted business for many years on the basis of the personnel policies that they had begun to use by the end of the 1820s, they stood little chance, in the longer run, of gaining support for these policies from their many colleagues with native families. Although "halfbreed" officers and applicants were effectively kept from high-ranked positions until the late 1840s or early 1850s, their numbers had been growing, several had shown themselves active and useful, and pressures to reward their services began to prove successful. Simpson himself modified his opinions of them in some instances. One who reached high rank was William Sinclair II. Much criticized by Simpson in 1832 (Williams 1975: 227), Sinclair had written in discouraged tones to his old colleague Edward Ermatinger on 1 August 1835 that he was "getting heartily tired of the Concern. The Country that gave me Birth is against my promotion and more so this Year than Ever in Consequence of the Half Breeds of Red River and my Brother at the head of them having given some trouble to the *Great Men*" (Ermatinger Papers, ser. 2, vol. 1). In 1844, however, his service earned him a chief tradership, and in 1850 he was made a chief factor.

The Gladman brothers, George and Joseph, neither of whom found much favour with Simpson in 1832, also later reached commissioned rank. George became a chief trader in 1836 and might have risen higher had he not retired from the service from 1846 to 1849 and again in 1853. Joseph became a chief trader in 1847, the year after James Anderson had strongly complained in a private letter that prejudice and "Interest" had held him back, and a chief factor in 1864 (Williams 1975: 208–209n). Native-born sons of the Christie, Hardisty, and other families also began to rise toward high ranks in this period and later. By the 1850s, then, the barriers against native-born officers were not as insuperable as before. But closer examination also suggests that a Red River educational background combined with part-Indian ancestry still proved a severe handicap; so far as known, these officers had all had at least some of their education in the "civilized world." Racial origin alone was perhaps receding in importance, leaving bias to be focused more narrowly, as James Anderson observed, against those native-born sons who were educated in the settlement.

This persisting bias, however, was not only unjust, but doubtless as "impolitic" as Anderson thought it to be, particularly in the 1850s. In the

1820s and 1830s Red River had still been a small, dependent, company-run colony. Although harbouring numbers of individuals with little love for the company, it was in no position to challenge company rules and policies. William Sinclair II had observed to Edward Ermatinger in June 1832 that Red River was "one of the last places I would choose for a residence . . . people there who call themselves freemen are just as much under subordination as any of those who are under [company] Contract" (Ermatinger Papers, ser. 2, vol. 1). But by the 1850s, population growth, the advocacy of Alexander Isbister and others in London, and other developments had brought new attention and even a measure of autonomy and freer trade to the colony.

A majority in the colony at this time was of mixed Indian-white descent. Although still divided between the largely French and Canadian métis of old North West Company background and the "English halfbreeds" of Hudson's Bay origin who tended to reside in distinct parts of the colony, they could unite effectively in support of certain causes, as for example in the 1849 trial of Guillaume Sayer for illicit trafficking in furs with the Indians. Sayer was found guilty of the charges, but so large and unruly a crowd gathered to observe the trial that the authorities did not attempt to hold and punish him. Upon his leaving the court, one of its own jurymen shouted, "Le commerce est libre!"—a cry taken up by the crowd and believed by many thereafter (Ross 1972: 376). Company claims of trade monopoly subsequently became less credible and still less easy to enforce.

The developments of the 1860s demonstrate that Red River moved a long way toward becoming a separate, non-company, and self-asserting community in the years between 1849 and 1869. In 1861 a native-born writer noted,

> the half castes or mixed race, not only far outnumber all the other races in the colony put together, but engross nearly all the more important and intellectual offices—furnishing . . . the sheriff, medical officer, the postmaster, all the teachers but one, a fair proportion of the magistrates and one of the electors and proprietors of the only newspaper in the Hudson's Bay territories (McNaught 1969: 142).

Clearly numbers of native-born sons who had not found company outlets for their ambitions were beginning to find them in Red River. And in 1868-69, some found a new cause. Once relieved of company rule, Red River residents came under similarly arbitrary and unresponsive control from Canada. They reacted promptly, first blocking the entry of a new governor sent to rule them without their consultation or consent and later resorting to unsuccessful but dramatic military actions under the leadership of Louis Riel: "We *may* be a small community, and a Half-breed community at that—but we are men, free and spirited men, and we will not allow even the Dominion of Canada to trample on our rights" (ibid., 143). Many of them later contributed to the expansion of Red River as it grew from a company-ruled colony to the substantial city of Winnipeg. For the Hudson's Bay Company, it became impractical to confine qualified native-born members of its families to its lower ranks arbitrarily.

DAUGHTERS IN THE NEW COMPANY

The changing situations of native-born company daughters from the 1820s to 1860s show interesting parallels with those of fur trade sons. In the first half of the period, there appeared a ready tendency in some newly dominant circles to prejudge native-born women in much the same way as their brothers, while later developments suggest a regained social standing and assimilation.

In the 1820s and 1830s, the social standing of officers' country wives and daughters was at the least problematic. Their numbers were far greater than the incoming white women and wives, and the vast majority of the commissioned officers and clerks of both companies had already taken such mates. And although some country wives, being the daughters of Indians or of tradesmen or voyageurs, had married upward by European as well as fur trade definitions, many were the daughters of older officers. Identified, like their brothers, by their parentage rather than racial grouping, they were accepted by many traders as the equals of their officer husbands, known as the highest ranked lady or "Bourgeoise" of the posts or districts over which their husbands presided and dignified by the title of "Mrs." By 1821, the fur trade social world encompassed numerous native wives and daughters of high standing, established as firmly as they could be in the still rather informal institutional settings of their respective companies.

The first real threats to these women's rank and position came from the protestant and Roman Catholic clergy who entered the Red River area in 1818–20. In tracing and reconstructing the family histories and names of company officers and country wives in the years before the merger, it comes as a slight (but illuminating) shock to discover in the early mission records that the clergy consigned these women to virtual anonymity unless or until married according to Christian rite. In the baptismal registers of John West and his successors, a few country wives of traders (mothers of baptized children) were listed as "Agatha, his reputed wife" or "Betsey, his reputed wife." But many other parents were listed under the name of the father and the added phrase "and a halfbreed woman" or "and an Indian woman," even when they were still both living and together, the wife's identity well known, and her standing long acknowledged. Interestingly, mixed-blood males whose children were baptized in these years were individually named and escaped the label of "halfbreed" (or the more rarely used term, "half-caste"). But unchristianized wives of officers were typically classed according to broad racial category, losing both identity and rank. Neither John West nor the Roman Catholics were prepared to accept customary marriages as valid; West declared that he would enforce Christian marriage "upon all, who are living with and have children by half-caste, or Indian women" (Thompson 1970: 49). Possessing little patience or persuasiveness, he managed to alienate many of his would-be parishioners by his strict evangelical Christianity and rigid stands, much as Anglican Herbert Beaver did at Fort Vancouver in the 1830s.

In categorizing native-born wives in this fashion, these incoming clergy were in general agreement with Simpson, his younger relatives, and those close colleagues who came under his influence. Both groups, though otherwise contrasting, tended to classify all native-born women as of a lower caste, whatever their rank and repute in the fur trade country. At the same time as judgments about race and character were preventing the advancement of mixed-blood men, criteria of race, religion, and morality relegated their sisters to lower ranks.

Race and colour were not the sole issues; they were aligned with other criteria to sharpen social distinctions. "Halfbreed" women were not only part-Indian and largely lacking in the education or civilized arts that respectable European ladies were assumed to possess; they were also the daughters and partners of unchristianized unions and had matured in circumstances in which their chastity seemed unprotected. In British society, all such women were certainly of the lower classes, or no more than mistresses or prostitutes, suited to serve the sexual desires of gentlemen but not to be considered as marital partners. Newcomers to the fur trade could make the same assumptions about mixed-blood women—and even some older traders used such grounds, one suspects, to avoid "entanglements" with women whose rank and virtue were suspect by British if not fur trade standards. Implicitly encouraged by clergymen's critical judgments and categorizations of native-born women, the Simpson cousins and several of their associates took advantage of some of these women, taking them as partners until their fortunes allowed them to claim sheltered and well-connected white wives from Britain or Canada.

These developments show some interesting parallels with nineteenth-century Cuba. Both Cuba and the Canadian Northwest after 1821 were characterized by a markedly stratified social order accompanied by a lack of consensus about its legitimacy and, hence, a constant bidding by the lower ranks for advancement (Martinez-Alier 1974: 128–29). In the fur trade country, perhaps even more than in Cuba, lack of consensus was pervasive; the 1820s to 1840s were years of sharp schisms and much confusion and variation regarding social values and ranking. Officers' native-born offspring, backed by parental support and by pre-1821 precedents, did not willingly accept the lower standing to which Simpson, the clergy, and certain others tended to consign them. Yet their ability to maintain their old social positions in the face of new challenges was at the same time weakened by defectors and waverers from the old order. Encouraged by Simpson's influence and example and by social pressures already inhering in their own familial backgrounds, certain former North Westers modified their behaviour and personal relationships after 1821, "betraying" in the eyes of some others the country wives with whom they had long resided (for example, the instances of William Connolly and John George McTavish). Like those Cuban whites who had extensive and well respected family connections and were expected to honour them, these traders uneasily recalled or decided that they should seek wives on whose rank and respectability no possible doubt could be cast. Conversely, Hudson's Bay men and others with few or no high-ranked relatives were less susceptible to such considerations—like the Cuban white who had "no known parents nor relatives whom he could tarnish" by marrying a *parda* (ibid., 20–21).

Problems of consensus extended still deeper than this, however, causing social divisions even within old North West circles and between North Westers and their kin, as in the instances of P.S. Ogden's and Samuel Black's estate disputes. The central problem was to define the rank and marital status of officers' native-born country wives. If they were universally of inferior social standing and not in fact married, as Simpsonian and missionary values and actions implied, then all their unions with company officers could be viewed simply as consensual unions of the type that Simpson enjoyed before marrying his English cousin in 1830. Given the pressures toward marrying within one's own status group, gentlemen's common understandings of the time about the social and sexual subservience of lower-class women in general, and a double standard that urged the good repute of a man of gentlemanly standing, officers could not be required to take their country wives in Christian marriage, if these women were simply ranked as lower-class paramours. If they did still choose to Christianize these alliances, thus defined, then they could be interpreted as doing so out of charity, gratitude, love, Christian sentiment, or perhaps a regard for a father-in-law's property and/or feelings, despite a supposed resultant decline in their own rank.

The matter was complicated by the fact that, whether or not officers viewed their country marriages as informal unions, there was also disagreement on the role and authority of the newly arrived clergy, unlike societies such as Cuba which possessed one highly institutionalized church. A Scottish Presbyterian or a Roman Catholic might reject the dictates of an Anglican minister (for example, John McLoughlin's rebuffs of Herbert Beaver), and free thinkers might reject all three sects.

An officer's rejection or acceptance of the Christian sacrament of marriage could accordingly mean several different things. Rejection might symbolize that he indeed viewed his fur trade alliance as consensual and transient and his partner as of low rank and was concerned to maintain his own rank and that of his kin (Simpson, McTavish, and ultimately, John Stuart). Or it might mean that he rejected the jurisdiction and authority of the particular clergy available, or of clergy in general. He might in fact assert the pre-existing *de facto* legitimacy of the union, using established fur trade or Indian custom or perhaps even the secular Scottish marriage laws (Van Kirk 1975: 252) as his authority and precedent, resenting and resisting any aspersions on his wife and affirming her equal standing.

Acceptance of the Christian marriage sacrament could also come at different points and for various reasons. An officer might accept it gladly because of strong Christian beliefs as soon as it became available to him (some officers accepted John West's ministrations as soon as he arrived in the country); or he might later be converted or rejoin his home sect upon retirement and reconfirm in Christian terms a marriage he had long viewed as binding, accepting the authority and advice of his clergy. Or he might decide to reinterpret a union that he had previously treated as consensual, for such motives as sentiment, charity, and gratitude.

The advent of clergy, the settling of Red River, and the start of Simpson's régime together provided occasions for differences of interpretation and attitude to be articulated and collide, as pressures developed toward a more highly formalized and regulated social order. The two companies had tended toward somewhat similar social patterns and solutions to problems of life in the fur trade country—toward the proliferation of fur trade families and customary marriages. But they had not come to share a fully unitary social order with consensus on values and behaviour by the time of the merger, despite areas of overlap and shared understandings. The arrival of new influences and pressures brought these differences to the surface as officers, whatever their personal backgrounds and predilections, were obliged to give them conscious consideration and make decisions about their marital loyalties. During this period of confusion and uncertainty, the position of native-born women was unclear and precarious. Nevertheless, as in the case of native-born sons, Simpson and his associates, even if implicitly aided by the clergy and their definitions of the situation, failed in the longer run to gain wide acceptance of their view on the social standing of company daughters, as shown by developments from the mid-1840s to the 1860s. Supported by officer parents and husbands, many maintained their social and marital standing in the company and in Red River.

In this they were helped by the fact that they constituted a majority. Several British wives had arrived in the fur trade country by about 1840, but officers who took white wives soon sought posts as near as possible to the "civilized world," finding their brides lonely, unhappy, and ill-suited to life at the posts or in Red River. By 1850, it was accepted that these officers would scarcely be able to handle post duties in remote places. In the mid-1850s, Chief Trader

James Anderson, stationed in the Mackenzie River district, briefly considered suggesting that his colleague Hector McKenzie would make a good officer for the area, but then dismissed the idea: "as he is married to an European Lady, it would be a sentence of death to send her here" (PAC, Anderson Papers, vol. 1, file 4).

In the same period, younger generations of company daughters were augmenting their education and learning civilized arts in the schools of Red River and elsewhere, so that they could not be readily disqualified from marrying officers, any more than their brothers could justly be denied candidacy for clerkships. They were also being Christianized and protected; one picturesque observation of the 1840s depicted the female pupils of the Red River academy to be "as strictly guarded from communication with other people as the inmates of a Turkish Seraglio" (Van Kirk 1975: 269). And James Anderson's letters of the 1850s noted that some of his young officers expected to find suitable wives in Red River.

A few of their mothers also gained important social positions. Anne Thomas, daughter of an old Hudson's Bay officer, had become the country wife of Alexander Christie by 1815 (HBCA, B. 59/z/1: 186). In the early 1830s, Simpson considered Christie for the post of governor of Assiniboia (Red River), but he first rejected him as unsuitable on account of his native family. When he finally decided Christie was still the best candidate, Anne became one of the first ladies of Red River (Van Kirk 1975: 377–78). On 10 February 1835, the Anglican clergyman at Red River formally married the Christies, with George Simpson as one of the witnesses.

Most other officers of the new company continued to find their wives among native-born daughters—a pattern deplored by James Hargrave and unattractive to the Simpsons and their friends, but one that nonetheless persisted. Former North West clerk James Douglas married a daughter of William Connolly and his Cree wife in 1828, and when he became governor of the Crown Colony of Vancouver Island in 1859, she became its first lady. In 1853, Donald A. Smith, later Lord Strathcona and the governor of the company, married Isabella, the daughter of Hudson's Bay officer Richard Hardisty and the native-born Margaret Sutherland in Labrador while serving as a clerk under her father.

Other mixed-blood women occupied high social positions elsewhere in the Northwest, although one went through a difficult ordeal in Red River. The standing of Mrs. John Ballenden, daughter of Alexander Roderick McLeod and wife of the officer in charge of company affairs at Red River in mid-century, was damaged by charges of immorality originating in allegations spread by another officer's white wife and by white women associated with the clergy. These charges, which seemed motivated by jealousy of Mrs. Ballenden's position as well as suspicions about her marital fidelity, demonstrated that white women arriving in the Northwest could still have divisive effects along social-racial lines (ibid., ch. 7). But despite this setback, the growth of large company families, along with extensive intermarriage between incoming employees and daughters educated in Red River and elsewhere, caused racial distinctions to lose significance as social barriers between white and native families of officers faded.

Contributing to this shift was the fact that families of part-Indian descent were becoming physically less distinct from whites as well as culturally more distant from Indians. Fur traders in both old companies had tended to shift away from Indian wives even before the 1821 merger, as policies changed and as the pool of eligible mixed-blood women rapidly grew. Many Indian groups had become socially separate and dependent enclaves of low rank, and Indian alliances were strongly discountenanced in most parts; those of Richard Grant and Bernard Ross caused repeated concern to their respective colleagues, James Hargrave and James Anderson. Those officers in the far west who still chose Indian wives, for example, clerk Alexander Lattie and Captain James Allan Scarborough in the Columbia district (Vaughan 1963; Barker 1948: 323–24), were now exceptional.

FATHERS AND MOTHERS, RACES AND RANKS: CONCLUDING PERSPECTIVES

"Strangers in blood" has a double meaning in this book. In British law, it served to describe any relationship, even familial, that the law refused to admit as legitimate. But it also provides one way of characterizing the meetings of whites and Indians—two groups with long separate racial histories—in the fur trade of northern North America.

The diversity of the Indian groups in these encounters has been recognized by many. The white traders may appear more homogeneous, but in fact they too must be viewed in the contexts of their distinctive "tribes" (companies) and home societies if the social complexities of the fur trade are to be understood. The story does not end with them, however. Hundreds of fur trade alliances, according to the somewhat variable customs of the country, produced a biracial population whose members followed widely varying careers and left their marks on later history. And looking backward, it is possible to see how differing company backgrounds and correspondingly diverse parental interactions and familial relationships had already begun to steer those progeny into diverging social groups and categories—Indian, white, and métis or "halfbreed"—before the coalition of 1821.

The biracial ancestry of many Hudson's Bay Indians has already been remarked. Subject as Home Indians to the paternalism of that company and isolated from the descendants of North Westers and Canadian freemen and from the conflicts over Red River, the mixed-bloods among these groups were not impelled to seek a non-Indian political or ethnic identity. Many of their descendants still reside today, often bearing English and Scottish surnames, in Indian bands in the old Hudson's Bay Company areas along the Bay and inland, and in other enclaves in Manitoba and westward. The mission records of the Red River "Indian Settlement" (St. Peter's Anglican Church) as well as of other churches of the area list several Indians bearing old Hudson's Bay names; evidently numerous descendants had been subsisting around the posts as hunters, trappers, or small-scale fur trade suppliers, until drawn to the colony. Still others, once two or three generations removed, became known mainly by Indian or clergy-conferred names, although they retained traditions about their company ancestors as did James Settee. And one Plains Cree group, the Parklands People, long recognized as Indian, traces its ancestry to eighteenth-century Hudson's Bay man George Sutherland (Mandelbaum 1940: 167). Isolated from the new company social order of the nineteenth century, these people remained remote from the problems that their fellow mixed-bloods were facing within it.

The passing of fur trade offspring into the other categories—white and halfbreed or métis—began on a small scale before 1821; earlier chapters have traced a few Hudson's Bay natives who became English and the larger numbers of North West descendants who began to assert or be assigned a distinct mixed-blood identity in this period. These developments were much accelerated after the coalition. In the following decades, the rule of a unified company-government provided what might be described as a hothouse atmosphere in which social distinctions seemed to grow and flourish. Pressed to economize and to increase the efficiency of company operations, and wielding strong monopoly powers, the new governor and his associates were able, for a time, to sort and simplify the fur trade population into classes of people distinguished by their race on one hand and their membership in kin-friendship networks on the other, directing them along different career paths. Because this new social system was relatively closed and stratified and undergoing genuine economic strain and because of disruptive changes and influences that suddenly accentuated its internal dissensions and ambivalences, the new social and racial distinctions at first became a basis for policy with little challenge.

These changes, however, soon roused strong opposition from those traders whose familial attachments were permanent, since they in fact strongly challenged enduring personal loyalties. To separate people on the basis of race was, particularly in officers' ranks, to separate father from child (and grandchild) and husband from wife in too many cases and to threaten the rank and prospects of too many men of "gentlemanly" standing and their native-born wives and offspring.

Numerous officers thus began more actively to maintain and defend personal familial ties. Their dominant defence tactic is distinctive enough to merit its own term—patrifocality—whereby fathers involved themselves in considerable social, economic, and emotional commitments toward the proper upbringing, education, and placement of offspring. Such fathers were not necessarily any more egalitarian in ideology than a Governor Simpson; nor were they always free of tendencies to generalize, in moments of discouragement, about mixed-bloods and their seeming faults as a class. But they devised means, effective in many instances, of working within the system to assure their children's standing so that they could escape the racial bias being promoted in the fur trade country. Patrifocal fur trade families were characterized by the presence of the father not only as head of the family but also as the figure central to its internal relationships, who played an active role in the upbringing, education, and placement of his offspring. Sometimes a grandfather became the central figure, as when Hudson's Bay Chief Factor Kennedy arranged for the education of A.K. Isbister in the Orkneys.

The strongest expressions of patrifocality appear in the efforts of company fathers to educate and place their children in Canadian and British society, efforts attended with much expense, hardship, and anxiety. Although several officers had attempted such placements in the years before 1821, their increasing numbers in following decades reflected not only improved opportunities in Britain and Canada but also the worsening conditions in the fur trade. In the relatively larger and more diversified societies of these countries, company offspring could acquire respectable schooling, professions, and trades and escape the company that, as Archibald McDonald said, had proved "so bad" to so many of them. While all faced the risk of sinking below gentlemanly rank, those who left the fur trade seemed to escape the racial bias that had been grafted onto its ranking system.

Some of those offspring who remained within the Northwest also benefited from paternal support, although often to less effect. Many officers spent considerable sums in Red River itself in attempts to provide education for their children and to keep them in range of their own supervision, only to realize that between the 1820s and the 1850s, these expenditures did not always ensure that their children reached the economic security and standing that they had hoped for. Nonetheless, as Red River grew, several of these offspring were later able to claim prominent positions in the colony, although some took up the cause of Louis Riel and the métis. Still others, although fewer, continued to find niches in company service. Aware of their distinctive fur trade and part-Indian ancestry, some of their descendants describe themselves simply as Rupertslanders, recalling the old Hudson's Bay Company name for its territories (interview with Mrs. Ruby Johnstone and Miss Barbara Johnstone, 8 July 1972, Selkirk, Manitoba). A few such kin groups, conspicuous for the numbers of their members linked by employment and marriage with the company, were noted as company families. A 1923 article in the company periodical, *The Beaver,* recorded that between 1809 and 1920, eight members of the Christie family served the concern for a total of 238 years (see also HBC Library, Roderick MacFarlane file). Many members of these families of mixed descent, both men and women, also became important residents of the growing settlements of the Northwest in later years (for examples, see Healy 1923 and Lugrin 1928).

Those company offspring who lacked either paternal resources or direction or both usually remained as halfbreeds or métis in the Northwest. These mixed-bloods were to some extent divided along old company lines. Many lower-ranked Hudson's Bay Orkneymen and other servants had retired to Red River, and their descendants, known as "Scotch" or "English halfbreeds," were said by some observers to be more settled and more oriented toward acquiring education and civilized ways than the métis with their taste for the more free and "improvident" life of the Indians (Hind 1971: 179), although the two overlapped somewhat.

In contrast, since very few Scottish North Westers had made their homes in Red River, most mixed-bloods of that company who gravitated to the settlement were of voyageur and French background or, if Scottish, they lacked paternal ties. As buffalo hunters, suppliers, or workers in other sub-servient capacities, they tended to constitute the lower classes of the fur trade, while maintaining a separate group consciousness that went back to the earliest days of Red River.

It is interesting that in forging a distinctive political identity, some métis began to attach special importance to their maternal ancestry. James Ross of Red River defiantly asked, "What if mama were an Indian?" (Van Kirk 1975: 412), and others asserted a double claim to the Northwest through both their Indian mothers and trader fathers. The sympathies of the typical métis man were said to be "all towards his Indian mother, squaw, and especially his (belle mère) mother-in-law" (Spry 1968: 169). Louis Riel effectively emphasized the role of Indian mothers in contributing to métis uniqueness:

> It is true that our savage origin is humble, but it is meet that we honor our mothers as well as our fathers. Why should we concern ourselves about what degree of mixture we possess of European or Indian blood? If we have ever so little of either gratitude or filial love, should we not be proud to say, "We are Métis!"? (Howard 1970: 46).

Lacking upward mobility, these mixed-blood descendants of the fur trade joined a common cause that emphasized their maternal descent, in contradistinction to the dominantly patrilineal and patrifocal familial structures that, with their orientation toward the "civilized world," had guided many of their peers toward higher social standing as whites and gentlemen. Their matrilineal orientation showed consistency with the relative weakness of many older North Westers' fur trade family ties; and it was surely, at least in part, a consequence of those traders' frequent tendency not to assume an active paternal role.

It is clear that the community lives of the different categories of fur trade progeny came to differ widely. Some remained enmeshed in Indian life. Some preserved no shared communal existence; patrifocality led to their mobility, dispersal, and assimilation in larger white communities. For the métis, in contrast, their efforts to seek and protect their rights in the Red River region helped to lead to their survival as an entity in Western Canada, albeit with persisting economic and political problems. The buffalo resource failed them and Louis Riel was defeated, but métis communities persisted as reminders of the Canadian fur trade, of the Indian women who had befriended, tolerated, or endured the white strangers who came for furs, and of the social and racial distinctions that began to pervade the Northwest in the early to mid-1800s.

References

Unpublished and Primary Sources

London. Public Record Office. PROB 11/1238 18857.

Montreal. McCord Museum. Robert McVicar Papers.

Ottawa. Public Archives of Canada.

    James Anderson Papers (transcripts). MG19, A29.
    Charles Napier Bell Collection. MG19, A30.
    Andrew Bulger Papers. MG19, E5.
    Canada. Governor General's Office. RG7, G1, vol. 78.
    Duncan Clarke Papers. MG19, A39.
    Edward Ermatinger Correspondence. MG19, A2, ser. 2, vol. 1.
    William Falconer Journals and Observations, Severn House. MG19, D2.
    Simon Fraser Papers and Journal (photocopies). MG19, A9, vols. 2, 4.
    James Hargrave Correspondence. MG19, A21.
    Hudson's Bay Company, Minutes of Council, Northern and Southern
        Departments. MG19, G supplementary, ser. 2, vols. 1, 2.
    James Keith Papers. Microfilm A-676.
    John Henry Lefroy Letters. MG24, H25.
    Miles Macdonell Papers. MG19, E4.
    Donald Ross Correspondence, Norway House. MG19, D7.
    Baron Strathcona and Mount Royal (Donald Alexander Smith) Papers
        (photocopies). MG19, A33, box 3.

St. Louis. Missouri Historical Society. Wilson Price Hunt Papers.

Toronto. Archives of Ontario.

    Nicol Finlayson Letters.
    John McDonald Le Borgne Letters.
    John Macdonell Papers.
    Donald McKay Journal, 1799–1806 (microfilm).
    James McMillan file (c/o Hugh MacMillan, archives liaison officer).
    Moose Factory register of baptisms, marriages, burials (microfilm).
    St. Gabriel Street Presbyterian Church registers, Montreal (microfilm).

Toronto. Metropolitan Toronto Library.

George Nelson Papers.

Victoria. Provincial Archives of British Columbia.

James Anderson Papers. A B40, An32.

Winnipeg. Hudson's Bay Company Archives (also available to 1870 on micro-film in the Public Archives of Canada, Ottawa).

Section A. 1/42, 47, 48. Minutes of London Committee.
6/16, 17. London correspondence outwards.
11/116–118. London correspondence inward from posts.
30/4–12. Servants' lists.
34/1–2. Servants' characters and personnel records.
36/1–15. Officers' and servants' wills.
44/1–4. Court probate and estate records.

Section B. Post records.
3. Albany.
59. Eastmain.
135. Moose.
155. Osnaburgh House.
239. York.

Section D. 4. Governor George Simpson: correspondence outwards.

———. Hudson's Bay Company Library. Employees' files.

———. St. John's Cathedral (Anglican). Red River registers of baptisms, marriages, burials.

———. Provincial Archives of Manitoba.

Peter Fidler's notebook, and Red River journal 1814–15 (transcript from Selkirk Papers).
William Kennedy Papers.
Red River court records.
Alexander Ross Papers.

Published and Secondary Sources

Abegglen, James G.
  1958   *The Japanese factory: Aspects of its social organization.* Glencoe,
          IL.: Free Press.
Aborigines' Protection Society
  1848   *The colonial intelligencer; or, aborigines' friend,* vol. 2. London.
Arthur, M. Elizabeth
  1970   General Dickson and the Indian liberating army in the north.
          Ontario History 62(3): 151–62.
  1978   Angelique and her children. *Thunder Bay Historical Museum
          Society Papers and Records,* vol. 6, pp. 30–40.
Axtell, James
  1975   The white Indians of colonial America. *William and Mary Quar-
          terly,* ser. 3, 32(1): 55–88.
Bailey, F.G.
  1969   *Stratagems and spoils: A social anthropology of politics.* New
          York: Schocken Books.
Bailey, Patrick
  1971   *Orkney.* Newton Abbott: David and Charles Ltd.
Barker, Burt Brown
  1948   *Letters of Dr. John McLoughlin written at Fort Vancouver
          1829–1832.* Portland: Binfords and Mort for the Oregon His-
          torical Society.
Barth, Fredrik
  1973   Descent and marriage reconsidered. In *The character of kinship,*
          ed. by Jack Goody. Cambridge: Cambridge University Press.
The Beaver
         1923   The Christie family and H.B.C. August, pp. 417–19.
The Beaver Club
  1819   *Rules and regulations.* Montreal.
Binns, Archie
  1967   *Peter Skene Ogden, fur trader.* Portland, OR: Binfords and Mort.
Bishop, Charles A.
  1972   Demography, ecology, and trade among the northern Ojibwa
          and Swampy Cree. *Western Canadian Journal of Anthropology*
          3(1): 58–71.
  1976a The emergence of the northern Ojibwa: Social and economic
          consequences. *American Ethnologist* 3(1): 39–54.
  1976b The Henley House massacres. *The Beaver,* autumn, pp. 36–41.
Bolus, Malvina
  1971   The son of I. Gunn. *The Beaver,* winter, pp. 23–26.

Bowsfield, Hartwell
 1974*a* Alexander Christie, *Dictionary of Canadian Biography,* vol. 10, pp. 167–68. Toronto: University of Toronto Press.
 1974*b* James Anderson. Ibid., p. 629.
Brown, Jennifer S.H.
 1975 Two companies in search of traders: Personnel and promotion patterns in Canada's early British fur trade. *Proceedings of the 2d Congress,* Canadian Ethnology Society, vol. 2. National Museum of Man, Mercury Series, Ottawa, paper no. 28, pp. 623–45.
 1976*a* Changing views of fur trade marriage and domesticity: James Hargrave, his colleagues, and "the sex." *Western Canadian Journal of Anthropology* 6(3): 92–105.
 1976*b* A demographic transition in the fur trade country: Family sizes and fertility of company officers and country wives, ca. 1750–1850. Ibid. 6(1): 61–71.
 1977 James Settee and his Cree tradition: An Indian camp at the mouth of Nelson River Hudsons Bay. *Proceedings of the 8th Algonquian Conference.* Ottawa: Carleton University.
 1979 Linguistic solitudes and social categories in the fur trade. In *Old Trails and new directions: Papers of the third North American Fur Trade Conference,* ed. by A.J. Ray and Carol Judd. Toronto: University of Toronto Press. Forthcoming.
 in press *a* George Atkinson; Isaac Batt; Malchom Ross; George Sutherland. *Dictionary of Canadian Biography,* vol. 4. Toronto: University of Toronto Press.
 in press *b* Charles Isham; William Richards. Ibid., vol. 5.
————, and Sylvia Van Kirk
 in press George Barnston. Ibid., vol. 11.
Burpee, L.J.
 1919 A forgotten adventurer of the fur trade. *Queen's Quarterly* 26(4): 363–80.
Campbell, Marjorie Wilkins
 1957 *The North West Company.* New York: St. Martin's Press.
Campbell, Robert
 1887 *History of the Scotch Presbyterian Church.* Montreal.
Chapin, Jane Lewis
 1936 McLoughlin letters, 1827–49. *Oregon Historical Quarterly* 37 (1): 45–75.
Cline, Gloria Griffen
 1974 *Peter Skene Ogden and the Hudson's Bay Company.* Norman: University of Oklahoma Press.

Clouston, J.S.
   1936   *Orkney and the Hudson's Bay Company. The Beaver,* December,
           pp. 4–8.
Cominos, Peter T.
   1963   Late Victorian sexual respectability and the social system. *Inter-
           national Review of Social History* 8: 18–48; 216–50.
Connolly v. Woolrich and Johnson et al.
   1867   Superior court, 9 July 1867. *Lower Canada Jurist* 11: 197–265.
Coser, Lewis A.
   1973   Servants: The obsolescence of an occupational role. *Social
           Forces* 52(1): 31–40.
Coues, Elliott
   1897   *New light on the early history of the greater northwest. The
           manuscript journal of Alexander Henry, fur trader of the North
           West Company, and of David Thompson, official geographer
           and explorer of the same company, 1799–1814. Exploration and
           adventure among the Indians on the Red, Saskatchewan, Mis-
           souri, and Columbia Rivers.* 3 vols. New York.
Cowie, Isaac
   1913   *The company of adventurers.* Toronto: William Briggs.
Cox, Ross
   1832   *Adventures on the Columbia River, including the narrative of a
           residence of six years on the western side of the Rocky Mountains
           among various tribes of Indians hitherto unknown: together with
           a journey across the American continent.* New York.
Craig, Joan
   1974   John Newton; Robert Pilgrim. *Dictionary of Canadian Bio-
           graphy,* vol. 3, pp. 482–83; 520–21. Toronto: University of
           Toronto Press.
Crozier, Michel
   1964   *The bureaucratic phenomenon.* Chicago: University of Chicago
           Press.
Cummings, Peter A., and Neil H. Mickenberg
   1972   *Native rights in Canada.* 2d. ed. Toronto: The Indian-Eskimo
           Association of Canada in association with General Publishing
           Co.
Davidoff, Leonore
   1974   Mastered for life: Servant and wife in Victorian and Edwardian
           England. *Journal of Social History* 7(4): 406–28.
Davies, K.G.
   1963   *Northern Quebec and Labrador journals and correspondence,
           1819–35.* London: Hudson's Bay Record Society, vol. 24.

1965   *Letters from Hudson's Bay, 1703–40.* Ibid., vol. 25.

1966a   From competition to union. *Minnesota History* 40(4): 166–77.

1966b   John Nixon. *Dictionary of Canadian Biography,* vol. 1, pp. 518–20. Toronto: University of Toronto Press.

Dempsey, Hugh A., ed.

1977   *The Rundle journals 1840–1848.* Calgary: Historical Society of Alberta, vol. 1.

Diamond, Sigmund

1961   An experiment in "feudalism": French Canada in the seventeenth century. *William and Mary Quarterly,* ser. 3, 18(1): 3–34.

Dobbs, Arthur

1744   *An account of the countries adjoining to Hudson's Bay.* London.

Doughty, Arthur G., and Chester Martin, eds.

1929   *The Kelsey papers.* Ottawa: Public Archives of Canada and Public Record Office of Northern Ireland.

Drage, Theodore S.

1748–49 *An account of a voyage for the discovery of a North-West passage by Hudson's Streights to the western and southern ocean of America performed in the year 1746 and 1747, in the ship California.* 2 vols. London.

Drake, Michael

1972   Perspectives in historical demography. In *The structure of human populations,* ed. by G.A. Harrison and A.J. Boyce. Oxford: Clarendon Press.

Eccles, W.J.

1969   *The Canadian frontier 1534–1760.* New York: Holt, Rinehart and Winston.

Elliott, T.C.

1922   Letters of Dr. John McLoughlin. *Oregon Historical Quarterly* 23(4): 365–71.

1935   Marguerite Wadin McKay McLoughlin. Ibid. 36(4): 338–47.

Ellis, Henry

1748   *A voyage to Hudson's Bay.* London.

Fallers, Lloyd A.

1967   *Immigrants and associations.* The Hague: Mouton.

Ferris, Joel E.

1957   Ranald MacDonald, the sailor boy who visited Japan. *Pacific North West Quarterly* 48(1): 13–16.

Fisher, Robin

1977   *Contact and Conflict: Indian-European Relations in British Columbia, 1774–1890.* Vancouver: University of British Columbia Press.

Fleming, R. Harvey
    1940   *Minutes of Council, Northern Department of Rupert Land, 1821–31.* Toronto: Champlain Society for the Hudson's Bay Record Society, vol. 3.

Flexner, James Thomas
    1959   *Mohawk Baronet: Sir William Johnson of New York.* New York: Harper and Brothers.

Fort William *Times-Journal*
    1965   Article on Susan, Cree mother of Simon and Joseph McGillivray, 23 March. Fort William [Thunder Bay], Ontario.

Foster, John E.
    1975   The Indian-Trader in the Hudson Bay fur trade tradition. In *Proceedings of the 2d Congress,* Canadian Ethnology Society, vol. 2. National Museum of Man, Mercury Series, paper no. 28, Ottawa, pp. 571–85.
    1976   The origins of the mixed bloods in the Canadian west. In *Essays on western history,* ed. by Lewis H. Thomas, pp. 71–80. Edmonton: University of Alberta Press.

Fox, Edward Whiting
    1972   *History in geographic perspective: The other France.* New York: W.W. Norton and Co.

Franklin, John
    1823   *Narrative of a journey to the shores of the Polar sea, in the years 1819, 20, 21, 22.* London.

Fraser v. Pouliot et al.
    1881   Superior Court. *Q.L.R.* 7: 149–62.
    1884   Superior Court. *La Revue légale* 13: 1–39.
    1885   Court of Queen's Bench, 8 May. Ibid., pp. 520–63.

Frisch, Rose E.
    1975   Demographic implications of the biological determinants of female fecundity. *Social Biology* 22(1): 17–22.

Galbraith, John S.
    1957   *The Hudson's Bay Company as an imperial factor.* Berkeley and Los Angeles: University of California Press.
    1976   *The little emperor: Governor Simpson of the Hudson's Bay Company.* Toronto: Macmillan of Canada.

Garry, Francis N.A., ed.
    1900   Diary of Nicholas Garry, deputy-governor of the Hudson's Bay Company: A detailed narrative of his travels in the north west territories of British North America in 1821. Royal Society of Canada, *Proceedings and Transactions.,* 2d. ser., vol. 6, sec. 2, pp. 73–200.

Gates, Charles M.
  1965   *Five fur traders of the northwest* (rev. ed.). St. Paul: Minnesota
          Historical Society.
Giraud, Marcel
  1945   *Le métis canadien.* Paris: Institut d'Ethnologie.
Glazebrook, G.P. de T.
  1938   *The Hargrave correspondence, 1821–43.* Toronto: Champlain
          Society, vol. 24.
Goody, Esther N.
  1973   Delegation of parental roles in West Africa and the West Indies.
          Paper presented at the 9th International Congress of Anthropo-
          logical and Ethnological Sciences, Chicago.
Graham, Henry Grey
  1971   *Social life of Scotland in the eighteenth century* (1st ed. 1899).
          New York: Benjamin Blom.
Graham, I.C.C.
  1956   *Colonists from Scotland: Emigration to North America 1707–
          1783.* Ithaca: Cornell University Press.
Great Britain. Parliament. House of Commons.
  1749   *A short state of the countries and trade of North America claimed
          by the Hudson's Bay Company.* London.
Grignon, Augustin
  1857   Seventy-two years' recollections of Wisconsin. *Collections of the
          State Historical Society of Wisconsin* 3: 197–295. Madison.
Hallowell, A. Irving
  1963   American Indians, white and black. *Current Anthropology* 4:
          519–31.
Hammick, James T.
  1887   *The marriage law of England: A practical treatise* (2d. ed.).
          London.
Hartz, Louis
  1964   *The founding of new societies.* New York: Harcourt Brace and
          World.
Healy, W.J.
  1923   *Women of Red River, being a book written from the recollec-
          tions of women surviving from the Red River era.* Winnipeg:
          Russell, Lang and Co.
Hickerson, Harold
  1966   Review of Saum, *The fur trader and the Indian. American
          Anthropologist* 68(3): 822–24.
Hind, Henry Youle
  1971   *Narrative of the Canadian Red River exploring expedition of*

1857 and of the Assiniboine and Saskatchewan exploring expedition of 1858. Edmonton: Hurtig.

Honigmann, John
    1953   Social organization of the Attawapiskat Cree Indians. *Anthropos* 48: 809–16.

Hopwood, V.G.
    1957   New light on David Thompson. *The Beaver,* summer, pp. 26–31.

Houghton, W.E.
    1957   *The Victorian frame of mind, 1830–1870.* New Haven: Yale University Press.

Howard, Joseph Kinsey
    1970   *The strange empire of Louis Riel* (1st ed. 1952). Toronto: Swan Publishing Co. Ltd.

Illick, Joseph E.
    1975   Child-rearing in seventeenth century England and America. In *The history of childhood,* ed. by Lloyd deMause. New York: Harper Torchbooks, Harper and Row.

Innis, Harold A.
    1970   *The fur trade in Canada* (1st ed. 1930). Toronto: University of Toronto Press.

Jessett, Thomas E.
    1959   *Reports and letters of Herbert Beaver, 1836–38.* Portland, OR: Champoeg Press.

Johnson, Alice M.
    1966   Charles Bayly; William Bond; George Geyer; Nehemiah Walker. In *Dictionary of Canadian Biography,* vol. 1, pp. 81–84; 107; 328–29; 666. Toronto: University of Toronto Press.
    1967   *Saskatchewan journals and correspondence, 1795–1802.* London: Hudson's Bay Record Society, vol. 26.
    1974   Thomas McCliesh; Richard Norton. In *Dictionary of Canadian Biography,* vol. 3, pp. 414–15; 489–90. Toronto: University of Toronto Press.

Johnstone et al. v. Connolly
    1869   Court of Appeal, 7 September. *La Revue légale* 1: 253–400.

Kane, Paul
    1968   *Wanderings of an artist among the Indians of North America* (1st ed. 1859). Edmonton: Hurtig.

Kipling, Rudyard
    n.d.   Baa, baa, black sheep. In *Wee Willie Winkie and other stories.* New York: Grosset and Dunlap.

Knox, H.C.
    1956   Alexander Kennedy Isbister. Historical and Scientific Society of Manitoba, *Transactions* series 3(12).
———, and Olive Knox
    1944   Chief Factor Archibald McDonald. *The Beaver,* March, pp. 42–46.

Krause, John T.
    1973   Some implications of recent work in historical demography. In *Applied historical studies: An introductory reader,* ed. by Michael Drake. London: Methuen, in association with the Open University Press.

Lamb, W. Kaye
    1957   *Sixteen years in the Indian country, the journal of Daniel Williams Harmon 1800–1816.* Toronto: Macmillan Company of Canada Ltd.
    1966   *The letters and journals of Simon Fraser 1806–1808.* Ibid.

Laslett, Peter
    1965   *The world we have lost.* New York: Charles Scribner's Sons.

Lewis, Oscar
    1970   The effects of white contact upon Blackfoot culture (1st ed. 1942). In *Anthropological essays.* New York: Random House.

Lewis, William S., and Naojiro Murakami
    1923   *Ranald MacDonald 1824–1894.* Spokane: Eastern Washington State Historical Society.

Lugrin, N. de Bertrand
    1928   *Pioneer women of Vancouver Island, 1843–1866.* Victoria: Women's Canadian Club of Victoria, British Columbia.

MacKay, Douglas
    1936   *The honourable company: A history of the Hudson's Bay Company.* Toronto: McClelland and Stewart.

Mackenzie, Alexander
    1911   *Voyages from Montreal through the continent of North America . . . in 1789 and 1793* (1st ed. 1801). 2 vols. Toronto: Courier Press Ltd.

Mackenzie, Cecil W.
    1937   *Donald Mackenzie: "King of the northwest."* Los Angeles: Ivan Deach Jr.

MacLeod, Margaret A.
    1947   *The letters of Letitia Hargrave.* Toronto: Champlain Society, vol. 28.
———, and W.L. Morton
    1974   *Cuthbert Grant of Grantown: Warden of the plains of Red River*

(1st ed. 1963). Toronto: McClelland and Stewart, Carleton Library no. 71.

McNaught, Kenneth
    1969   *The Pelican history of Canada.* Harmondsworth: Penguin Books.

Mandelbaum, D.G.
    1940   *The Plains Cree.* Anthropological Papers of the American Museum of Natural History, vol. 37, pt. 2. New York.

Manitoba Library Association, compiler
    1971   *Pioneers and early citizens of Manitoba.* Winnipeg: Peguis Publishers.

Marcus, Steven
    1966   *The other Victorians: A study of sexuality and pornography in mid-nineteenth century England.* New York: Basic Books.

Martinez-Alier, Verena
    1974   *Marriage, class, and colour in nineteenth-century Cuba: A study of racial attitudes and sexual values in a slave society.* Cambridge: Cambridge University Press.

Massicotte, E.-Z.
    1933   Note sur John Thomson. *Bulletin des recherches historiques* 39: 495–96.

Masson, Louis F.R.
    1960   *Les bourgeois de la compagnie du Nord-Ouest: Récits de voyages, lettres, et rapports inédits relatifs au Nord-Ouest canadien* (1st ed. 1889–90). 2 vols. New York: Antiquarian Press.

Mattison, Ray H.
    1965   Kenneth McKenzie. In *The mountain men and the fur trade of the far west,* vol. 2, ed. by LeRoy R. Hafen. Glendale, CA: Arthur H. Clarke Co.

Merk, Frederick
    1968   *Fur trade and empire, George Simpson's journal 1824–25.* Cambridge: Belknap Press of Harvard University Press.

Meyer, Duane
    1961   *The Highland Scots of North Carolina 1723–1776.* Chapel Hill: University of North Carolina Press.

Mitchell, Elaine Allan
    1973   The Camerons of Timiskaming. *Nor'Wester, the journal of the North West Company* 2(1): 11–13.
    1974   Angus Cameron. *Dictionary of Canadian Biography,* vol. 10, pp. 114–15. Toronto: University of Toronto Press.
    1977   *Fort Timiskaming and the fur trade.* Toronto: University of Toronto Press.

Morgan, Edmund S.
  1966   *The Puritan family* (1st ed. 1944). New York: Harper Torch-
          books, Harper and Row.

Morice, Adrian G.
  1929*a* A Canadian pioneer: Spanish John [Macdonell]. *Canadian His-
          torical Review* 10(3): 223–35.
  1929*b* Sidelights on the careers of Miles Macdonell and his brothers.
          Ibid. (4): 308–32.

Morton, Arthur S.
  1929(ed.)   *The journal of Duncan M'Gillivray of the North West Company,
             1794–1795*. Toronto: Macmillan Company of Canada Ltd.
  1944   *Sir George Simpson, overseas governor of the Hudson's Bay
          Company*. Portland, OR: Binfords and Mort for the Oregon His-
          torical Society.
  1973   *History of the Canadian West to 1870–71* (1st ed. 1939). Toronto:
          University of Toronto Press.

Morton, W.L.
  1966   The North West Company: Pedlars extraordinary. *Minnesota
          History* 40(4): 157–64.

Munnick, Harriet D.
  1971   The Ermatinger brothers. In *The mountain men and the fur trade
          of the far west,* vol. 8, ed. by LeRoy R. Hafen. Glendale, CA:
          Arthur H. Clarke Co.

Myers, J.A.
  1919   Jacques Raphael Finlay. *Washington Historical Quarterly* 10(3):
          163–67.

Nakane, Chie
  1970   *Japanese society*. Berkeley and Los Angeles: University of Cali-
          fornia Press.

Nerlove, Sara B.
  1974   Women's workload and infant feeding practices. *Ethnology*
          13(2): 207–14.

Nicks, John
  1979   Orcadian servants of the Hudson's Bay Company in the era of
          competition, 1780 to 1821. In *Old trails and new directions:
          Papers of the third North American fur trade conference,* ed.
          A.J. Ray and Carol Judd. Toronto: University of Toronto Press.
          Forthcoming.

Nicks, Trudy
  1979   Iroquois in the northwestern fur trade. In ibid.

Nute, Grace Lee
  1922   Diary of Martin McLeod. *Minnesota History* 4(7–8): 351–439.
  1923   James Dickson: A filibuster in Minnesota in 1836. *Mississippi*

Valley Historical Review 10(2): 127–39; 174–81.

1931 *The voyageur.* New York: D. Appleton and Co.

1969 Pierre Esprit Radisson. *Dictionary of Canadian Biography,* vol. 2, p. 538. Toronto: University of Toronto Press.

Oerichbauer, Edgar S.

1979 Interim report of the 1970 and 1978 archaeological excavations at a North West Company wintering post, Burnett County, Wisconsin. Typescript. Museums Division, The State Historical Society of Wisconsin, Madison.

O'Meara, Walter

1950 An adventure in local history. *Minnesota History* 31(1): 1–10.

1968 *Daughters of the country: The women of the fur traders and mountain men.* New York: Harcourt, Brace and World.

Paine, Robert, ed.

1971 *Patrons and brokers in the East Arctic.* Newfoundland Social and Economic Papers no. 2, Institute of Social and Economic Research, Memorial University of Newfoundland. Toronto: University of Toronto Press.

Peterson, Jacqueline

1977 Prelude to Red River: A social portrait of the Great Lakes métis. Paper presented to the American Society for Ethnohistory, Chicago.

Plumb, J.H.

1975 The new world of children in eighteenth-century England. *Past and Present* 67: 64–95.

Porter, K.W.

1930 Jane Barnes, first white woman in Oregon. *Oregon Historical Quarterly* 31(2): 121–35.

Pryde, George S.

1935 Scottish colonization in the Province of New York. *Proceedings of the New York State Historical Association* 16: 138–57.

Quaife, Milo Milton, ed.

1944 *Growing up in southern Illinois 1820–61,* by Daniel Harmon Brush. Chicago: Lakeside Press, R.R. Donnelley and Sons.

1968 *Voyage to the northwest coast of America,* by Gabriel Franchère. New York: Citadel Press.

Raven, Simon

1961 *The English gentleman: An essay in attitudes.* London: Anthony Blond.

Rich, E.E.

1938 *George Simpson's journal of occurrences in the Athabaska Department and report 1820–21.* Toronto: Champlain Society for the Hudson's Bay Record Society, vol. 1.

1939   *Colin Robertson's letters, 1817–1822.* Ibid., vol. 2.

1945   *Minutes of the Hudson's Bay Company 1679–1684.* London: Champlain Society for the Hudson's Bay Record Society, vols. 8, 9.

1947   *George Simpson's 1828 journey to the Columbia.* London: Hudson's Bay Record Society, vol. 10.

1948   *Hudson's Bay Company letters outwards, 1679–1694.* Ibid., vol. 11.

1949   *James Isham's observations and notes, 1743–49.* Toronto: Champlain Society for the Hudson's Bay Record Society, vol. 12.

1955   *Samuel Black's Rocky Mountain journal.* London: Hudson's Bay Record Society, vol. 18.

1956   *London correspondence inward from Eden Colvile, 1849–1852.* Ibid., vol. 19.

1957   *Hudson's Bay Copy Booke of letters commissions instructions outward, 1688–1696.* Ibid., vol. 20.

1961   *History of the Hudson's Bay Company 1670–1870.* 3 vols. New York: Macmillan.

———, and A.M. Johnson

1951   *Cumberland House journals and inland journals 1775–82.* 2 vols. London: Hudson's Bay Record Society, vols. 14–15.

1954   *Moose Fort journals, 1783–85.* Ibid., vol. 17.

Robson, Joseph

1752   *Account of six years' residence in Hudson's Bay.* London.

Ross, Alexander

1855   *The fur hunters of the far west.* 2 vols. London.

1972   *The Red River settlement: Its rise, progress, and present state* (1st ed. 1856). Edmonton: Hurtig.

Ruggles, Richard I.

1977   Hospital boys of the Bay. *The Beaver,* autumn, pp. 4–11.

Saum, Lewis O.

1965   *The fur trader and the Indian.* Seattle: University of Washington Press.

Saunders, Richard M.

1939   The emergence of the coureur de bois as a social type. In Canadian Historical Association, *Report,* pp. 22–33. Toronto.

Scott, W.R.

1912–13   The trade of Orkney at the end of the eighteenth century. *Scottish Historical Review* 10(4): 360–68.

Shorter, Edward

1971   Illegitimacy, sexual revolution, and social change in modern Europe. *Journal of Interdisciplinary History* 11(2): 237–72.

1973 Female emancipation, birth control, and fertility in European history. *American Historical Review* 78(3): 605-40.

Skinner, Alanson
1911 *Notes on the eastern Cree and northern Saulteaux.* Anthropological Papers of the American Museum of Natural History, vol. 9.

Smith, Dorothy Blakey
1971 *James Douglas, father of British Columbia.* Toronto: Oxford University Press.

Smith, Raymond T.
1956 *The Negro family in British Guiana.* London: Routledge and Kegan Paul Ltd.

Smith, Shirlee A.
in press Ferdinand Jacobs. *Dictionary of Canadian Biography,* vol. 4. Toronto: University of Toronto Press.

Southesk, Earl of
1969 *Saskatchewan and the Rocky Mountains: A diary and narrative of travel, sport, and adventure, during a journey through the Hudson's Bay Company's territories in 1859 and 1860.* Edmonton: Hurtig.

Sprenger, G. Herman
1972a An analysis of selective aspects of Métis society, 1810-1870. M.A. thesis, University of Manitoba, Winnipeg.
1972b The Métis nation: Buffalo hunting vs. agriculture in the Red River settlement (circa 1810-1870). *Western Canadian Journal of Anthropology* 3(1): 158-78.

Spry, Irene M.
1968 The papers of the Palliser expedition, 1857-1860. Toronto: Champlain Society.
1976 William Sinclair Jr. *Dictionary of Canadian Biography,* vol. 9, p. 722. Toronto: University of Toronto Press.
in press Matthew Cocking. Ibid., vol. 4.

Stevens, Wayne E.
1926 *The northwest fur trade 1763-1800.* University of Illinois Studies in the Social Sciences 14(3). Urbana: University of Illinois Press.

Sweet, Louise E., ed.
1975 Early mercantile enterprises in anthropological perspectives. *Proceedings of the 2nd congress,* Canadian Ethnology Society, vol. 2. National Museum of Man, Mercury Series, paper no. 28, Ottawa, pp. 491-663.

Thompson, Arthur N.
1970 John West: A study of the conflict between civilization and the

fur trade. *Journal of the Canadian Church Historical Society* 12(3): 44–57.

Thomson, Edward William
   1895   Great Godfrey's lament. In *Old man Savarin and other stories*. Toronto: William Briggs.

Thorman, G.E.
   1966   Henry Sergeant. *Dictionary of Canadian Biography,* vol. 1, pp. 605–6. Toronto: University of Toronto Press.

Thwaites, Reuben Gold, ed.
   1911   A Wisconsin fur-trader's journal, 1803–04, by Michel Curot. *Collections of the State Historical Society of Wisconsin* 10: 396–471. Madison.

Trigger, Bruce G.
   1969   *The Huron: farmers of the north.* New York: Holt, Rinehart and Winston.

Trudel, Marcel
   1973   *The beginnings of New France, 1524–1663.* Toronto: McClelland and Stewart.

Tyrrell, J.B., ed.
   1911   *Samuel Hearne's journey from Prince of Wales's Fort in Hudson's Bay to the Northern Ocean 1769–1772.* Toronto: Champlain Society, vol. 6.
   1934   *Journals of Samuel Hearne and Philip Turnor, 1774–92.* Ibid., vol. 21.

Van Kirk, Sylvia M.
   1972   Women and the fur trade. *The Beaver,* winter, pp. 4–21.
   1974a   The custom of the country: An examination of fur trade marriage practices. Paper presented at the meetings of the Canadian Historical Association, Toronto.
   1974b   Thanadelthur. *The Beaver,* spring, pp. 40–45.
   1975   The role of women in the fur trade society of the Canadian west. Ph.D. diss., Queen Mary College, University of London.
   n.d.   The coming of white women to fur trade society. Manuscript version of Van Kirk 1972.

Vaughan, Thomas, ed.
   1963   Alexander Lattie's Fort George journal, 1846. *Oregon Historical Quarterly* 64(3): 197–245.

Wallace, William S.
   1933   Notes on the family of Malcolm Fraser of Murray Bay. *Bulletin des recherches historiques* 34: 267–71.
   1934(ed.) *Documents relating to the North West Company.* Toronto: Champlain Society, vol. 22.

1954   *The present state of Hudson's Bay,* by Edward Umfreville (1st ed. 1790). Toronto: Ryerson Press.

Warner, Mikell de L. W., and Harriet Munnick

1972   *Catholic church records of the Pacific northwest:* Vancouver volumes 1 and 2 and Stellamaris Mission. St. Paul, OR: French Prairie Press.

Williams, Glyndwr

1969(ed.)   *Andrew Graham's observations on Hudson's Bay 1767–91.* London: Hudson's Bay Record Society, vol. 27.

1975(ed.)   *Hudson's Bay miscellany 1670–1870.* Winnipeg: Hudson's Bay Record Society, vol. 30.

1978   The puzzle of Anthony Henday's journal, 1754–55. *The Beaver,* winter, pp. 40–56.

Wrigley, E.A.

1966   Family limitation in pre-industrial England. *Economic History Review* 19 (2nd ser.): 82–110.

Index

In order to make more accessible the differences between the Hudson's Bay Company and the North West Company discussed in the text, entries in the index have been flagged with the initials HBC (Hudson's Bay Company) and NWC (North West Company) wherever relevant. In the case of fur traders' names, the initials indicate the primary company allegiance of the trader.